# **MEDIA**MORPHOSIS

**JOURNALISM AND COMMUNICATION FOR A NEW CENTURY: THE PINE FORGE PRESS SERIES**

*Consulting Editors: Shirley Biagi, Marilyn Kern-Foxworth, Duncan McDonald, Meg Moritz, and Leonard Teel*

*Facing Difference: Race, Gender, and Mass Media* by Shirley Biagi and Marilyn Kern-Foxworth

*Mediamorphosis: Understanding New Media* by Roger Fidler


**PINE FORGE PRESS TITLES OF RELATED INTEREST**

*A Guide to Field Research* by Carol A. Bailey

*Media/Society: Industries, Images, and Audiences* by David Croteau and William Hoynes

*The Production of Reality: Essays and Readings on Social Interaction*, 2nd ed., by Jodi O'Brien and Peter Kollock

*The McDonaldization of Society*, Rev. Ed., by George Ritzer

# **MEDIA**MORPHOSIS
## UNDERSTANDING *new* MEDIA

### Roger Fidler

KENT STATE UNIVERSITY

**PINE FORGE PRESS**

Thousand Oaks, California ■ London ■ New Delhi

*For information, address:*

 **Pine Forge Press**
A Sage Publications Company
2455 Teller Road
Thousand Oaks, California 91320
(805) 499-4224
E-mail: sales@pfp.sagepub.com

**Sage Publications Ltd.**       **Sage Publications India Pvt. Ltd.**
6 Bonhill Street              M-32 Market
London EC2A 4PU              Greater Kailash I
United Kingdom              New Delhi 110 048 India

*Production:* Dusty Davidson, The Book Company
*Copy Editor:* Betty Berenson
*Interior Designer:* Lisa Mirski Devenish
*Compositor:* The Cowans
*Cover Designer:* Paula Shuhert and Graham Metcalfe
*Print Buyer:* Anna Chin

*Printed in the United States of America.*

97 98 99 00 01 10 9 8 7 6 5 4 3 2 1

Library of Congress Cataloging-in-Publication Data

Fidler, Roger F.
   Mediamorphosis : understanding new media / Roger Fidler.
      p.    cm. -- (Journalism and communication for a new century)
   Includes bibliographical references (p.   ) and index.
   ISBN 0-8039-9086-3 (alk. paper)
      1. Mass media--History.    2. Mass media--Technological innovations.
   3. Mass media--Forecasting.    I. Title.   II. Title: Media morphosis.
   III. Series.
   P91.F467 1997
   302.23'09--dc21                                        96-52540
                                                              CIP

*For Ada,*
*who made it possible with love,*
*and*
*to the memory of James K. Batten,*
*journalist, mentor, friend*

# About the author

Roger Fidler is a professional in residence and coordinator of the Information Design Laboratory at the Kent State University School of Journalism and Mass Communication in Ohio. He is an internationally recognized electronic publishing visionary and pioneer.

He has worked in the newspaper business for more than 34 years as a journalist, designer, and technologist and has been actively involved in new media development since 1979. In 1981 he conceived the tablet newspaper concept and developed the initial prototype ten years later as a Freedom Forum Media Studies Fellow at Columbia University. From 1992 to 1995, he directed the Knight-Ridder Information Design Laboratory in Boulder, Colorado. He also founded PressLink, the first on-line computer service to serve the newspaper industry, in 1985 and the Knight-Ridder Graphics Network (now KRT Graphics), the first computer graphics network for newspapers, in 1983. From 1979 to 1983, he was a key member of the Knight-Ridder videotex development team and served as the first director of design for the company's commercial service called Viewtron.

His newspaper career began in 1961 doing "a little bit of everything" for a weekly newspaper in Eugene, Oregon, to help pay his way through the University of Oregon. Since then he has worked for the Eugene *Register-Guard*, Everett *Herald*, *Pacific Stars and Stripes* (Tokyo), St. Petersburg *Times*, Detroit *Free Press*, and Knight-Ridder. His positions have included science writer, reporter, copy editor, Sunday magazine editor, graphic artist, photographer, art director, graphics editor, design director, newsroom systems manager and corporate consultant. Between 1974 and 1984, he redesigned more than 30 newspapers. He is a founding member of the Society of Newspaper Design (SND).

# About the publisher

Pine Forge Press is a new educational publisher, dedicated to publishing innovative books and software throughout the social sciences. On this and any other of our publications, we welcome your comments. Please call or write us at:

Pine Forge Press
A Sage Publications Company
2455 Teller Road
Thousand Oaks, CA 91320
(805)499-4224
E-mail: sales@pfp.sagepub.com

Visit our new World Wide Web site, your direct link to a multitude of on-line resources: http://www.sagepub.com/pineforge

# contents

*chapter two*

# domains of communication media • 31

*chapter three*

# the mediamorphic role of language • 53

*chapter four*

# technologies of the third mediamorphosis • 81

*chapter five*

# the cultural context of the third mediamorphosis • 109

*chapter six*

# lessons from failure • 139

*chapter seven*

# mediamorphosis within the interpersonal domain • 167

*chapter eight*

# mediamorphosis within the broadcast domain • 195

This decade's big puzzle is new media. What is it, people and companies ask. Is there anything people want from media that our current saturated level of media does not provide? What kind of shape will it take? Can new media businesses be built and, if so, how long will it take? The questions go on and on.

Today money is being made in new media. But it is being made by trade show impresarios, conference organizers, lawyers, and a few others, including a handful of authors who promise the answers. Roger Fidler, in *Mediamorphosis: Understanding New Media*, comes as close as any author I know to answering the questions.

Today's new media conundrum is the Internet. The Internet is expensive to access, artistically primitive, painfully slow, and overpopulated with garbage. And it is wonderful. It gives voice to those who don't have a radio or TV frequency or a printing press. It transcends boundaries; while some contend that it is a source of disunity, if you are thinking globally, it is a source of unity. It breaks down "entry barriers" to business; today, media are very expensive, but with a little money and quite a bit of ingenuity, you have a chance to start an Internet business that, at the instant of launch, is distributed internationally. Without the need to buy land, construct buildings, and install expensive equipment, modest investments in the programming and its marketing will, with increasing frequency, be enough.

Finally, the new media have helped people leave the density of our cities where the bulk of our seemingly intractable problems exist, and either commute by networked computers or start a business that is not place-dependent. Independence from place not only liberates individuals, but provides beginning answers to the maldistribution of population.

So what will be the future shape of this wonderful development? Frankly, those who do most of the talking, who have the biggest megaphones, don't know. We are treated to "hyper-cyber" by people who write stories without knowing or outlining the slightest bit of context. Roger Fidler has not made that mistake.

He has a fertile mind, a rich database of experiences, and treats us to some very expansive thinking about the future. Roger takes us into "Metaverses," where we can use personal agents, video mail, electronic currency, and other dazzling new personal tools. His future might be right; certainly nobody has had a better laboratory to think about the new media in the next century than Roger Fidler, although as he admits, some of his theories will turn out to be just that—theories.

Where Roger's research and writing take a particularly helpful turn is in giving us all an immensely helpful context for thinking about the future of media. He not only presents us with a future filled with imagination, but also one filled with context. He knows that, while many show little concern for media history, answers are not available without understanding the metamorphosis of the media. He sketches beguiling 21st century scenarios colliding with inertia. Any person seriously interested in new media must know both sides.

*Alfred C. Sikes*
Former FCC Chairman and President
Hearst New Media and Technology

# preface

**me•di•a•mor•pho•sis** (me'de-a-môr'fa-sis) n. *The transformation of communication media, usually brought about by the complex interplay of perceived needs, competitive and political pressures, and social and technological innovations.*

When I coined the word *mediamorphosis* in 1990[1] to serve as a working title for an article about the future of newspapers, I never expected to see it as a book title. So, I was pleasantly surprised when Craig LaMay, the editor who commissioned the article,[2] told me he thought the term was worth retaining and suggested that I expand the concept. At the time, my focus was solely on emerging information technologies and their potential influence on newspapers, but the scope of mediamorphosis soon proved to be much broader.

The following year, the Freedom Forum Foundation (formerly the Gannett Foundation) awarded me a fellowship to explore the mediamorphosis idea and to begin writing this book at its Media Studies Center at Columbia University. After more than a dozen years of pioneering on the electronic media frontier, often appropriately referred to as the "bleeding edge," I found myself looking forward to what I assumed would be a relatively relaxing academic interlude. All I needed to do, or so I naively thought, was to put into writing the lessons I had learned from my experiences with some of the first consumer videotex and online computer services in the United States, gather additional supportive material from the libraries at Columbia University and the Media Studies Center, and then describe my vision for the future of newspapers. But I quickly

---

[1]A recent search of periodical archives turned up several prior uses of *mediamorphosis* dating back to 1972. However, all were used in a political context to describe the influence of the media on a politician's image (for example, "the mediamorphosis of George Bush").

[2]The article, "Mediamorphosis, or the Transformation of Newspapers into a New Medium," appeared in the Fall 1991 issue of *Media Studies Journal.*

discovered that the transformations I was attempting to describe involved the whole human communication system and that mediamorphosis was not a simple concept. The more I delved into the history of communication and the technologies that were obviously converging, the more I sensed that we were in the midst of what might be the greatest transformation of human communication since the emergence of written language.

By the time I completed my fellowship year, I found that many of my original ideas had undergone their own metamorphosis and that the book was still far from complete. Any hope that I might have an abundance of free time for writing was soon dispelled by a sudden and dramatic resurgence of interest in new forms of communication. Everything from CD-ROMs and multimedia computer systems to personal digital assistants and the Internet emerged almost simultaneously as potential threats and opportunities for established media and telecommunication companies. All of this activity seemed to confirm my feeling that enormous changes were about to take place.

Even though *Mediamorphosis: Understanding New Media* is about technological change within the human communication system and contemporary media businesses, it is not a technical book. My purpose has been to demystify emerging media technologies as much as possible and to provide a structure for understanding their potential influences on the popular forms of mainstream media—newspapers, magazines, television, and radio.

While this book explores many of the ideas and insights that have come from my research and experiences, I do not claim to possess any secret or absolute knowledge of the future. All I can offer are my interpretations of the data I've gathered. I also cannot claim to be totally unbiased. I have spent more than three decades working as a professional journalist, designer, and "technologist" within the newspaper business, so my experiences and loyalties are certain to have influenced my perspectives.

The vision of digital print media presented in Chapter 9 is one that I have been intimately involved with since the beginning of the 1980s, when I first began to recognize the publishing opportunities afforded by flat-panel displays. I knew at the time that any practical application of this technology for publishers was at least a decade or two away, but the vision it inspired of digital print media was too compelling to put aside. An invitation from the Associated Press Managing Editors (APME) Association to submit a paper about the future of newspapers in 1981 gave me the first opportunity to write about the tablet medium and to create several page mockups.[3]

Throughout the 1980s, I continued to refine my vision while developing other new media opportunities within Knight-Ridder. Variations of the "Mobile Digital Document Reader" scenario, which I originally created in 1988 for an American Press Institute publication,[4] have appeared in several books and magazines. Since 1992, I have been actively pursuing the development of tablet publishing systems, first as the director of Knight-Ridder's Information Design Laboratory (IDL) in Boulder, Colorado, and more recently as a consultant and professional in residence at Kent State University in Ohio. Although my various involvements with new media prolonged completion of this book, they also contributed greatly to the development of the mediamorphosis concepts.

Despite the many pessimistic prognostications that are so common today, my outlook for the future of journalism and print media remains optimistic. My hope is that the stories and explanations I've presented will serve to encourage and inspire those who have more than a passing interest in the future of contemporary media, and, most of all, in the written word.

## Acknowledgments

*Mediamorphosis: Understanding New Media* would not have been possible without the funding, time, and nurturing environment provided by Knight-Ridder and The Freedom Forum Foundation. I am particularly indebted to the late James K. Batten, Knight-Ridder's chairman and chief executive officer, for his unwavering support and trust, and to Everette Dennis, the Media Studies Center's former executive director, for providing invaluable assistance and greatly expanding my horizons. I also owe a sincere debt of gratitude to Jane Coleman, Craig LaMay, Mark Thalhimer, Shirley Gazsi, Deborah Rogers, and all the other members of the Media Studies Center staff. Each of the fellows with whom I shared the sabbatical experience in New York enriched my life, but I am especially devoted to Cleveland and Frances Wilhoit for their help and friendship.

---

[3]This article appeared in Associate Press Managing Editors Special Report, *Newspapers in the Year 2000* (New York: Associated Press, Fall 1981).

[4]"Plugging into the News," in *Newspaper Design 2000 and Beyond.* Reston, VA: American Press Institute, 1988, pp. 36–41.

In the course of my research, I met with many leaders of media and technology companies, all of whom deserve a sincere thanks. I owe a special thanks to John Seely Brown, the director of Xerox PARC, for taking the time to share his views on the role of documents in society. I would also like to express my appreciation to George Gilder, the author of *Life after Television,* for his contributions to my vision of mediamorphosis.

Thanking the publisher—Steve Rutter—for his confidence and patience, and the editors—Rebecca Smith, Duncan McDonald, Shirley Biagi, and Meg Moritz—who have worked with me throughout this laborious process is, of course, obligatory, but in this case they are all especially deserving. Without them, I seriously doubt that this book would have been completed. They have contributed much, and whatever success this book may have is as much their doing as mine. Thanks also to the following reviewers, commissioned by Pine Forge Press, whose insights and help on the manuscript were invaluable: Carolyn Cline, University of Southern California; Pam Creedon, Kent State University; Joan Deppa, Syracuse University; Greg Lisby, Georgia State University; Susan Lucarelli, University of Tennessee; John Pavlik, Columbia University; Susanna Hornig Priest, Texas A&M University. I would like to offer particular thanks to Kathleen A. Hansen from the University of Minnesota who read the manuscript over multiple drafts and who forced me to write a much better book. Even though Arnold Ismach, former dean of the University of Oregon School of Journalism and Mass Communication, was not one of the assigned editors, he never shied from giving various stages of the manuscript a close read and providing me with insightful suggestions. To all, I am forever indebted and grateful.

The acknowledgments for this book would not be complete without thanking three very special friends, Barrie Hartman, Dave Emery, and Roy Paul Nelson, who helped divert me from astronomy to mass communication while I was a student at the University of Oregon. And finally, I'd like to express my warmest gratitude to the most important contributor to this book—my best friend, partner, and wife, Ada Vigo.

*Roger Fidler*
rfidler@saed.kent.edu

# principles of mediamorphosis

Change is not something most people look forward to or are particularly good at predicting. Even for the inventors and innovators who stimulate technological and social changes, visualizing the future presents an enigmatic problem. Yet, despite the anxieties often caused by change, humans seem to have a remarkable propensity for rapidly assimilating new ideas, products, and services once they are perceived to fit into their personal and cultural definitions of reality. While no one, it seems, is ever completely prepared for change or able to accurately predict outcomes, we can all begin to discern probable shapes of the future by learning to recognize the historic patterns and mechanisms of change. This chapter introduces several frameworks for assessing change and evaluating new **media**[1] technologies. It also lays a foundation for understanding the mediamorphic process, which will be built upon in the following chapters.

## Coping with change

New technologies are assimilated so rapidly in U.S. culture that historic perspective is often lost in the process. For example, on a recent visit to a newspaper, I met a young artist who was creating an explanatory diagram on an Apple Macintosh computer. As we casually talked about news graphics, he paused now and then to

---

[1]Terms that appear in **boldface** in the text are defined in the Glossary/ Index at the back of the book.

reflect on what I had just said and then returned his attention to the computer screen. Finally, he let go of the **mouse** he was using to draw shapes, and gave me a serious look. "You know," he said, "I can't even imagine how you could create news graphics without a computer."

His comment demonstrates just how quickly radical new technologies and concepts can become commonplace in people's minds. In 1984, when I was establishing the Knight-Ridder Graphics Network,[2] few newspaper artists I spoke with could imagine creating graphics *with* a computer. Most were openly skeptical and some were even hostile when I confronted them with this new tool. Yet, despite the initial resistance, computers replaced mechanical drawing implements in nearly every art department around the world in less than 10 years.

Today, more **informational graphics**—maps, charts, graphs, diagrams, and so on—are published by more newspapers and magazines than was conceivable or even possible before the introduction of computer graphics systems. Computers have done more, however, than simply increase the quantity of graphics. They have also brought about fundamental changes in the content, timeliness, form, and quality of graphics, as well as in the role and status of news artists.

Prior to computers and laser printers, artists relied on tools that had not changed significantly in nearly a century. Every word included within a graphic had to be hand lettered or typeset and carefully pasted in place. Adding textures and colors required artists to manually prepare overlays that had to be photographically manipulated before a graphic was suitable for printing. The whole process from conception to completion often required a full day for a single graphic.

## *The influence of personal computers*

Computers did not appreciably reduce the amount of time artists needed to render original graphics. Nor did they require less skill and talent to use than the old-fashioned drawing tools. Their great-

---

[2]I founded and directed the Knight-Ridder Graphics Network (KRGN) until 1988. KRGN was the world's first syndicated service to produce and electronically distribute daily news graphics drawn with the assistance of personal computers. In 1988, the service merged with the Chicago Tribune

est contributions were in their ability to eliminate time-consuming, labor-intensive production steps and to permit fast editing and updating of graphics, often within minutes of a deadline.

Because of the time and effort required to alter or correct hand-drawn art, editors had been reluctant to request news graphics requiring text or details that might change before deadline. Consequently, the vast majority of art that appeared in newspapers and magazines before the introduction of computers were simple "mood" illustrations and cartoons that incorporated little or no textual information. After computers, there was a dramatic shift toward graphics with meaningful and useful content. My analysis of graphics appearing in Knight-Ridder's newspapers revealed that in the five years between 1984 and 1989, the average number of graphics published each day nearly tripled, and informational graphics went from about 10 percent of the total to nearly 90 percent. A random sampling of other U.S. newspapers showed a similar trend.

The influence of computers upon the artists was equally profound. Before 1985, their status and salaries were comparatively low. In the decade that followed, those who mastered the computer systems and could produce informational graphics were quickly elevated to respected positions within the news and feature departments. Their salaries rose dramatically, and many came to be regarded as graphic journalists. Of course, not all artists successfully made the transition. Many were, in fact, replaced by those who had gravitated directly to computers, bypassing the mastery of mechanical drawing tools. And unfortunately for those left behind, such displacements have become an expected consequence of changing technologies.

### Yesterday's future, today's past

Much of what is now taken for granted has, in fact, only recently emerged. Just one human generation ago, at the beginning of the 1970s, electronic pocket calculators were just starting to compete

---

*(Continued)*

Graphics Service and was renamed Knight-Ridder Tribune Graphics (KRT Graphics). It is now a division of KRT Information Services based in Washington, DC, and is syndicated by Tribune Media Services and its worldwide affiliates.

with slide rules and mechanical adding machines; computers were big and impersonal; and AT&T was still a monopoly that leased nearly all private telephones in the United States. Portable communicators and voice interaction with computers only existed in the imaginary twenty-third-century universe of the original "Star Trek" television series.

Twenty-five years ago, electronic media were confined to broadcast radio and television. **Lasers** and **fiber-optic networks,** miniature video cameras and handheld television sets, compact disc players and music CDs, **digital fax** machines, **cellular phones,** and laptop computers were all unknown outside of a few research and development laboratories.

**Information retrieval** was something one only did in libraries with printed books and periodicals, or microfilm, using pencils and paper. The **Internet** and **electronic mail** (e-mail) were still confined to the rarefied and generally secret world of defense-related research.

Newspapers and magazines had just begun converting their newsrooms from mechanical typewriters to electronic text-editing systems and their composing rooms from **hot-type** to **cold-type** technologies. Few journalists then could have imagined the electronic news gathering and production technologies that are common today or foreseen **desktop publishing** and the explosion of news graphics made possible by personal computers.

A mere decade ago, few people could have imagined that by the mid-1990s digital fax machines, electronic mail services, and miniature cell phones would be routinely used to communicate just as easily and inexpensively with individuals in distant countries and rural communities as within large cities and office buildings. In the mid-1980s, most publishers abandoned **consumer online services** (then called **videotex**) after collectively losing several hundred million dollars and promptly declared that electronic publishing would not emerge as a viable business until well into the next century. Who then would have envisioned the frenzy of activity that now surrounds consumer online services and the **World Wide Web?**

The social and political changes of the past 10 years have been no less dramatic and surprising. Even the Central Intelligence Agency didn't anticipate the sudden collapse of the Berlin Wall and the reuniting of East and West Germany, the abrupt demise of apartheid and white minority rule in South Africa, or the rapid breakup of the Soviet Union and apparent ending of the Cold War.

# Visions of future media

The preceding examples serve to illustrate one of the cardinal maxims of prognostication—always expect the unexpected. Another equally important maxim is also readily discernible from past experiences—be skeptical of popularized visions.

Back in the 1930s and 1940s, artist renderings of future aircraft, as envisioned by famous aviators and designers, appeared with great frequency in newspapers, magazines, and books. Present-day samplings of these once popular visions reveal that most experts of that time correctly foresaw that by the 1960s commercial airplanes would routinely carry hundreds of passengers to distant locations in mere hours. But, beyond that, their visions all went astray, especially when it came to predicting just how this amazing feat would be accomplished. Instead of the jumbo jets that are now commonplace, their "aeroships of the future" either had gigantic wings with as many as 10 prop engines or they were rocket-propelled.

## *Missing the future*

Many similar flights of fancy have been published about future information and entertainment technologies dating back at least to the invention of the electric telegraph in the 1830s. For example, not long after photography became popular in the last century, some diviners predicted that photographic images would ultimately replace printed newspapers. Early in this century, television was often portrayed in futuristic visions as a video-telephone or as a public entertainment medium to be housed primarily in theaters. Seers in the 1930s and 1940s envisioned homes equipped with facsimile machines that would deliver up-to-the-minute newspaper editions directly to subscribers and thereby render large printing plants and manual delivery networks obsolete. Some might argue that these visions of the future were not wrong, just premature in their predicted time frames.

There are, however, many dramatic examples of seemingly credible predictions that have missed the future entirely. For example, until the mid-1980s, a popular vision of the future was a world controlled by fewer than a dozen monster computers. Screen writers and novelists often gave these computers a sinister, humanlike intelligence and foresaw a bleak future in which humans would be pitted against supercomputers in a struggle for dominance and survival. Instead, within the span of a single decade, microcomputers shifted control from centralized **temples of iron**[3] in the hands of a few to powerful personal computers in the hands of the many.

## Information superhighways and teleputers

Since the early 1990s, communication sages have been predicting that in the next decade so-called **information superhighway networks** will routinely bring an ever expanding universe of interactive information, entertainment, shopping, and personal services to nearly everyone through some form of what futurist George Gilder has called a **teleputer**—a new device that will blend attributes of television and telephony with a personal computer.[4]

No one seems to doubt the technological feasibility or the wisdom of building such networks and devices. Dozens of communication companies are, in fact, already investing tens of billions of dollars to rewire the world with high-speed fiber-optic cables that are capable of carrying vast volumes of data. And nearly all computer and consumer electronics companies are actively developing their own versions of the anticipated teleputer.

Nor does anyone appear to doubt that every institution and every business is about to be challenged and altered by emerging forms of electronic media—forms that know no local or national boundaries and have the capability of empowering individuals to seize control of information and entertainment from the traditional **gatekeepers**.

***The opposite extremes.*** However, the visions that describe what people will actually do with these networks and the services the networks will provide are widely divergent. Many of these visions are

---

[3]As computers grew in complexity and power, they came to be known as "temples of iron" because of their huge size and iron cores. The religious symbolism was further reinforced by the white-jacketed operators who took on the mystical persona of a priesthood as they maintained the computers and controlled their communications with the outside world. Time with these centralized mainframe computers was so precious through the end of the 1970s, that elaborate time-sharing systems and digital communication networks had to be devised.

[4]A more detailed description of the teleputer concept can be found in George Gilder, *Life after Television: The Coming Transformation of Media and American Life* (rev. ed.). New York: Norton, 1994. See pp. 52-70.

linear extensions of existing media technologies or are concepts that bear a striking resemblance to the aircraft envisioned with 10 prop engines. One example, which has persisted for more than six decades, is of home presses (fax machines or computer printers) producing custom-printed editions of newspapers and magazines for every subscriber. Another is the video-on-demand technology foreseen for more than three decades as the future of television.

At the opposite extreme are the more technologically aggressive prophecies. Like the visions of rocket planes in the 1930s and 1940s, these expect sudden, bold leaps. Some in this category go so far as to predict that by the time today's teenagers reach middle age, video images will have replaced written and spoken words as the principal conveyers of messages and that people will "experience" events, as opposed to merely viewing, hearing, or reading about them, through some advanced form of **virtual reality** (VR).

Equally diverse are assumptions about the social, political, and economic implications of new systems for human communication and commerce made possible by these global networks and hybrid devices. Popularized visions of the future often foresee, for example, the replacement of traditional banking and monetary systems by **online** financial services and digital cash; the return to a participatory form of democracy built upon the concepts of electronic town meetings and computerized polling and voting systems; the demise of mass production and mass media brought about by the emergence of custom production systems and personal information and entertainment services.

***The only certainties.*** Even though the experts espouse many differing and often conflicting ideas about the future that awaits us, all agree as to the only certainties—society and the human communication system will change together and in often unexpected ways. Some of the changes that will occur in the next century will undoubtedly conflict with present-day social values and standards. Popular forms of communication media may be called by different names, and they may be used in different ways. But however society and media may change, we can be reasonably assured that they will continue to embody and build upon the experiences of the past, as they always have. By letting history be our guide, we will see that the forces shaping our future are essentially the same forces that have shaped our past.

## The 30-year rule

While we may never be able to foretell the outcomes of technological change with a high degree of precision, we can sharpen our focus. To do so, we must first enlarge our perspective and discard most of our commonly held assumptions, particularly about the speed of change.

Changes may seem to be occurring more rapidly in the world today, but studies of historical records have shown that this is a common misconception. Paul Saffo, a director at the Institute for the Future in Menlo Park, California, posits that the amount of time required for new ideas to fully seep into a culture has consistently averaged about three decades for at least the past five centuries. He calls this the **30-year rule.**

As a **new media** forecaster, Saffo has learned from experience that our short human memories all too often confuse surprise with speed. When it comes to emerging technologies, he finds that the slowness of change is the rule rather than the exception. Most ideas take much longer to become "overnight successes" than anyone is ever prepared to admit. The lesson he says we most often forget is:

> You should never mistake a clear view for a short distance. It's that sense of standing on a ridge, looking out across a great forest at a distant mountain goal. The peak is so close it seems you could reach out and touch it. That is, until you get in among the trees and start beating your way towards the mountain.[5]

The reason life feels so much more rapid today, Saffo contends, is not that individual technologies are accelerating at a faster rate or that things are happening more quickly than they have in the past. What's actually occurring is that "more technologies are coming up at the same time. It is the unexpected cross-impact of maturing technologies that creates this powerful acceleration that we all feel."[6] **Cross-impacts** are also the variables, he says, that make new media forecasting so difficult.

---

[5] "Paul Saffo and the 30-Year Rule," *Design World,* 24 (1992): 18.
[6] Ibid., p. 23.

### Stages of development

There is, however, a relatively consistent pattern of accelerated development that takes place as each new technology moves from laboratory to marketplace. Saffo has identified three typical stages within the 30-year rule. "First decade: lots of excitement, lots of puzzlement, not a lot of penetration. Second decade: lots of flux, penetration of the product into society is beginning. Third decade: 'Oh, so what?' Just a standard technology and everybody has it."[7]

**Which development stage are we in?** As we attempt to peer into the future of communications, it would seem, therefore, that the critical question to be asked with regard to emerging media technologies is, Which development stage are they in? But, as we will discover, the answer to such an apparently simple question is not always obvious. To know the stage, we must also have some idea of when the clock started, and how innovations are likely to be affected by other technological and social developments, which are not easily determined in the midst of change.

**Example: Xerox's Alto.** When the first **personal computer** designed specifically for nontechnical users was switched on at the Xerox Palo Alto Research Center (PARC) in the early 1970s, most of the underlying ideas and technologies had been under development for one to three decades. The scientists who created the Alto, as this early computer was called, believed they were already in the second stage and that their invention could quickly penetrate the office market, but the company's senior executives and market researchers were unconvinced.[8]

While Xerox's decision not to immediately begin marketing Alto systems is often held up as an example of corporate incompetence, it may have been based on a more accurate assessment than the pundits have acknowledged. With the benefits of hindsight, we can now see that personal computing in the 1970s was still in its first stage. Beyond a small cadre of scientists and amateur enthusiasts,

---

[7]Ibid.

[8]The story of Xerox's development of the first personal computer system is told by Douglas K. Smith and Robert C. Alexander in *Fumbling the Future: How Xerox Invented then Ignored the First Personal Computer.* New York: Morrow, 1988.

few people then were ready to believe they might soon have a practical use for their own desktop computer. Additionally, many of the component and manufacturing technologies needed to make personal computers affordable to general consumers were not yet available.

Another decade would pass before a personal computer system comparable to the Alto would enter the consumer marketplace. And even in the 1980s there was uncertainty as to which stage personal computers were in. Many financial bets were made on the assumption that they were then in the third stage, only to be lost when the market for home computers faltered toward the middle of the decade. What we can see only now is that the cross-impacts of video game, electronic mail, online information, and Internet technologies coupled with faster and cheaper telecommunications and a growing home office market in the 1990s finally thrust personal computers into the third stage.

### Restating the rule

The 30-year rule may not be foolproof, but it does put the development of new technologies into a more realistic perspective. We need to remember, however, that this rule is not intended to fix a precise time frame for the widespread adoption of new technologies. Saffo's essential point is that impressions of spontaneous technological advancements are generally wrong. This rule can be restated in two different ways: (1) Laboratory breakthroughs and discoveries nearly always take longer than anyone expects to become successful commercial products or services. (2) Technologies that appear to have suddenly emerged as successful new products and services have been under development for much longer than anyone admits.

### The dangers of technomyopia

While the time required for new technologies to migrate from laboratories to store shelves may span several decades, Saffo also cautions industry leaders against complacency. History, he says, shows that once consumers perceive a new technology to be useful and affordable, widespread adoption can take place rather quickly. Yet, despite the frequent repetition of this pattern, he has found that people are still nearly always caught by surprise.

The relatively flat, slow ramp followed by a steep, rapid climb is the growth model upon which most start-up companies build their business plans. But that model can be misleading. The actual pattern for enterprises attempting to exploit new technologies rarely conforms to a smooth ascending curve. More often than not, the typical, real-life trend line resembles a roller coaster. Several moderate ups and downs generally precede the final grand ascent to market success, although there are never any assurances that there will, in the end, be a final grand ascent.

This tendency to undergo several initial ups and downs may contribute to the surprise factor when a new technology finally does take off. Typically, a great deal of publicity will follow the announcement of a discovery or new invention. But when the first rush of excitement is dampened by disappointments and setbacks, we usually treat future growth phases with skepticism. Saffo calls this affliction **technomyopia:**

> [Technomyopia[9]] is a strange phenomenon that causes us to overestimate the potential short-term impacts of a new technology. And when the world fails to conform to our inflated expectations, we turn around and we underestimate the long-term implications. First we over-shoot and then we under-shoot.[10]

***Example: The video game roller coaster.*** The development of video game technology illustrates this phenomenon. Beginning in 1972 with two simple ball-and-paddle games called Odyssey and Pong, video games quickly captivated the minds, and wallets, of teenagers and young adults. A steady stream of popular video arcade games, such as Pac Man and Space Invaders, followed in the late 1970s. Within 10 years, Americans were spending more money on home video game systems and at video arcades than they spent on movies and music—a total of more than $11 billion. Then, even more suddenly, the market collapsed. By 1985 total sales of home video game systems had dropped from more than $3 billion at its peak to only $100 million.[11]

---

[9]Saffo referred to this affliction as *macro-myopia* in the 1992 *Design World* article. However, he now prefers to use the term technomyopia, which I agree is more appropriate and so I have taken the liberty of substituting it in this chapter.

[10]"Paul Saffo and the 30-Year Rule," p. 18.

[11]Steven Lubar, *InfoCulture: The Smithsonian Book of Information Age Inventions.* Boston: Houghton Mifflin, 1993, p. 274.

The crash forced nearly all U.S. video game companies into other computer businesses or bankruptcy. Most industry executives and analysts saw this as a sign that video games were merely a fad. But just as the U.S. market was collapsing, **Nintendo,** a Japanese toy company, introduced a new game system in Japan called Famicon. And two years later, Nintendo swept across the Pacific with the speed and power of a tsunami. Armed with a wider selection of fast-action games that incorporated sophisticated graphics, Nintendo quickly revived interest among those who had become bored with earlier systems and attracted a new generation of players as well. By 1989 Nintendo controlled 80 percent of the U.S. video game market, which had recovered to its $3 billion precrash level. By the beginning of the 1990s, one out of every five U.S. households owned a Nintendo set.

## Criteria for adopting new technologies

Saffo's 30-year rule incorporates elements of the early 1980s work of media scholar Everett Rogers. As a Stanford professor, Rogers formulated an explanation of the process by which innovations are adopted and implemented within a society, which he called the **diffusion theory.** He proposed that the characteristics of an innovation, as perceived by members of a society, determine its rate of adoption. The five attributes of an innovation defined by Rogers are: (1) relative advantage, (2) compatibility, (3) complexity, (4) reliability, and (5) observability.[12]

### *The example of cellular telephones*

The adoption of cellular telephones from their introduction in the early 1980s through their rapid **diffusion** into the general consumer market 10 years later provides an instructive example of how these attributes apply. However, to understand the process of adoption, we need to know a few things about cellular technology.

Cellular communication is just one of the many services made possible by the integration of communications with computers. Telephone switching systems had been computerized in the United States since the 1960s, but it wasn't until AT&T was broken up two

---

[12]Everett M. Rogers, *Communication Technology: The New Media in Society.* New York: Free Press, 1986.

decades later that phone companies began using their switches in new and different ways.

Cellular technology, which relies on many low-powered receiving-transmitting stations with overlapping service areas called cells, opened the mobile phone market by significantly reducing the amount of the radio spectrum that had been required for wireless communications. With radio-telephones, the market was always limited by the scarcity of frequencies that could be assigned to customers. Because cellular systems can reuse the same frequencies many times, they are capable of providing access to virtually everyone.

*Relative advantage.* The perceived relative advantages of wireless cellular phones over existing wired telephones and radio-telephones have been increased mobility and greater efficiency. Instead of being tethered to a telephone line in a building or carrying a standard telephone mounted on a large battery pack with a radio receiver-transmitter, lightweight and compact cell phones can be carried in coat pockets or purses. The freedom to make and receive telephone calls from a car, restaurant, street corner, or even while hiking in the mountains was quickly seen as an essential requirement and enormous time saver by salespeople and others who felt a need to be in touch at all times. Cellular phones provide an enhanced sense of convenience and security.

*Compatibility.* Because cellular services are connected with established telephone networks and use standard dialing systems, communications between cell phones and wired phones are perceived to be relatively seamless. Cordless phones, which are primarily used within homes, have also boomed in recent years and contributed to the widespread acceptance of phones without wires.

*Complexity.* The operation of cell phones is similar to the operation of ordinary wired phones. They can be used without special training or any significant modifications to already well-understood procedures and skills. The overall level of **complexity** is generally perceived to be quite low.

*Reliability.* Before receiver-transmitter stations for cellular phones finally covered most densely populated regions at the beginning of 1990s, customers were often frustrated by annoying interruptions in cellular communications and by limitations in their ability to use the phones. But, since then, most people have come to perceive cellular communications as relatively ubiquitous and reliable. However, as cell phones have become more popular throughout the world, the lack of a secure system for protecting privacy and preventing the piracy of cell phone identification codes has raised new concerns relating to reliability that will need to be resolved.

*Observability.* Stories about cellular technology in mainstream media during the 1980s helped to inform and excite people about this innovation, but the decisions to adopt or reject it, in Rogers's view, have been most influenced by contacts with early adopters, interpersonal networks, and observations of people actually using cell phones. Rogers suggests that the more that people are seen using a new technology and are perceived to be benefiting from it, the more likely someone is to form or change an attitude about his or her own need to adopt the technology.

## The importance of early adopters

The identification and courting of potential early adopters, Rogers contends, is essential to the overall marketing strategy for any new consumer product or service. Early adopters are the people who enjoy being first on the block with a new gadget, perceive immediate uses for something new, and are willing to take risks. They usually have a high degree of tolerance for initial limitations and inconveniences, provided that the innovation imparts some measure of status, respect, or attention from their peers and cohorts. Rogers found that early adopters gradually convince the opinion leaders in their companies, institutions, or communities to adopt an innovation through word-of-mouth evangelizing and eager demonstrations. The opinion leaders, in turn, convince those in their interpersonal networks to become adopters.

Rogers's research has demonstrated that all **diffusion curves** for new ideas are S-shaped, with the rate of adoption accelerating rapidly when a product or service has diffused into 10 to 25 percent of its potential market.[13] Early adopters, he believes, provide the initial thrust needed to arrive at that takeoff point (see Exhibit 1.1).

---

[13]Ibid.

**Exhibit 1.1** Adoption curve and diffusion.

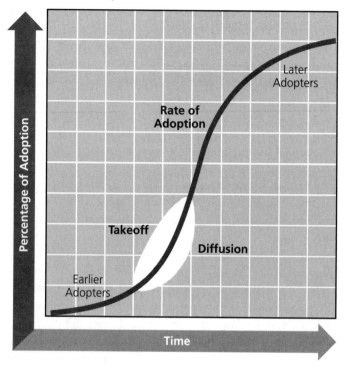

## *Bridges of familiarity*

The five attributes of innovations that Rogers lists in his diffusion theory suggest that the success of any new form of communication is dependent upon how comfortably and easily it fits into people's lives. While I agree with his arguments, I have come to believe that a sixth attribute is equally critical to the comfortable and easy fit of new media within the general consumer market—*familiarity*.

*Links to the past.* In the history of the human communication system, new forms have rarely been adopted without familiar links to earlier or existing forms. As revolutionary as the inventions of the printing press and movable type may seem today, early printers did not make a sudden break with the past. For decades, they replicated almost exactly the traditional letter forms and formats of documents produced by hand. Printing was referred to as artificial writing, as opposed to natural writing, well into the sixteenth century and was used primarily as a low-cost means of fulfilling the growing demand for Bibles, ancient texts, and papal indulgences. (A growing market for popular novels and risqué books also contributed to the rapid growth of printing presses in Europe.)

The development of modern books and periodicals was a gradual, evolutionary process. The first newspapers, which emerged more than 150 years after Johann Gutenberg produced the first printed Bibles, took as their model the established forms of newsletters and newsbooks. Even with the introduction of industrial age technologies, traditional newspaper format did not change significantly until the end of the nineteenth century.

***Crossing the bridge.*** Modern forms of communication media have demonstrated similar patterns. For example, photography was readily adopted because it was based on familiar ways of seeing and of representing vision.[14] It emerged just as improved transportation was providing greater mobility and, consequentially, increasing demand for keepsake images of distant relatives and friends. Itinerant artists were already traveling from town to town attempting to fulfill people's desires for portraits when the effect of light on silver salts was discovered and used to create the first photographic images in the 1830s. Initially, photography was seen as a more efficient and reliable means of producing portrait and landscape art. More creative uses had to wait until this **bridge of familiarity** had been crossed.

Silent films owed their quick acceptance to familiarity with photography and vaudeville shows. The recording of images and mechanical music boxes provided the familiar bridges for the phonograph and recorded sound. Commercial radio initially took for its content model recorded music and live stage productions, such as concerts, plays, and vaudeville acts. Radio and audio recordings, in turn, provided the connections for rapid acceptance of the "talkies"—films that synchronized pictures with voices and sounds. Television was anticipated and quickly accepted as radio with moving pictures.

Over time, each new form of communication has evolved from its origins as a recognizable extension of an earlier form into a distinct form all its own. This continuum of transformations and adaptations, as we shall see, is actually a complex process comparable in

[14]See Lubar, *InfoCulture*, p. 53.

many ways to the evolution of species. Successful forms of new media, just as new species, do not emerge spontaneously from nowhere. They have all required links with the past.

### The power of metaphors

Computer hardware and software companies have only recently come to realize that familiar, bridging metaphors can be a powerful tool for gaining market acceptance. The idea of using a visually recognizable "face" to communicate with computers was first proposed by Douglas Engelbart early in the 1960s, but most of his peers failed to recognize its value. Almost 10 years passed before scientists were able to create the first fully functional **graphical user interface (GUI)** based on Engelbart's idea.

The original computer **interfaces** required users to communicate their requests through an array of cryptic codes and complex instructions that had to be entered from a keyboard precisely as indicated in the manuals. An error in typing or the use of an incorrect code could result in a significant loss of time, or worse, a loss of vital data.

*The desktop metaphor.* GUIs (pronounced "gooeys") have overcome this problem by providing users with recognizable visual and aural clues. For example, in most contemporary GUI designs, computer directories are displayed as file folder icons. With a mouse or other pointing device, a user is able to open a **directory** by simply pointing and clicking on the appropriate "folder." To move a "document" from one folder to another, a user merely has to select the document to be moved and visually "drag" it into another folder by holding down a button on the mouse.

Steven Jobs, the cofounder and former chairman of Apple Computer, introduced one of the first commercial GUIs with the company's Lisa computer in 1982, and in 1984 enhanced it for the more popular Macintosh. Most dedicated computer users and engineers initially scoffed at the concept. For them, the idea of using icons and familiar visual cues was a waste of precious computing power and unsuited to "serious" computing. *Real* computers, they argued, were supposed to be difficult to use.

Fortunately, Apple's vision of "computers for the rest of us" found a ready market among publishers and graphic artists. From these early adopters, the Macintosh with its "user-friendly" GUI spread steadily into the general consumer market. In the past dozen years, the **desktop metaphor** introduced by Apple has become the recognized GUI standard throughout the world for personal computing.

*The village metaphor.* Computer and telecommunications companies have been pursuing a similar GUI for **interactive television** and online computer services based on the so-called **village metaphor.** The underlying idea is to graphically depict a town containing familiar buildings that represent certain activities. A post office, for example, is where users would expect to send and receive electronic mail, a library is where they would logically go for reference information, a video store or theater is where movies could be viewed on demand, and a newsstand is the place to buy electronic editions of newspapers and magazines.

## Technological accelerators and brakes

Rogers's diffusion theory is perhaps the simplest model for visualizing the historic adoption patterns of established technologies, but it only partially explains why a new media technology will suddenly diffuse into the general consumer market and attain a dominant position. Early adopters may encourage others to try a new technology, but they alone have not been shown to provide the energy needed for rapid acceleration, or to have sufficient influence to significantly affect the introduction and diffusion of a technology.

The diffusion theory cannot adequately explain, for example, why FM radio (which was invented in the early 1930s and provided a far superior means of broadcasting than the original AM radio technology) floundered for three decades and then, in less than 10 years, managed to dethrone its rival all across North America. What was the accelerator? And what had applied the brakes for so long? These are the questions that Brian Winston, a journalism professor at the University of Wales, has attempted to answer.[15]

---

[15]Brian Winston, "How Are Media Born and Developed?" in John Downing, Ali Mohammadi, and Annabelle Sreberny-Mohammadi, eds., *Questioning the Media: A Critical Introduction.* Thousand Oaks, CA: Sage Publications, 1995, pp. 54–74.

Winston blends a strong cultural perspective with the history of media technologies to arrive at a comprehensive explanation of how new media are born and developed. His ideas are based on the following convictions:

- Social, political, and economic forces play powerful roles in the development of new technologies.

- Inventions and innovations are not widely adopted on the merits of a technology alone.

- There must always be an opportunity as well as a motivating social, political, or economic reason for a new technology to be developed.

### Supervening social necessities

In Winston's view, the accelerators that push the development of new media technologies are what he calls **supervening social necessities**. He defines these as "the interfaces between society and technology."[16] They derive from the needs of companies, requirements of other technologies, regulatory or legal actions, and general social forces. In the case of FM radio, the supervening social necessities that emerged in the 1960s fit into all four categories.

***Needs of companies.*** Competition with television was cutting deeply into the profits of large established AM stations, and their future seemed in doubt. By contrast, the dramatically lower costs associated with FM broadcasting made the operation of smaller stations that targeted niche audiences quite profitable and appealing to media companies, entrepreneurs, and investors. Manufacturers were also attracted to FM because it created a new and potentially even larger market for radios.

***Requirements of other technologies.*** Advances in recording and playback technologies, significant improvements in home equipment, and the growing popularity of hi-fi and stereo recordings created the need and demand for high-quality broadcasting technology, which FM readily provided.[17] Stereo, introduced on FM in 1961,

---

[16]Ibid., p. 68.
[17]Lubar, *InfoCulture*, p. 237.

offered radio audiences yet another incentive to switch. The miniaturization of electronic components also made it possible for radio manufacturers to combine AM and FM technologies in more compact receivers, which, in turn, increased the demand for FM stations and new equipment.

*Regulatory and legal actions.* The resolution in the mid-1960s of patent infringement suits finally removed a serious legal impediment to FM's development. But even more important was the 1967 Public Broadcasting Act. This regulatory action established National Public Radio (NPR) as a production center for educational and public affairs broadcasting and reserved space on the FM dial for new public radio stations.

*General social forces.* However, FM owes a great deal of its ultimate success to rock 'n' roll music and to teenagers in the late 1950s and 1960s. Because of AM's broad reach and large undifferentiated audiences, stations tended to broadcast only Top 40 popular music and avoid so-called underground recordings, such as rock 'n' roll, jazz, and blues. The smaller FM stations could afford to target niche audiences, which allowed them to satisfy the musical tastes of teenagers and to provide an outlet for small, independent recording studios.

The increasing popularity of FM music stations among teenagers helped drive demand for new portable and car radios with FM receiver technology. It also attracted advertisers who were trying to reach the affluent young audience, which was rapidly becoming a social and economic force to be reckoned with. By 1969, the average FM listener was about 10 years younger than the average AM listener, and more than half of all Americans listening to radio were tuned to FM stations.

## The law of suppression of radical potential

The law of suppression of radical potential, in Winston's view, applies the brakes that slow the disruptive impact of a new technology upon the social or corporate status quo.[18] Brakes arise from the same four broad categories identified with supervening social neces-

---

[18]Winston, "How Are Media Born and Developed?" p. 69.

sities. The law helps us understand why FM radio took so long to succeed in the general consumer market despite its obvious technical and economic superiority over AM broadcasting.

***Needs of companies.*** In 1933, when Howard Armstrong demonstrated his FM prototype to David Sarnoff, president of the powerful Radio Corporation of America (RCA), AM radio was already well established and generating high profits for manufacturers and broadcasters. Sarnoff recognized that FM represented a revolutionary new radio technology that was far better than AM, but he was not eager to disrupt RCA's substantial profits from AM radio, especially in the midst of the Great Depression.

***Requirements of other technologies.*** In the 1930s RCA was also investing heavily in the development of television, and many of the company's patents involved using the same portion of the radio spectrum that Armstrong was proposing for FM radio. Sarnoff saw television as RCA's next great opportunity and marshaled the company's resources to protect its position.

***Regulatory and legal actions.*** When Armstrong realized that RCA would not back his invention, he decided to push its development on his own. After the **Federal Communications Commission (FCC)** allocated a small range of the radio spectrum for FM broadcasting, he secured licenses to build several stations and begin manufacturing FM radios. Buoyed by his early success, he confidently predicted in 1940 that the existing AM broadcast system would be largely superseded by FM within five years.

But, however farsighted he was about technology, Armstrong underestimated the interest Sarnoff and other broadcasters had in maintaining the status quo, as well as their political clout, particularly with the FCC.[19] At the insistence of RCA and the network broadcasters, the FCC began hearings in 1944 into the appropriate spectrum allocations for television and other **broadcast** technologies that were poised to take off as soon as the war ended. Using dubious evidence to justify its decision, the FCC in 1945 approved the recommendations of the broadcasters to move FM to a different

---

[19]Tom Lewis, *Empire of the Air: The Men Who Made Radio.* New York: HarperCollins, 1991, pp. 300–301.

location in the radio spectrum and give TV broadcasters the portion previously allocated to FM.[20]

With this one ruling, the FCC rendered all of Armstrong's installed FM broadcast equipment and radios obsolete and useless. At the time, there were more than 50 FM broadcast stations and half a million FM radios in operation in the United States.[21]

*General social forces.* The 1929 stock market crash and subsequent global depression significantly reduced consumer demand for new radio sets and caused a shakeout in the radio manufacturing business. Enthusiasm for a new radio technology that would require replacement of existing sets and broadcast equipment was understandably low.

However, even with the financial constraints posed by the Depression, Armstrong managed to attract a credible number of early adopters and investors. Unfortunately, just as FM broadcasting was poised to take off, its commercial development and expansion were abruptly halted by the United States's entry into World War II. After the war, FM technology still had a strong following, but the obsolescence caused by the FCC's change of radio spectrum allocations seriously inhibited continuing support. Moreover, by the end of the 1940s, TV was already rapidly drawing consumer and investor attention away from both AM and FM radio.

## The mediamorphic process

While the preceding hypotheses are integral to the process I call **mediamorphosis**, they only provide general insights into the pacing and timing of technological developments. Before we can even begin to make reasonable judgments about emerging technologies and the future of mainstream media, we need to acquire a broad, integrated knowledge of human communications and the historic patterns of change within the overall system. This knowledge is central to our understanding of the mediamorphic process, which I have defined as: *The transformation of communication media, usually brought*

---

[20]Ibid., pp. 302–303.
[21]Ibid.

*about by the complex interplay of perceived needs, competitive and political pressures, and social and technological innovations.*

Mediamorphosis is not so much a theory as it is a unified way of thinking about the technological evolution of communication media. Instead of studying each form separately, it encourages us to examine all forms as members of an interdependent system, and to note the similarities and relationships that exist among past, present, and emerging forms. By studying the communication system as a whole, we will see that new media do not arise spontaneously and independently—they emerge gradually from the **metamorphosis** of old media. And that when newer forms of communication media emerge, the older forms usually do not die—they continue to evolve and adapt.

The example of FM's delayed success and radio's transformation from a mass-audience medium to a niche-audience medium can also be used to illustrate this key principle of mediamorphosis. As TV began its grand ascent, general-audience radio went into a steep decline that led some analysts to predict the eminent death of the medium. But radio didn't die. Nor was AM entirely subsumed by FM. Instead, AM adapted and through the adoption of new technologies and marketing strategies has steadily become more competitive with FM. Since the beginning of the 1990s, AM radio has been showing strong signs of revival in the United States and elsewhere.

The rapid diffusion of TV also brought about significant transformations within the newspaper, magazine, and film industries, which will be elaborated upon in subsequent chapters. Each was declared a dying medium without the capacity to compete with TV's immediacy and compelling images, yet each proved to be more resilient and adaptable than expected. This also illustrates an important corollary to the **metamorphosis principle:** Established forms of communication media *must* change in response to the emergence of a new medium—their only other option is to die. The metamorphosis principle, as well as several other key principles of mediamorphosis, derive from three concepts—coevolution, convergence, and complexity.

## *Coevolution*

All forms of communication are, as we shall see, tightly woven into the fabric of the human communication system and cannot exist independently from one another in our culture. As each new form emerges and develops, it influences, over time and to varying degrees, the development of every other existing form. **Coevolution** and coexistence, rather than sequential evolution and replacement, have been the norm since the first organisms made their debut on the planet. The wealth of communication technologies we now take for granted would not have been possible if the birth of each new medium had resulted in the simultaneous death of an older medium.

**Communicatory codes.** Specific forms of media, as with species, have life cycles and eventually do die out, but most of their defining traits will always remain part of the system. Just as biological characteristics are propagated from one generation to another through genetic codes, media traits are embodied and carried forward through **communicatory codes** that we call languages. Languages have been, without compare, the most powerful **agents of change** in the course of human evolution.

As we will discover in chapter 3, the development of spoken language and written language brought about two great transformations, or mediamorphoses, within the human communication system. Each of these two classes of language has been responsible for reordering and greatly expanding the human mind in ways that made modern civilization and culture possible. Countless **transforming technologies** affecting all aspects of human life and communication have been inspired and energized by these two agents of change.

Now a third great mediamorphosis resulting from the recent development of a new class of language is poised to once again radically influence the evolution of communication and civilization. For the past two centuries, industrial age and information age technologies have been conjointly contributing to the rapid development and spread of this language, which has only become known to most people in the past two decades. This new class of language is called **digital language**. It is the *lingua franca* of computers and global telecommunication networks.

**Communication domains.** Since the origin of written language, the forms of media have coevolved along three distinct paths that I refer to as domains. These domains, which will be described in the next chapter, have propagated specific sets of media traits that have remained relatively stable for nearly six millennia. But, as we will discover, digital language is already transforming the existing forms of communication media. It is the agent of change most responsible for the present blurring of distinctions between the historic domains of communication.

## Convergence

Nearly every personal computer sold today offers users the ability to play CD-ROMs that blend text and still images with audio and video clips, as well as the opportunity to conveniently dial into global networks and access vast stores of textual and audio/visual information. This is just one of the more obvious examples of the concept known as media **convergence**. The idea that diverse technologies and forms of media are coming together now seems almost commonplace, but not so long ago it was considered quite visionary.[22]

In 1979, when Nicholas Negroponte began popularizing the concept in his lecture tours to raise funds for a building to house the Media Lab at the Massachusetts Institute of Technology, few people had any comprehension of convergence. Audiences were often astonished by Negroponte's revelation that "all communication technologies are suffering a joint metamorphosis, which can only be understood properly if treated as a single subject."[23] To illustrate this concept, Negroponte drew three overlapping circles labeled "broadcast and motion picture industry," "computer industry," and "print and publishing industry" (see Exhibit 1.2). Since then, the notion that these industries are coming together to create new forms of communication has shaped much of the thinking about the future of **mass media** and human communications.

*Multimedia forms of communication.* Negroponte and others at MIT are credited with being among the first to recognize that this convergence of media industries and digital technologies would ultimately lead to new forms of so-called multimedia communication. **Multimedia,** or mixed media as it is also known, is generally defined as any medium in which two or more forms of communication are integrated.

---

[22]For a more detailed explanation of convergence, see John V. Pavlik and Everette E. Dennis, "The Coming of Convergence and Its Consequences," chapter 1 in Pavlik and Dennis, eds., *Demystifying Media Technology: Readings from the Freedom Forum Media Studies Center.* Mountain View, CA: Mayfield, 1993, pp. 1–4.

[23]Quoted in Stewart Brand, *The Media Lab: Inventing the Future at MIT.* New York: Viking Penguin, 1987, p. 11.

**Exhibit 1.2** The MIT Media Lab's construct of convergence.

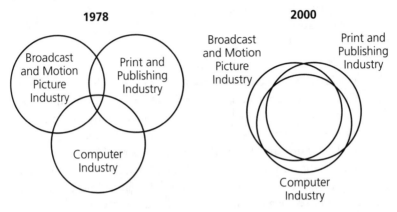

Within the broadest definition of the term, most printed newspapers and magazines qualify as forms of multimedia because they convey information through a blend of written words, photography, and graphics displayed on a paper medium. However, the visions of multimedia popularized in the past two decades have tended to dismiss paper as an "old" medium. The preferred "new" medium for displaying blended content is the electronic screen. With an electronic display medium, such as a computer monitor or television screen, new multimedia systems are capable of conveying information through various blends of full-motion video, animation and sounds, as well as still images and written words.

*Misinterpretations of convergence.* While the concept of media convergence, as promoted by Negroponte and the MIT Media Lab, has provided a popular and useful tool for comprehending some of the changes now taking place within established media businesses, it has also been prone to misinterpretation. Common assumptions that the present convergence will lead to fewer forms of communication, or ultimately to the demise of established forms such as newspapers and magazines, are not supported by historic evidence. Everett Rogers and other media scholars have clearly shown that "the history of communication is the story of 'more.'"[24] Rather than consolidating or replacing older forms, newer forms have tended to

---

[24]Rogers, *Communication Technology,* p. 26.

diverge and add to the media mix. To be fair, when Negroponte drew the three overlapping circles, he was not attempting to predict outcomes as some people have suggested. He was merely pointing out regions of potential opportunities for new media development.

Two other common misinterpretations are the beliefs that convergence is something new to this period of time and that it primarily involves **mergers**. Convergence has, in fact, always been essential to evolution and the mediamorphic process. Large-scale convergences as we are now seeing within the media and telecommunication industries may occur only occasionally, but the forms of media that exist today are actually the result of innumerable small-scale convergences that have occurred frequently throughout time. Even though merger and convergence are often used synonymously, they do not mean the same thing. A merger implies that two or more entities (for example, companies, technologies, or media) are coming together to form a single, integrated entity. Convergence is more like a crossing of paths or marriage, which results in the transformation of each converging entity, as well as the creation of new entities.

### Complexity

During periods of great change, such as we are now experiencing, everything around us may appear to be in a state of chaos and, to a large extent, it is. **Chaos** is an essential component of change. Without it, the universe would be a dead place and life would be impossible. Out of chaos comes the new ideas that transform and vitalize systems.

*Chaos theory.* A central tenet of contemporary chaos theory is the notion that seemingly insignificant events or slight initial variations within **chaotic systems,** such as the weather and the economy, can trigger cascades of escalating, unpredictable occurrences that ultimately lead to consequential or catastrophic events. This aspect of the theory is often illustrated by the example of a butterfly flapping its wings in China and causing a hurricane to develop off the coast of Florida.

Chaotic systems are essentially anarchistic. That is, they exhibit nearly infinite variability with no predictable long-term patterns, which explains why precise long-range weather and national economic forecasts are all but impossible. It also explains why no one will ever be able to accurately predict which specific new media technologies and forms of communication will ultimately succeed and which will fail.

The importance of chaos to our understanding of mediamorphosis and the development of new media is actually less in the theory than in its connection to another related concept—complexity. In this context, *complexity* refers to the events that take place within certain apparently chaotic systems. The study of complexity has been fostered by a group of scientists from different disciplines who founded the Santa Fe Institute in New Mexico in the mid-1980s.

Chaos and order, like birth and death, are opposite extremes of all complex, or so-called *living systems*. According to physicist Mitchell Waldrop, the edge of chaos is "where new ideas and innovative genotypes are forever nibbling away at the edges of the status quo."[25]

**Complex, adaptive systems.** Research conducted at the Santa Fe Institute has led to several insights central to the mediamorphic process. As scientists studied the behavior of complex systems, they discovered that the richness of the interactions that occur within living systems allows them to undergo *spontaneous self-organization* in response to changing conditions. In other words, complex systems are *adaptive*, in that "they don't just passively respond to events the way a rock might roll around in an earthquake. They actively try to turn whatever happens to their advantage."[26]

By recognizing that the human communication system is, in fact, a complex, adaptive system, we can see that all forms of media live in a dynamic, interdependent universe. When external pressures are applied and new innovations are introduced, each form of communication is affected by an intrinsic self-organizing process that spontaneously occurs within the system. Just as species evolve for better survival in a changing environment, so do forms of communication and established media enterprises. This process is the essence of mediamorphosis.

---

[25]M. Mitchell Waldrop, *Complexity: The Emerging Science at the Edge of Order and Chaos.* New York: Touchstone, 1992, p. 12.

[26]Ibid., p. 11.

# Principles of mediamorphosis in perspective

This chapter furnishes a number of general insights into the adoption and implementation of new media technologies that are used in subsequent chapters to guide our thinking about the next stage in the transformation of mainstream media and emerging computer-mediated communications. The following *six fundamental principles of mediamorphosis* flow from the hypotheses discussed in this chapter:

1. *Coevolution and coexistence:* All forms of communication media coexist and coevolve within an expanding, complex adaptive system. As each new form emerges and develops, it influences, over time and to varying degrees, the development of every other existing form.

2. *Metamorphosis:* New media do not arise spontaneously and independently—they emerge gradually from the metamorphosis of older media. When newer forms emerge, the older forms tend to adapt and continue to evolve rather than die.

3. *Propagation:* Emerging forms of communication media propagate dominant traits from earlier forms. These traits are passed on and spread through communicatory codes called languages.

4. *Survival:* All forms of communication media, as well as media enterprises, are compelled to adapt and evolve for survival in a changing environment. Their only other option is to die.

5. *Opportunity and need.* New media are not widely adopted on the merits of a technology alone. There must always be an opportunity, as well as a motivating social, political, and/or economic reason for a new media technology to be developed.

6. *Delayed adoption:* New media technologies always take longer than expected to become commercial successes. They tend to require *at least* one human generation (20–30 years) to progress from proof of concept to widespread adoption.

The next chapter defines the three primary domains within the human communication system and examines the relationships and inherent traits that exist among the various forms. By combining the principles of mediamorphosis with an understanding of the attributes that have shaped the development of communication media in the past, we can gain valuable insights into the new forms that may emerge early in the next century as well as the ways in which existing forms may adapt and continue to evolve.

# domains of communication media

Not so many generations ago, family trees were used within nearly all cultures to establish a person's role and place in the world as well as to reveal his or her most probable future path. And even though individual genealogies are no longer taken as seriously as they once were, they continue to provide valuable clues to people's present and future condition. We know, for example, that distinguishing characteristics and the predisposition to a variety of diseases and afflictions can be genetically propagated from generation to generation. Through photo albums, letters and stories, medical histories, and relatives, people have been able to gain a great deal of knowledge about themselves and possible health problems they may face in the future.

As we will discover in this chapter, family trees and histories can be just as valuable to our understanding of mediamorphosis and the continuing evolution of human communications. But, to reveal the probable paths of existing and emerging media, we need to group the contemporary forms of communication according to their familial relationships and then determine which of their traits have been and are most likely to continue being propagated.

## Categorizing the forms of communication

Numerous terms are routinely and interchangeably used to identify various groupings of media. Newspapers and magazines, for instance, can be grouped under such headings as Print Media, Typographic Media, Information Media, News Media, The Press, Periodicals, and Mass Media. The possible category headings for radio, television, film, and other popular forms of communication media are no less extensive. While each is valid, all, in my view, are too exclusive and limiting for comparative purposes. Print and Broadcast Media, for example, only include relatively recent forms even though older, closely related forms are still part of the contemporary media mix.

I have therefore chosen to construct a three-part classification scheme loosely based upon a new system for classifying living creatures proposed by Carl Woese, a biologist at the University of Illinois.[1] In this scheme, the individual forms of communication are grouped into three domains, or primary branches, according to their inherent dominant traits, which are identified later in this chapter. I have labeled the domains the interpersonal, broadcast, and document.

The **interpersonal domain** includes those forms that involve two-way exchanges of information, as in face-to-face conversation and telephony. This is the only domain that offers the possibility of unmediated communication. Although the term *interpersonal* suggests communication between individuals, I have extended the definition to include those interactive communications between humans and computers where the computer program assumes the role of a surrogate human.

The **broadcast domain**, in this scheme, encompasses more than radio and television. I have taken the liberty of expanding the contemporary definition of broadcast beyond modern electronic media to include all forms of mediated communication that involve the dissemination to audiences of structured aural/visual content, such as art, film, theater, and public speeches. By audiences, I mean individuals or groups who are cast in the role of spectators or observers.

The **document domain** includes all mediated forms that involve the dissemination of structured handwritten or typographic and visual content to individuals primarily through portable media, such

---

[1]Instead of grouping all living things into five kingdoms based on fundamental characteristics, Carl Woese developed a three-part classification scheme in 1990 that organizes life forms according to the genetic code contained in their DNA. In Woese's scheme, the tree of life divides into three primary branches, or domains, which he has labeled as Bacteria, Archaea (primitive microbes that dwell in extreme environments), and Eucarya (everything else from amoebas and protozoa to plants and animals).

as newspapers, magazines, and books. Also included are the page-based forms that reside on computer networks, such as the World Wide Web.

Although scientists can only speculate about the origins of human communication, they are certain that the primordial, non-linguistic forms were interpersonal. The emergence of speech and spoken language some 30,000 years ago greatly extended the inter-personal domain and also caused the first major branching, which would ultimately lead to the development of broadcast forms. The second major branching occurred about 6,000 years ago with the emergence of written language. This branch grew rather quickly and gave shape to the document domain.

The family tree of communication media, as it exists today, can be visualized as a complex structure with many minor branches in all three domains (see Exhibit 2.1). New branches have formed even more rapidly since the application of electricity to communication and the emergence of digital language in the nineteenth century. Given our present understanding of the mediamorphic process, we can be reasonably confident that the tree will grow vastly more com-plex in the twenty-first century. The evolution of the media domains is examined more extensively in chapters 3–4. In the remainder of this chapter, we examine the characteristics of the three domains and compare their distinctive traits.

## The interpersonal domain

Interpersonal forms have at their locus human speech and nonver-bal methods of exchanging information, such as facial expressions, sign languages, and physical contact. These are highly participatory and interactive forms that rely extensively on memory and context. People engaged in interpersonal communication do not draw so much from stored or recorded messages as they do from their own experiences and emotions.

All forms of communication included in this domain involve two-way exchanges of information between individuals or between individuals and computer programs acting as human surrogates. Interpersonal forms are set apart from all other forms by their near-ly total lack of human mediation. That is, they may employ tech-nological mediators, such as telephones and personal computers, as

**Exhibit 2.1** The family tree of communication media.

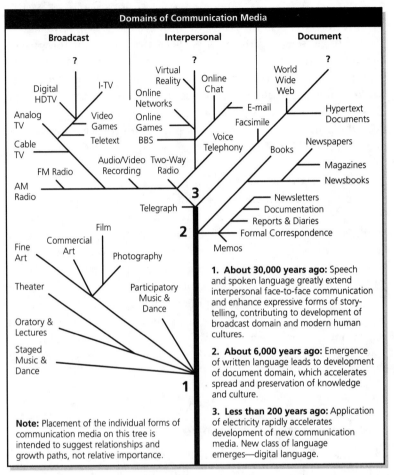

**Note:** Placement of the individual forms of communication media on this tree is intended to suggest relationships and growth paths, not relative importance.

1. **About 30,000 years ago:** Speech and spoken language greatly extend interpersonal face-to-face communication and enhance expressive forms of story-telling, contributing to development of broadcast domain and modern human cultures.

2. **About 6,000 years ago:** Emergence of written language leads to development of document domain, which accelerates spread and preservation of knowledge and culture.

3. **Less than 200 years ago:** Application of electricity rapidly accelerates development of new communication media. New class of language emerges—digital language.

well as language mediators, such as professional translators, to facilitate communication across time, distances, and cultures, but otherwise are devoid of external content control and manipulation.

Interpersonal communication tends to be loosely structured and does not need to be conveyed in a sequential or contiguous manner to be understood. Several threads of thought can be interwoven throughout single or multiple interchanges without losing meaning and context. In group conversations, for example, each person may respond to the specific questions or comments of other participants while also introducing or expanding on her or his own topics of interest. One participant may attempt to dominate the flow of a conversation, but the other participants are still capable of interrupting and changing the course of the conversation at any time.

Because interpersonal communication is highly spontaneous and often emotionally charged, the informational content tends to be of a more immediate and ephemeral nature than either the broadcast or document forms. Prior to the development of the telegraph, telephone, and sound recording systems, none of the forms within this family could be accurately preserved, replicated, or transported.

## Immediate and delayed forms of interpersonal communication

Interpersonal communication can be defined as either immediate or delayed. Immediate forms include face-to-face encounters and participatory interactions, such as jam sessions and karioke singing, that take place within the range of human senses and in real time. These are space- and time-bound forms. With immediate oral communications, for example, messages are gone the moment that last sound dies. Only the people who are actually present in the same place and time are able to hear and respond to the messages. The introduction of the telephone extended the reach of face-to-face interactions, but did not overcome the space and time constraints of immediate interpersonal communications.

Delayed forms of interpersonal exchanges occur when the two-way flow of information between participants is interrupted by significant gaps of time, as with voice, written, and electronic mail. The ancient Romans are credited with developing the essential infrastructure and procedures for regular mail service, which blends attributes of the interpersonal and document domains. The concept of technologically mediated, delayed interpersonal communication was introduced by the telegraph. But, unlike the telephone and written correspondence, the telegraph required skilled intermediaries to encode and decode the messages sent "by wire" between the participants.

## Twentieth-century forms of interpersonal communication

The forms of technologically mediated interpersonal communication have been greatly expanded in this century. Amateur shortwave radio, which blossomed in the 1920s, continues to offer two-way, immediate communication between individuals around the globe and is often used to assist in the wake of natural disasters. Citizens band (CB) radio, which suddenly became popular with a large segment of the general public in the late 1970s (and just as suddenly faded a few years later), continues to be used by ranchers and cross-country truckers. Digital fax has provided a convenient and popular form of delayed interpersonal communication since the early 1980s.

Early in the 1990s, "talk" radio and television programs, in which members of the audience are able to interact "on-the-air" via telephone with celebrity hosts, began attracting large regional and national audiences in the United States. While these popular shows are promoted as extended interpersonal conversations, they actually function as a broadcast form of entertainment. This form of communication might be more appropriately defined as "low-tech" interactive radio and television.

## Cyber media

After more than two decades of slow development, the exchange of electronic mail between computer users finally gained widespread acceptance, particularly for global business communications, in the mid-1990s. Variations of electronic mail, such as "online chat" and interactive **bulletin board services,** are becoming increasingly popular and have contributed significantly to the growth of consumer online services such as **America Online (AOL)** and **CompuServe,** as well as to the rise of so-called **cyber communities.** Even though electronic mail and **chat** involve the written word, they are fundamentally unstructured extensions of oral communication that provide a way for people to interact spontaneously without external human mediation.

The phenomenal expansion of the Internet and consumer online services has focused increasing attention on **computer-mediated communication (CMC)** and its implications for established media companies. With an estimated 50 million people interacting and exchanging information through CMC networks worldwide, this technology can no longer be dismissed as a fad or an underground network for techies.

While CMC was originally developed to facilitate information exchanges, new and generally unexpected forms of communication are emerging from the convergences of various computer and communication technologies. These forms, which I have placed into the **cyber media** family, now include **multiuser** games and virtual reality systems, as well as the various forms of electronic mail and bulletin boards.

As computer networks become faster and more powerful, they will have an increasing capacity to incorporate programs that function more like surrogate humans. With future cyber technologies, we may not know, or even care, if the "person" we are interacting with is another human or a digital entity.

## The broadcast domain

From this extended perspective, the broadcast forms can be seen as having evolved from nonlinguistic aural and visual communications, such as modulated sounds (for example, singing, chanting, and drum beats), ritual dances, and cave paintings. These are generally considered to be among the earliest forms of human communication, although more and more scientists are coming to believe that the development of speech and spoken language may actually have paralleled or even preceded their emergence.

This has historically been the least interactive and most receptively passive of the communication domains. Nearly all of the informational content is externally processed by mediators, such as clerics, artists, musicians, actors, and teachers, who control the production and selection of content, as well as the pacing, sequencing, and timing of its delivery. The development and spread of religious and political ceremonies, public storytelling, and staged performances encouraged the growth of large passive audiences and ultimately led to the twentieth-century notion of **mass communication.**

All forms of communication included in this domain involve essentially one-way transfers of mediated information from one individual or group to another individual or group. These forms, both ancient and modern, have tended to involve people at an emotional, sensory level. They generally convey feelings and thoughts connected to human experiences and spiritual beliefs.

## Linear and landscape structures of the broadcast domain

While exceptions can be found, particularly in art, most forms defined by this domain have historically presented their content in a linear, or sequential, manner. A movie, for example, is presented as an unvarying sequence of acts and scenes, telling its story the same way each time it is viewed. Consequently, most broadcast forms are time bound. That is, the segments of information are fixed by the producer and cannot be readily transcended or altered by individual members of an audience. For instance, we can only access broadcast television and radio news at the times assigned by the stations. But with newspapers and magazines, which belong to the document domain, we can read the news whenever we like. Furthermore, we can read a newspaper or magazine in any order we like, whereas with TV and radio we get the news in the order decided by someone else.

The predominantly visual forms of the broadcast domain appear to have derived most of their underlying structure and shape from nature. Stages in theaters and concert halls, for example, present audiences with rectangular frames that are wider than they are tall. This permits panoramic, three-dimensional views that simulate outdoor landscapes and real-life environments. Most works of art and photographs that depict scenes from nature or groupings of people have historically been defined by rectangular shapes that also have a greater width than height. As film and television evolved, they, too, took on the classic landscape orientation of theater and art.

## Problems with preservation of broadcast information

Like interpersonal communication, broadcast forms have not, until recently, been easily preserved, replicated, or transported. Expressive devices, such as poetry, legends and myths, prayers, and theatrical and dance narratives, have been developed by all oral cultures to facilitate the memorization of long, complex stories and human records.[2] But even with these devices, oral communications

---

[2]Annabelle Sreberny-Mohammadi, "Forms of Media as Ways of Knowing," in John Downing, Ali Mohammadi, and Annabelle Sreberny-Mohammadi, eds., *Questioning the Media: A Critical Introduction*. Thousand Oaks, CA: Sage Publications, 1995, p. 28.

have been inherently unreliable for preserving information across time and distance. Much of oral history has been lost to future generations by breaks in the chains of trained story "rememberers" and cultural upheavals. Art forms, particularly paintings and sculptures, would seem to be exceptions; but, without understandable written explanations, they, too, have tended to quickly lose their original meaning and social context.

Even though modern sound and image recording technologies, such as music CDs, film, and video tape, have extended our ability to preserve, replicate, and transport the broadcast forms, none of the storage and presentation media used today is expected to survive or to be decipherable for more than a few centuries without frequent copying. Many important films have already faded or crumbled into dust. Most video tapes and color photographs begin to deteriorate within a few years, and digital data stored on optical compact discs (CDs and CD-ROMs) are not expected to be readable for more than 30 years due to technological obsolescence and materials decay.[3]

## *Electronic broadcast media*

Until the middle of the nineteenth century, staged performances, music, dance, and art changed only gradually, and then only because of changing tastes and styles within societies. But an explosion of technological and social innovations in the latter half of the nineteenth century and first half of the twentieth led to widespread mediamorphosis within the broadcast domain. Several new forms were born, each adapting the content of earlier forms. Photography developed to fill an increasing demand for portrait and landscape art. Sound recordings extended access to musical performances and public speakers. Silent film employed elements of theater and art (photography). The "talkies" were an outgrowth of silent film and sound recording. Radio also drew upon the theater, musical performances, and public speakers for its content. Television, in turn, borrowed heavily from radio, film, and theater.

With the emergence of electronic **broadcast media**, the size of audiences was greatly expanded. Instead of performing for a few hundred people at one time, an entertainer or speaker could potentially be seen and heard simultaneously, or nearly simultaneously, by

---

[3]Jeff Rotherberg, "Ensuring the Longevity of Digital Documents," *Scientific American* (January 1995): 42–47.

tens of millions of people across nations and even around the globe. The power of radio and television to influence the interests and tastes of large audiences, as well as individual buying decisions, was not missed by politicians and commercial enterprises.

Since the 1970s, computer technologies have begun to introduce elements of the interpersonal and document forms into electronic broadcast media. For example, broadcast **teletext** services can display "pages" of information on TV screens using a special decoder technology and remote control. All electronic forms of the broadcast domain are expected to become less passive and more **interactive** with the further development and application of digital language.

## The document domain

The **document** domain emerged with the development of written languages, which makes it the most recently evolved of the three domains. Documents combine a distinctive set of attributes with a number of qualities drawn from the interpersonal and broadcast domains. Like the broadcast domain, most forms within this category transfer information from one to many or few to many, but they give the individual audience members more active control over the communication process, as in the interpersonal domain. This is a significant difference that sets books, newspapers, and magazines apart from television, radio, and film.

Among the most important distinctive attributes of the document forms have been portability, convenience, simplicity, and reliability. Nearly all documents can be easily shared and read in practically any location, in any way, and at any time that is convenient and comfortable for the reader. No other forms of communication have, so far, been able to surpass documents in their ability to reliably preserve, replicate, and transport information across distances and time. However, because of the time required to compose and deliver written documents, all communication within this domain has historically been delayed.

### Reader control of documents

In most cases, the informational content of documents is externally processed by mediators who control the production and selection but, unlike the broadcast forms, the individual readers retain control over the pacing, sequencing, and timing. Instead of passively observing, readers of documents are actively seeking information.

Reading a document is much like driving a car. Readers, like drivers, can determine their own routes and travel at their own pace, on their own schedules. By comparison, watching or listening to most broadcast forms is like taking a bus or train—control of the speed, route, and schedule is in the hands of someone else.

The structure and flow of information in document forms can be either linear or nonlinear. Traditionally, written stories are sequentially structured by authors and editors, whereas reference materials are designed primarily for nonsequential reading. However, readers do not have to process written material as the producers have intended. Readers can scan and jump from one point to another within a sequentially written story or set of stories, as with newspapers and magazines, or read a reference book in a linear manner if they choose to do so.

## Abstract representations of document information

In the document domain, content and context are conveyed abstractly through phonetic alphabets or pictographic characters rather than through natural sounds and images. Readers must interpret the written words and symbols and give them meaning. Consequently, reading and browsing written information requires a greater amount of internal analytic processing by receivers than do most broadcast forms. Documents can affect people on an emotional level but they tend to be most effective in their ability to stimulate the imagination and facilitate abstract and analytical thinking.

Because most forms of documents have historically been defined by two-dimensional pages or surfaces, their content tends to be spatially (page) bound rather than time bound. While a reader may mentally assign a personal time commitment to a document based on the number of pages or length of a story, the actual time devoted to the content is variable and totally within the reader's control.

## Portrait orientation of documents

Documents appear to have taken most of their underlying structure and shape from the physical characteristics of humans (see Exhibit 2.2). While there is no consensus as to why the rectangular pages of

**Exhibit 2.2** Comparison of portrait and landscape orientations.

Landscape (horizontal)

Portrait (vertical)

documents are predominantly portrait oriented (taller than they are wide), the reason, as the word *portrait* suggests, may have something to do with the shape of the human face and body.

When people communicate face-to-face, they do so in close proximity to one another. In this situation, the eyes tend to focus on the vertical, rectangular image of the person in front of them. Thus, there is no need for people to make use of horizontal parallax (provided in humans by the spacing between their horizontally set eyes) or peripheral vision to discern distance and movement in three-dimensional space, as they do when viewing panoramic landscapes or staged performances from afar. There is some evidence that dealing at close range with the density of information contained in most documents may require the eyes to focus more narrowly on relatively small, vertical segments. Readability and eye-tracking studies, for example, have frequently shown that people tend to read more quickly and comfortably when columns of text are set in relatively narrow widths, as they are in most newspapers and magazines.

For whatever reasons, the portrait orientation of documents is firmly rooted in human cultures—it is a standard humans seem to have preferred since the beginning of written history. Other shapes and orientations have been tried, but documents that rely mainly on the written word and page-based structures have been predominantly rectangular and portrait oriented in nearly every culture. Even ancient clay tablets and scrolls were mostly designed to be read as vertical (portrait-oriented) pages.

## Print media

Until Johann Gutenberg invented a simple tool for casting reusable, movable type in the mid-1400s, document technologies had remained relatively stable. The most significant technological changes had been in the materials upon which documents were written and in the methods of binding the materials together. With the spread of printing presses, new forms of documents, such as newspapers, magazines, and novels began to emerge. While these forms were primarily extensions of earlier hand-written newsletters, newsbooks, and narratives, the development of **print** technology brought about a great change in the frequency and the number of copies that could be economically produced and distributed.

Publishing technologies introduced in the nineteenth century vastly increased the quantity and variety of documents in the world and made modern **print media** possible. By the middle of the twentieth century, printing technologies had evolved to the point where newspapers and magazines could regularly provide large numbers of readers with vast amounts of timely information, graphic material, and high-quality color. The introduction of computer technologies in the late 1960s brought further improvements in quality and efficiency, but they had no direct influence on the physical form. The form and content of documents remained confined, as they had always been, to two-dimensional pages defined by their width and height.

## Hypertext and hypermedia documents

Only since the introduction of personal computers in the 1980s have documents begun to take on a third dimension—depth—through the use of a technology known as **hypertext**.[4] With hypertext documents, elements of pages can be linked directly to other pages in a

---

[4]The term *hypertext* is generally credited to Ted Nelson. While in graduate school in 1960, Nelson became thoroughly frustrated with his efforts to keep track of his notes on file cards. For him, all methods of using paper to manage information seemed inadequate and imposed restrictions that masked the true structure of his ideas. While most contemporary computer systems and online computer networks have adopted many of the hypertext concepts that Nelson developed in his long quest, none has yet fully realized his larger vision of a world where "instantaneous electronic literature," as he calls it, is universally available. A more detailed explanation of this hypertext vision can be found in *Literary Machines* by Theodor Holm Nelson. This book is self-published and is frequently updated.

•

nonsequential manner. For example, a reader can click on a person's name and immediately receive a biography and picture of that person. A more advanced version, called **hypermedia,** has added a fourth dimension—time—by incorporating links to audio and video elements. When selected, a still photo or graphic, for instance, can turn into a full-motion **video clip.**

Hypertext and hypermedia represent the first significant changes within the document domain brought about by the influence of digital language. These concepts are now frequently used by publishers for electronic books distributed on CD-ROMs and floppy disks, as well as for electronic editions of publications developed for the World Wide Web and online computer services.


## Inherited media traits

Now that we have broadly described the three primary branches of this classification scheme, we can begin to identify and compare the distinctive traits that are shared by specific forms of media within the human communication system. By learning to recognize and apply these traits, we can gain insights not only into how forms of communication media have evolved in the past but also into how they may be transformed in the future.

As with human families, some traits can be easily recognized through many generations, whereas others may disappear in one generation and reappear in another. Because the forms of media are not strictly isolated from one another within the human communication system, coevolving forms from different domains can occasionally converge and produce new forms that exhibit a blend of traits from each domain. Although genetic models cannot precisely determine which traits will be exhibited by individual offspring, they can be used to narrow the range of possibilities and provide valuable clues to the probable future path of each family. This is essentially the approach I have taken for evaluating the future direction of communication media in chapters 7–9.

For comparative purposes, I have listed in Table 2.1 some of the defining traits within each media domain. Three criteria have been used for comparing the domains: (1) content flow and control; (2) presentation and format; and (3) reception and constraints. The following explanations include insights that I have arrived at independently through observation and research.

**Table 2.1** Dominant traits of media domains

| | Media Domains | | |
|---|---|---|---|
| | **Interpersonal** | **Broadcast** | **Document** |
| Flow and control | Unmediated | Mediated | Mediated |
| | Two-way | One-way | One-way |
| | Participants | Producers/ Spectators | Editors/ Seekers |
| | Unscheduled | Scheduled | Scheduled |
| Presentation and Format | Oral/expressive | Aural/visual | Textual/visual |
| | Unstructured | Structured | Structured |
| | Nonlinear/linear | Linear | Nonlinear/ linear |
| | Portrait (human faces) | Landscape (3-D panoramas) | Portrait (2-D pages) |
| Reception and Constraints | Spontaneous | Immediate | Deliberate |
| | Interactive | Passive | Active |
| | Time/space bound | Time bound | Space bound (surface) |
| | Mobile | Fixed location | Portable |

**Note:** The terms used in this table are intentionally generalized to facilitate comparisons.

## Flow and control of communication

This category focuses on the content and delivery of messages. It compares traits that influence the information contained in messages and the process of dissemination, as well as the relationships between senders and receivers.

*Mediation.* In face-to-face conversations, the content and flow of messages are controlled directly by sender and receiver. Because no intermediaries are involved, this is classed as an *unmediated* form of communication. However, nearly all of the broadcast and document forms employ intermediaries who do have the power to influence the content and flow of messages. For this reason, they are collectively regarded as *mediated* forms.

*Direction.* Even though an individual may dominate a conversation, all interpersonal communications are fundamentally *bidirectional.*

With the broadcast and document forms, messages generally flow from senders to receivers without the expectation of a response. Audiences may provide feedback through letters, surveys, or monitoring systems that influence future content, but the message flow remains essentially *unidirectional.*

*Gatekeepers and audiences.* Among the interpersonal forms, senders and receivers are usually equal participants in the exchange of messages. With the exception of moderated meetings and debates, no one is assigned the task of controlling a conversation's flow or content.

Within the broadcast and document domains, so-called gatekeepers control which stories will be told, as well as how and when. These gatekeepers are the managers, aggregators, and distillers of information and entertainment. The relationships between gatekeepers and audiences, however, are not the same in both domains.

Nearly all broadcast forms are based on a producer–spectator relationship. Producers are expected to actively control the communication process and spectators are expected to passively accept that control. In practice, spectators are not quite so passive, but they still tend to defer control of broadcast "events" and messages to the producers.

Most document forms are based on an editor–seeker relationship. Editors are primarily assigned the task of validating, filtering, organizing, and presenting content on behalf of their audiences who are typically active seekers of information and entertainment. Seekers tend to be more involved in the communication process and more selective than spectators.

*Scheduling and timing.* The scheduling and timing of communications within the interpersonal domain tend to be unplanned and are usually jointly determined by the participants. Within the broadcast and document domains, the producers and editors generally schedule the delivery times. But with documents, readers can determine when they will read and for how long.

## Presentation and format of communication

This category compares traits that influence the structure and presentation of content and communications.

**Language.** Interpersonal forms of communication rely on the spoken word and nonlinguistic expression, such as body language, physical contact, and participatory music and dance. Even though memos, faxes, and electronic mail involve written language, they are extensions of oral forms of interpersonal presentation. Broadcast forms, as defined in this scheme, convey their content primarily through aural and visual media. They tend to appeal more directly to the senses than either interpersonal or document forms of communication. Documents rely almost exclusively on written (handwritten and printed) language. But they also often include visual elements, such as photographs and illustrations.

**Structure.** While established social courtesies impose some structure on interpersonal communication, it is essentially unstructured. Structure is imposed on the content of broadcast and document forms by the requirements and constraints of their particular media technologies, as well as by the mediators.

**Content.** All forms of the broadcast domain, with the exception of art forms, have historically presented their content in a sequential, or linear, fashion. Each scene or set follows one after the other from beginning to end. Viewers or listeners cannot easily skip ahead to see or hear what's coming next, or individually alter the sequences. With interpersonal and document forms, content can be presented in either a linear or nonlinear fashion. Informal conversations often digress and weave multiple thoughts together nonsequentially. Newspapers intentionally package their content to facilitate nonlinear browsing even though stories are generally written in a linear style.

**Image orientation.** During face-to-face conversations, most participants focus their eyes on each other's face or body, where height is greater than width. Most forms of documents have historically used a similar "portrait," or vertical, orientation for the presentation of content. With few exceptions, the pages of newspapers, magazines, books, and letters are universally portrait oriented. Most visual forms of the broadcast domain, such as theater, film, and television, have adopted a "landscape," or horizontal, orientation to frame three-dimensional scenes and panoramic images.

## Reception and constraints of communication

This category compares traits that influence the way message receivers deal with communication media.

*Interactions.* All forms of interpersonal communication are interactive. That is, in nearly all cases, there is the expectation of a spontaneous and nearly instantaneous response.

The situation within the broadcast domain is far more complex. While there is an expectation of immediacy with nearly all broadcast forms, audience interactions with each form can be quite diverse. When people view a movie at a theater, for instance, the room is dark and the audience is expected to be silent. In this environment, film can take on a dreamlike quality and evoke strong emotional responses. The same movie viewed at home on a TV set tends to take on a more social quality. The degree of audience involvement in a home is affected by a variety of factors. If viewed on a commercial channel, intrusive ads fragment the experience and encourage channel switching or conversations that disrupt the mood. With premium satellite or cable channels, the film is not interrupted by commercials, but viewers must still arrange their schedules to match the times designated by the channel operators. Video cassettes and VCRs give viewers much more control and thus elicit a different set of responses. Some viewers, for example, use their VCRs to scan prerecorded movies much the way they scan books and periodicals, fast-forwarding through the dull scenes and replaying the exciting ones. (With more advanced digital recording and playback systems, such as digital versatile disk [DVD], viewers will have an even greater capacity for rapidly scanning and interacting with recorded video.) Viewers also interact differently when they are alone than they do with other people. However, despite this variability of interactions, a strong argument can still be made that audiences are *comparatively* more passive with these forms than with interpersonal and document forms of communication.

The act of reading requires active involvement and concentration on the reader's part. Even though documents are structured by authors and editors according to their requirements, readers can interact with documents as they chose. They can read documents in segments at different times, skip ahead to see what happens next or read the endings first, or read only those portions that match their interests.

*Limitations.* In the interpersonal domain, communication is constrained by time and space. Even with telephones, participants must be copresent at the same time and in the same virtual space. That is, they may be in different cities, but the medium effectively collapses the distance between them by creating the illusion of shared space. Even when there is a time delay, as with facsimile and electronic mail, there is a strong expectation of quick responses.

Nearly all broadcast forms, such as radio, television, and theater, are bound by time. Audiences can only listen to or view performances at the times and for the durations set by the producers. Recorded forms give audiences greater control over the times when they can listen or watch, but the duration time is still set by the producers.

Documents are essentially free of time and space constraints. Readers can interact with documents at any time and in any place that is comfortable and convenient for them. However, the size and number of pages are determined by the producer. If the content doesn't fit, the editor and/or author must fill or cut the material to the space allowed.

*Location.* Interpersonal forms allow for a high degree of mobility. Location is mutually determined by the participants. With most broadcast forms, location is relatively fixed. It is determined by the location of the device (TV set, radio, film projector) or by the venue (theater, concert hall, art gallery). The miniaturization of electronic devices has increased the mobility of some radios and TV sets, but they still require listeners and viewers to be within the broadcast range of the stations they prefer. Documents are, by design, portable. They can be easily read almost anywhere—on airplanes, in coffee shops, or on park benches.

## Domains of communication media in perspective

Organizing the forms of media into three domains—interpersonal, broadcast, and document—provides a means to readily identify and compare the inherent qualities that define each primary branch of the human communication system. These domains and their dominant traits can be summarized as follows:

- The interpersonal domain: Includes one-to-one forms of oral/expressive communication whose content is not structured or influenced by external mediators. Also includes communications between humans and computers where the computer program is a surrogate human.

- The broadcast domain: Includes mediated, few-to-many forms of aural/visual communication whose content is highly structured and presented to audiences sequentially from beginning to end in relatively fixed locations and in scheduled, predetermined periods of time.

- The document domain: Includes mediated, few-to-many forms of textual/visual communication whose content is packaged and presented to individuals primarily through portable media. Also included are page-based electronic forms that reside on computer networks, such as the World Wide Web.

As will be seen in subsequent chapters, the traits that define these domains have been shaped over the course of many thousands of years by two agents of change—spoken language and written language. With each great metamorphosis that followed the development and spread of these agents, new media emerged and existing media were transformed within each domain. Throughout this long and sporadic process, the distinctions among the domains have been maintained by the relatively predictable propagation of their dominant traits. But, since the 1970s, the swift spread of digital language within all three media domains has brought us to a new and radically different stage in the accelerating evolution and expansion of the human communication system—a stage that might be appropriately referred to as the era of digital engineering.

Just as genetic engineering offers the potential for creating new genotypes that blend characteristics of naturally incompatible species, digital engineering is likely to confront humankind early in the next century with a vast array of new communication that will combine the dominant attributes of the media domains in ways that are unimaginable for most people today. Furthermore, unlike past mediamorphoses, which required many generations and even millennia for new media technologies to permeate the majority of human societies, the technologies that will emerge in the twenty-first century can be expected to affect nearly everyone everywhere at about the same time. Although the hybrid traits emerging from digital engineering might make the media domains somewhat less distinct, or even lead to the creation of a fourth domain, they will still be affected by the principles of mediamorphosis. That is, the transformations will be affected by the complex interplay of perceived needs, competitive and political pressures, and social and technological innovation.

As we will discover in chapter 3, the patterns of adoption and implementation are deeply rooted in human culture. We will also observe how the media domains have been, and continue to be, shaped by spoken and written language and the transforming technologies each has inspired.

# the mediamorphic role of language

Ever since modern humans began walking the Earth some 4,000 generations ago, agents of change—the metamorphosing concepts that stimulate humans to think about themselves and their world in new ways—have been influencing the development of human social systems and cultures. The control of fire, the domestication of animals, the discovery of the wheel, the smelting of ores, and the harnessing of electricity are but a few of these agents of change. Once revealed by the human mind, each has acted as a powerful stimulant for specific inventions and innovations that have radically transformed and altered the course of civilization.

When discussing communication technologies, two agents of change stand out above all others—*spoken language* and *written language*. Each has vastly expanded the human communication system and played a central role in the advancement and spread of civilization. Now a new and quite different class of language—*digital language*—is emerging as yet another agent of change.

In this chapter, we will follow the evolutionary paths of the media domains from their emergence to modern times and apply the principles of mediamorphosis to understand the development of new media. We will also gain a basic understanding of digital language and the great mediamorphosis in progress. (For a chronology of significant events that have influenced the evolution of human communication, see Exhibit 3.1.)

## Expressive language and communication tools

While no one knows, or is ever likely to know, exactly when humans began to create uniform systems for interacting with one another,

**Exhibit 3.1** Time line of human communication.

| Years Ago (logarithmic) | Significant Events and Developments |
|---|---|
| | **Expressive Language\* and Communication Tools** |
| 100,000 | *Homo sapiens sapiens* (modern humans) |
| | **Spoken Language and the First Mediamorphosis** |
| | Cave paintings in southern Europe |
| 10,000 | End of last ice age |
| | Emergence of large-scale agricultural communities |
| | Bronze Age begins in Asia Minor |
| | **Written Language and the Second Mediamorphosis** |
| | Emergence of ancient empires |
| | Development of document technologies |
| | Handwritten books and libraries |
| B.C.–A.D. | Roman roads and mail services |
| | Development of printing and pulp paper in Asia |
| 1,000 | Development of pulp paper in Europe |
| | European Renaissance begins in Italy |
| | Commercial revolution |
| | Handwritten newsletters and newsbooks |
| | Development of printing in Europe |
| | Printed newspapers, magazines, and books |
| | Industrial revolution |
| | **Digital Language[†] and the Third Mediamorphosis** |
| | Application of electricity to communications |
| 100 | Wireless communication, moving pictures |
| | Long-distance telephone (transcontinental) |
| | Broadcast radio, radio facsimile machines |
| | Broadcast television |
| | Mainframe computers |
| | Cable television, first transatlantic telephone cable |
| | ARPANET (the Internet's predecessor), electronic mail |
| | Satellites, light-wave communication, video games |
| | Microprocessors, personal computers, VCRs |
| 10 | Digital facsimile machines, compact discs |
| | Digital radio and television |
| | Virtual reality and video conferencing systems |
| | World Wide Web |
| | Mosaic "net browsers" |

\* Expressive language includes signs and symbols as well as art, music, and dance.

† The origin of digital language is generally associated with the development of electronic computers in the 1940s, but the basic concepts, as we will see in chapter 4, can be traced back to the early decades of the nineteenth century.

the development of communal communication tools is generally accepted to be among the paramount achievements that differentiated *Homo sapiens sapiens* (modern human beings) from their hominid ancestors about 100,000 years ago. But, even though our knowledge of human activities and communication technologies prior to the relatively recent rise of agricultural civilizations is sketchy at best, most scientists are willing to concede that signs and signals, and other forms of expressive language, such as music and dance, have long been used by groups of humans to communicate.

The ability to communicate is not in itself unique to humans. We know, for example, that the complex songs and chatterings of whales, porpoises, monkeys, birds, and insects convey information over great distances to other members of their species with remarkable efficiency. There is little doubt that the primordial forms of human communication were inspired by other species. In fact, linguists studying groups of aboriginal peoples living in remote regions of the planet have found that their languages and rituals invariably include a mixture of sounds and movements acquired from the animals with whom they share their habitat. However, humans have not been content with just mimicking animal cries and behavior. Instead, they have embellished and manipulated such sounds and signals to give them an expanded meaning, presumably to satisfy some inner need for personal expression.

This uniquely human quality is the foundation of the interpersonal domain of communication media (see chapter 2), and is undeniably one of the linchpins of our culture. It has imbued human communication with its most distinctive characteristic—infinite variability in space and time.[1] The great diversity of languages, art, music, and dance, that has shaped our world views across millennia would not exist without the ability to consciously convey, change, and assimilate new ideas.

Another linchpin has been the intense curiosity modern humans have about the world in which they live and their indomitable drive to gather, exchange, and control information. But creativity and the drive for information could not by themselves have transformed human life and culture as dramatically as they have without a fortunate assist from nature—the physical evolution of the human

---

[1]Mario Pei, *The Story of Language* (rev. ed.). New York: Meridian Penguin, 1965, p. 26.

brain, skull, tongue, and voice box that made speech and linguistic communication possible.

## Spoken language and the first great mediamorphosis

Anatomical data gathered from fossilized skulls affirm that modern humans acquired the physical capability for speech between 90,000 and 40,000 years ago. Rudimentary forms of spoken language may have emerged quite early in this evolutionary process as an outgrowth of practical needs for interpersonal communication within familial and tribal groups. It seems probable that those humans who could more effectively communicate instructions and share their knowledge through spoken language gained a significant competitive advantage that improved their chances of survival.

Since no records exist, the origins of spoken language will be forever a matter of speculation. However, we can be certain that its diffusion among modern humans spanned many thousands of years. While this was a long period of time when compared to our present-day experiences with social and technological changes, it occupied only a brief moment relative to the four billion years that life has existed on this planet and the more than four million years that the human species has been evolving.

### The advantages of speech

With the rise of spoken language came the *first great mediamorphosis*[2] of the human communication system and the accelerated development of the interpersonal domain—and hence the rapid transformation of human existence. By mastering the use of words and other symbols, humans were able to cope with their physical and social environments in ways that would not have been possible during previous stages of their evolution.[3] Most notably, spoken language enabled people to organize themselves in larger groups and

---

[2]Melvin L. DeFleur and Everette E. Dennis refer to the development of speech and spoken language as the "first great communication revolution" in *Understanding Mass Communication* (4th ed.). Boston: Houghton Mifflin, 1991, p. 4.

[3]Melvin L. DeFleur and Sandra Ball-Rokeach, *Theories of Mass Communication* (5th ed.). White Plains, NY: Longman, 1989, p. 17.

to systematically deal with complex problems. The ability to encode information through spoken language provided a more efficient way to gather, process, and disseminate practical information.

In addition to being more efficient for external communication with other human beings, spoken language provided a more efficient means for internal communication, for thought. It has been well established that "the rules of thinking parallel the rules of talking."[4] That is, the ability to master the rules of language greatly enhanced the human capacity for reasoning, planning, and conceptualizing.

Finally, spoken language gave human beings a way to pass on their collective knowledge, experiences, and beliefs—in other words, their culture—to each succeeding generation. Media historian James Carey has suggested that human communications evolved to serve such purposes as well as to facilitate the exchange of information. In his view, some forms of communications are directed "not toward the extension of messages in space but toward the maintenance of society in time; not the act of imparting information but the representation of shared beliefs." Communication of this sort serves as "a symbolic process whereby reality is produced, maintained, repaired, and transformed."[5] It is possible to conclude (although this conclusion is not universally shared) that spoken language thus may actually have accelerated the development of non-linguistic rituals, symbolism, music, and art.

The principles of mediamorphosis introduced in chapter 1 apply even at this nascent juncture in the evolution of human communication. Despite the obvious superiority of spoken language, its spread did not eliminate earlier expressive forms. And when spoken language began transforming human communication, it adopted some of the well-defined, widespread traits of the dominant expressive forms.

### The emergence of the broadcast domain

The development of the broadcast domain also reflects the principles of mediamorphosis. During the initial stages of the first great mediamorphosis, the broadcast domain evolved slowly and intermittently in the shadow of the interpersonal domain. Unmediated,

---

[4]Ibid., p. 14.

[5]Quoted by Steven Lubar, *InfoCulture: The Smithsonian Book of Information Age Inventions*. Boston: Houghton Mifflin, 1993, p. 5.

one-to-one forms of spontaneous, interactive communication were gradually supplemented by mediated, planned, one-to-many forms.

The convergence of newer oral forms with older expressive forms clearly contributed to the development of embryonic broadcast traits. Prehistoric cave paintings, for example, were apparently meant to transmit to the group the artists' complex thoughts about important animals in the environment. Such thoughts could not have been formulated without the logical capacity induced by the development of spoken language. And the paintings themselves may have played a role in ritual, expressing the human relationship to prey and predator. Recent scientific dating of exquisitely executed cave paintings in Spain and southern France has provided compelling evidence that at least some groups of modern humans possessed advanced conceptualization and communication skills more than 30,000 years ago.

However, the broadcast domain probably did not become ascendant until human beings started concentrating in large-scale, multifamily agricultural communities. We know from observations of surviving Stone Age, oral societies that our prehistoric ancestors developed and enjoyed many forms of storytelling and ritual performance. Anthropologists have found that within small, generally isolated nomadic groups, nearly everyone participates in the recounting of experiences and events through coordinated dancing, music making, singing, and acting as well as speaking. Since stories are shared by everyone, there is little need for mediators or distinctions between performers and audiences.

Although these early blended forms of interpersonal and broadcast communication were diminished by ongoing developments in human communication and civilization, they endure in today's technologically advanced cultures in such forms as musical jam sessions, karioke singing, group dancing, and audience-participation theater. Interactive online games called **multiuser dungeons** (MUDs) have also contributed to an apparent revival of interest in communal storytelling and role playing.

### The differentiation of audiences and performers

As modern humans organized into larger and larger communities, broadcast communication became increasingly more important. The requirements of ancient empires for great assemblages of people to see and hear their leaders and priests created a supervening social necessity to develop technologies that could augment a person's presence and more broadly project spoken messages.

In their efforts to overcome the natural limitations of human sight and hearing, architects learned to design stages and seating (or standing) arrangements that could provide hundreds and even thousands of people with unobstructed views. They also learned to apply their growing knowledge of acoustics to amplify and focus sound.[6] Even today, we still marvel at the richness of sound projected from the stages of ancient amphitheaters and the daises of medieval churches.

An unavoidable consequence of these technological advances, however, was a steady decline in audience participation. Except for controlled group interactions, such as singing, chanting, and cheering, audiences in ancient civilizations were expected to be reverently passive recipients of broadcast messages (as they are today).

This development also contributed to the differentiation between audiences and performers and to the increasing power of mediators. The steady growth of agricultural societies and empires made it impractical for everyone to be involved concurrently in the telling of culturally relevant stories and the performing of rituals. Those with demonstrated talents for leading, communicating, and performing gradually became the gatekeepers and "rememberers" who controlled the content and flow of broadcast communications within each society.

## Staged performances and the broadcast domain

Once the roles of audience and performer were differentiated, broadcast forms became increasingly structured and standardized. The spontaneity and individual embellishments that had defined interpersonal communication and communal interactions since the emergence of spoken language metamorphosed into staged performances that were carefully orchestrated and uniformly presented. For the rulers of ancient empires, the consistency of stories, performances, and rituals, which were presented to the diverse audiences

----

[6]Information about the design and acoustical qualities of ancient and medieval structures was drawn from a variety of sources, including encyclopedias, newspapers, and magazines.

scattered throughout their realms, was essential to the maintenance of their legitimacy and power, as well as for cultural identity and cohesiveness.

The dominant traits of the broadcast domain, which we associate with modern theater and television, can therefore be seen as evolving from the needs of early large-scale agricultural societies and the institutions created to organize and control them. In the 10 millennia that civilization has been spreading around the globe, ancient staged performances have provided the foundation upon which nearly all forms of broadcast communication have been built.

Over time, every culture has adapted these concepts and evolved its own distinct styles of presentation. Operas and plays, Noh and Kabuki, magic shows and circuses, modern dances and ballets, concerts and recitals, public debates and orations, while different, are similar in that they have all furnished entertainment as well as information to large, relatively passive audiences. In each case, instructive religious, political, and cultural messages have been integrated into the content, as they still are today in films and television programs.

### The limitations of oral communication

Speech and spoken language obviously carried humankind a long way. But even though the oral forms of interpersonal and broadcast communication can be rich in detail and relevance, they are inherently unstable and unreliable across space and time. As stories are passed from one tribal group to another or from generation to generation, they tend to lose much of their original meaning and context, and ultimately become incomprehensible or metaphorical.

The ancient Homeric epics—the *Iliad* and the *Odyssey*—provide an instructive example. Nothing is actually known about Homer as an individual other than he was the foremost, if not the first, Greek poet. Described since antiquity merely as a blind beggar bard of Chios, most authorities today accept that he probably lived in Greek Asia Minor (now the Mediterranean coast of Turkey) sometime between 1000 and 800 B.C. and that, like most people of that time, he was illiterate. The present-day versions of these classic poems have descended from medieval and Renaissance manuscripts that were themselves copies of now-lost ancient manuscripts. No one knows when they were originally transcribed, but they were undoubtedly conveyed orally for many generations prior to the emergence of a written Greek language and for many generations thereafter.

Scholars since at least early Roman times assumed that the stories of the Trojan Wars and ancient places described by Homer were largely mythical and allegorical. However, in recent decades archeologists have uncovered convincing evidence that the city of Troy actually existed and that it was almost certainly destroyed in a battle that took place near the time when Homer is presumed to have created the epics. It therefore seems likely that he based his poems on historical facts as he knew them. But because they have passed through so many generations of oral retelling, we can never know how much of the poems are factual, or how much has been embellished and altered by later storytellers. In fact, every oral message is subject to the same sort of mutation.

## Written language and the second great mediamorphosis

The earliest attempts to reliably preserve knowledge and overcome the limitations of oral communication may have occurred in the period of the prehistoric cave painters. It seems plausible that these early humans also drew meaningful illustrations on animal skins or on other perishable materials, but no evidence other than their cave paintings has survived.

The oldest surviving evidence of uniform systems for recording and preserving information dates back about six thousand years to ancient Sumer and Egypt. At that point, the rapid growth of farming, commerce, and governance within these rising agricultural economies created an opportunity, as well as the motivating reasons, to seek and adopt new communication tools that would be more suitable than human speech and memory for maintaining dependable and accurate records across time.

The solution, which was discovered almost simultaneously by both cultures, was written language—the agent of change most integral to the defining of civilization as we know it today. This was the stimulus for the *second great mediamorphosis* and the subsequent branching of the document domain.

Written language and document technologies apparently emerged gradually from long-established methods for keeping track of transactions and information relevant to planting and harvesting. With symbols scratched and painted on stones or pressed into soft clay, the farmers, traders, and civil servants of ancient civilizations began to regularly record information about harvests and the seasonal flow of rivers, taxes and the exchange of goods, and the precepts for social and domestic harmony.

The early document technologies had a radical effect on human communication and thought. Linguists have found that as written language was developed and spread, spoken tongues and cultures attained much greater stability.[7] Exchanges of written messages did not require senders and receivers to be copresent, so communications were freed from their earlier time and space constraints. Written documents separated words from their speakers and their original context, diminishing the importance of memory and permitting a more detached and deliberate examination of message content. Written documents also made it possible for thoughts and ideas to live on long after the originators had died.

### The development of light, portable documents

With increasing mobility and sophistication came the need for a document technology that was easier to store and transport than the bulky stone and clay tablets, and that was able to conveniently display much larger amounts of information. The solution to this problem was discovered in Egypt about 45 centuries ago. By pounding and pressing crisscrossed strips of wet papyrus reeds until they formed thin solid sheets and then setting them in the sun to dry, the ancient Egyptians produced the first durable paper. Using brushes made from another plant and two colors of ink (black and red) to apply their symbols, scribes could create documents faster and more efficiently than ever before.

The length of a document was now relatively unrestricted because papyrus paper could be produced in continuous rolls. Even with long documents, weight and bulk were no longer significant issues. The acquisition of a light, portable document technology and a system of written symbols that could be produced quickly and read by scribes provided the necessary conditions for great social and cultural change.[8]

---

[7]Pei, *Story of Language*, p. 95.
[8]DeFleur and Ball-Rokeach, *Theories of Mass Communication*, p. 21.

During the next three thousand years, Egyptian glyphs and other pictographic forms of writing were largely replaced in Western civilizations by written languages based on phonetic symbols and modern alphabets. Papyrus scrolls also gave way to bound books with pages made from animal skins, and later to less expensive paper produced from rags and wood fiber. But despite these improvements, the production of books and other documents remained an onerous and time-consuming task until the beginning of the *typographic age* in the fifteenth century.

### The typographic age

The basic concepts of mechanical printing were developed in China and Korea about A.D. 600 but their cultures prevented the technology from being utilized as it would be by the Europeans some nine centuries later. That is, the imperial courts regarded printing as their exclusive technology and the symbol of their power, and thus evoked Brian Winston's "law of the suppression of radical potential."[9]

In the eighth and ninth centuries, the Arabs learned of the methods for printing documents, as well as the secrets for producing rag paper, through their various commercial dealings and military confrontations with the Chinese. They immediately recognized the advantages of rag paper and wood-block printing and did not hesitate to use them for producing books and religious documents. Because their Islamic faith encouraged the spread of knowledge and the teachings of Mohammed, printing on paper diffused quickly within their culture.

The Europeans were apparently aware of these document technologies for some time, but they showed little interest in adopting them until the fifteenth century. Although the first rag paper was produced in Europe about A.D. 1200, it didn't become a commodity until after a great disaster—the Black Death—swept across the continent in the later half of the 1300s. Between 25 and 40 million people—about one-third of the European population—died from plague within two decades. In addition to upsetting the feudal system and

---

[9]Brian Winston, "How Are Media Born and Developed?" in John Downing, Ali Mohammadi, and Annabelle Sreberny-Mohammadi, eds., *Questioning the Media: A Critical Introduction,* Thousand Oaks, CA: Sage Publications, 1995, p. 70.

contributing to the spread of Renaissance ideas, the Black Death created new wealth for many of the survivors and mountains of garments, bedding, and other articles made of cloth that were essentially useless.[10] Consequently, the processes for converting rags to paper diffused rapidly as the fourteenth century drew to a close. So many people entered the business that by the 1450s there was an enormous surplus of rag paper, which forced the price to a low level. This fortuitous situation occurred just as the Renaissance was creating a great demand for books and documents throughout Europe.

***Gutenberg's inventions.*** Johann Gutenberg did not invent printing, but he is credited with developing four key innovations that made it practical and economical to mechanically replicate high-quality documents in great numbers. One was a typecasting device that could quickly produce many copies of metal type that were durable and exactly the same. Previously, movable type was either engraved in metal or carved in wood. Both methods were laborious and lacked precision. His second innovation was an alloy of lead, tin, and antimony, out of which the cast letterforms were made. This mixture prevented oxidation and added the strength needed to withstand the pressures applied by the printing press. It is essentially the same alloy that has been used by hot-metal printers ever since. His third innovation was the mechanical printing press itself, which he adapted from the bookbinding presses that had been developed sometime earlier. The final innovation was a printing ink with an oil base that could be colored in various ways.[11]

Although little is known with certainty about the development of mechanical printing prior to 1500, its rapid spread across the continent no doubt evoked as much nervousness about the future of publishing as electronic technologies have in the latter half of the twentieth century. Literate Renaissance Europeans were obviously fascinated by the new technology, but they also struggled with how to properly define and value it. They first called Gutenberg's method for reproducing uniform copies of documents "artificial writing," as

---

[10]Charles Van Doren, *A History of Knowledge: The Pivotal Events, People, and Achievements of World History.* New York: Ballantine, 1991, p. 152.
[11]Ibid., pp. 153–154.

opposed to "natural writing."[12] Even though early printers devoted considerable effort to precisely replicating the page formats and letterforms popularized by scribes, their products were regarded as cheap imitations of hand-lettered documents for many decades. By 1470—just 15 years after the first Gutenberg Bibles were sold—the price of mechanically printed Bibles, which were carefully crafted, exact replicas of a manuscript Bible, had already dropped to one-fifth that of the copies produced by scribes.[13]

***Fulfillment of unmet needs.*** Gutenberg's inventions were originally seen as a way to increase the productivity of scribes who labored in the medieval manuscript-copying institutions called scriptoria. The monasteries in Europe had undertaken, after the collapse of the Roman empire, almost exclusively, the business of manually replicating and preserving ancient manuscripts. With the flowering of the Renaissance[14] and the spread of universities, demand for acceptable texts increased rapidly and began to overwhelm the capacity of the scriptoria. Media historian Anthony Smith suggests that, "Printing in Europe developed directly from this unfulfilled requirement for **text** in scribal society."[15]

With mechanical printing, scribes were able to avoid the laborious work of hand-lettering and comparing copies with the original texts to eliminate errors, which allowed them to devote their skills to embellishing pages with touches of color and "illuminations." This arrangement kept some scriptoria operating for many decades, but it soon became apparent that the world was entering a new era. By the end of the so-called incunabula[16] stage of printing in 1500, there were already more than 1,100 print shops in 200 European

---

[12]Everett M. Rogers, *Communication Technology: The New Media in Society.* New York: Free Press, 1986, p. 27.

[13]Anthony Smith, *Goodbye Gutenberg: The Newspaper Revolution of the 1980s.* New York: Oxford University Press, 1980, pp. 8–9.

[14]The intellectual and artistic revival known as the Renaissance originated in Italy in the fourteenth century and had spread throughout Europe by the end of the sixteenth century. This period, which marked the transition from medieval to modern times, unleashed the human spirit and encouraged the rise of commercial enterprise, scientific inquiry, and technological innovation.

[15]Smith, *Goodbye Gutenberg,* p. 7.

[16]The word *incunabula* comes from the Latin *cunae,* meaning "cradle." In this case, it refers to all books printed before the year 1500.

cities, in which some 12 million books, in 35,000 editions, had been produced.[17]

The continuing development of printing technologies and publishing enterprises quickly led to the standardization of written languages. Before the mass production of books and periodicals, spelling and the construction of sentences often were left to an individual's personal preferences. Not until publishers began insisting on uniform styles did dictionaries and rule books for grammar become a necessity.

## Literacy for the masses

While written language and document technologies have played an indispensable role in the creation and preservation of human knowledge, they have only recently found their way into the hands of most people. For most of their 6,000-year existence, they were viewed as sacred gifts to the ruling elites. It took five and a half centuries since Gutenberg's inventions for written documents to become relatively ubiquitous. And the idea that nearly everyone in a society should be literate didn't begin to catch on until the end of the sixteenth century and wasn't widely accepted in most Western cultures until the outset of the industrial revolution.[18]

*The birth of newspapers.* The rise of literacy provided a growing market for printed newspapers, which in turn further stimulated the spread of literacy. There is still some debate as to when and where the first newspaper was published, but the idea spread rather quickly throughout the European continent after the beginning of the seventeenth century. Newspapers originally functioned primarily as journals of commerce for the new merchant classes. Their content usually included announcements of ship arrivals and departures,

---

[17]Warren Chappell, *A Short History of the Printed Word.* New York: Dorset Press, 1970, p. 84.

[18]The industrial revolution is generally conceded to have begun in the middle of the 1700s, at least in England, but it did not have a significant impact upon other European countries and the United States until the beginning of the 1800s. In the British colonies of North America, the idea of universal literacy (among white males) was already well established by the time of the American Revolution.

cargo manifests, and the prices of goods, as well as a sprinkling of news items from foreign lands (see Exhibit 3.2).

The technology of newspaper printing changed slowly. Printers at the beginning of the nineteenth century were still manually assembling each story one letter at a time in forms called sticks and pressing each page one copy at a time, just as Gutenberg had done some 350 years earlier. Consequently, most newspapers were unable to publish more than a few hundred copies; those that could print more than a thousand copies were the exception. But a combination of new technologies and new ideas soon changed the nature of the medium.

***Industrial age printing.*** In 1833, a young printer by the name of Benjamin Day began publishing a newspaper in New York City called the *Sun,* which sold on the streets for only one cent. At the time, established New York newspapers sold for six cents a copy— a rather substantial fee when the average daily wage for nonfarm workers in the U.S. was about 75 cents. Within four months, Day was selling more than 5,000 copies per issue of the *Sun.* Two years later, he claimed a circulation of more than 15,000, which made it the largest newspaper in the United States.[19]

There were two secrets to Day's success. One was his ability to attract large audiences with a new, "popular" form of journalism that included a racy mix of crime, sex, and human interest stories. The other was his early adoption of industrial age technologies, which made it possible for him to cut costs and increase the number of copies he could economically print. Among the most powerful of these early transforming technologies was the steam-driven press.

Other enterprising publishers in North America and Europe quickly launched their own versions of the cheap, popular newspaper, which became known in the United States as the "penny press." For most historians, this was the genesis of modern mass media.

***The golden age of print media.*** Throughout the middle decades of the nineteenth century, an array of more advanced industrial age technologies contributed to an explosion of print media. But growth began to level off again in the 1870s, in part because the cost and time involved in the manual setting of type limited the number of pages that could be economically published.

---

[19]Mitchell Stephens, *A History of News: From the Drum to the Satellite,* New York: Viking Penguin, 1988, p. 203.

**Exhibit 3.2** The *London Gazette* in 1707.

Numb. 4354

# The London Gazette.

### Published by Authority.

From **Thursday** July 31. to **Monday** August 4. 1707.

*Windsor, August 1.*

THE humble Address of the Bishop, Dean and Chapter, and Clergy, of the Cathedral Church and Diocese of Chichester, has been presented to Her Majesty.

*To the QUEEN's most Excellent Majesty,*

Most Gracious Sovereign,

THough few of Your Majesty's Subjects are plac'd at so great a Distance as we are from the Borders of the Two late Kingdoms, (heretofore the unsociable Field of Rapine and Blood,) yet none are more sensible of the Blessings of the happy Union, or more sincerely thankful to Your Majesty for the Accomplishment of it. It was Your Zeal for the common Good of Your Subjects which gave Birth to that noble Design, and nothing but the Possession You have of their Hearts, and the Wisdom of Your own Councils, could, under God, have brought a Work of so great Difficulty to such a speedy Conclusion. Your Majesty has hereby establish'd an Union of Interests; and we, whose Function more particularly obliges us to promote Peace upon Earth, shall think our selves inexcusable to God, Your Majesty, and the whole Kingdom, if we endeavour not in our several Stations, as far as in us lies, daily to improve it into an Union of Hearts and Affections. May Your Majesty, by the special Care of the Divine Providence, long live to see and enjoy with us the blessed Fruits of so glorious an Undertaking; and may You successfully protect (as You have hitherto done) to preserve our Religion, to secure our Church, and to maintain the Succession of the Protestant Line against all the Attempts of Papists and their Adherents: Which is the hearty Prayer of Your Majesty's most dutiful, loyal Subjects.

Which Address Her Majesty received very graciously.

*Alicant, July 15. N. S.* Denia is besieg'd by 10000 Men, under the Command of the Chevalier d'Asfeldt, but, by Order of the Earl of Galway, has been so seasonably supply'd from hence with strong Reinforcements and great Quantities of Ammunition, that the Besieged have already held out above Twenty Days, and repuls'd the Enemy at Two general Assaults. The Fortifications are inconsiderable; but the Garison consisting chiefly of English and Dutch Troops, it is not doubted but they will make a very brave Defence. We are here so well provided with all manner of Necessaries, and have a Castle of so great Strength, that we are not at all apprehensive of the Enemy's Approach.

*Neufchatel, July 26.* Monsieur de Puisieux having written to the Four Cantons of Switzerland, allied to this Principality, in Favour of the French Competitors, Mr. Stanyan, the British Envoy, recommended in a Memorial to the Magistracy of Berne the Right of his Prussian Majesty, and afterwards set out for this Place, where he arriv'd the 2nd Instant. The next Day he notified his Arrival to the Governor and Council of State, as also to the Council of the City; each of which, by a separate Deputation, made their Complements to the Envoy, and express'd themselves with the highest Veneration and Zeal for Her Majesty's Person and Interests. The Clergy soon after sent Representatives on the same Occasion. The Envoy's Secretary presented a Letter from Her Majesty of Great Britain, and a Memorial, to the Council of State, in Behalf of his Prussian Majesty; and at the same time deliver'd Duplicates of that Letter and Memorial to the Council of the City, the Clergy, and Bourgeoisie of Vallangin. The last of these have also deputed Persons to congratulate the Envoy's Arrival; who, in a most thankful and submissive manner, have acknowledg'd Her Majesty's Care of their Privileges in this juncture. Her Majesty's Interposition hath already very much effac'd the Impressions which the French Ministers had made on the People, to the Prejudice of the King of Prussia. The Tribunal which is to decide this important Controversie is compos'd of 12 Persons, who are the States of the Country. It was so long deferr'd on the 28th Instant, but is put off to an indefinite Time, till a Competition between the Prince of Conti and Count Metternich a-

bout Precedency be adjusted. 'Tis thought this Pretence for suspending the Session is agreeable to each Party, and will be given up as soon as either thinks his Interest secure.

*Berlin, July 30.* The Count of Solms Braunfeldt was Installd Knight of the Order of the Prussian Eagle the Day after his Majesty's Birth-day. The Bishop of Spiga, who had resided here some time in Behalf of the Elector Palatine, but without any Publick Character, hath had a private Audience, wherein he press'd the King, by setting forth the present State of the Empire, to augment the Troops he had already design'd for the Service on the Rhine with Two Battalions of his Majesty's Guards. He hath been receiv'd with great Distinction in this Court; but finding he cannot obtain more than was before granted upon the Application of the British Ambassadors and other Ministers of Princes in the Alliance, he designs to leave suddenly this Place, and return to Hanover. A Swedish Minister in this Court speaks with Assurance of an amicable Composure of the Misunderstandings between the Emperor and his Master, his Swedish Majesty having approv'd the Expedient of delivering up the Adjutant who insulted the Swedes, and the paying 4000 Dollars, as a Reparation to those who were wounded or imprison'd on that Occasion. His Electoral Highness of Hanover hath answer'd his Majesty's Letter of Felicitation, upon accepting the Command of the Imperial Forces, in the most obliging Terms; and express'd his Intention of having a peculiar Regard to the Services of his Majesty's Troops, when his Electoral Highness shall put himself at the Head of that Army. The King hath acknowledg'd the Elector's Friendship in another Letter; wherein, after having consented that the utmost Precautions in this great Affair are very just, he urges his Electoral Highness to repair to the Army as soon as possible, where his Presence is so absolutely necessary, and would certainly produce an advantagious Change in the present Scene of Affairs. The Ladies of Monsieur Hermelin and Monsieur Cederhelm have pass'd through this Place to Retin, whither the Countess Piper is expected to follow in few Days. The Chief Ministers of Sweden having sent away their Families, is a Circumstance which makes us believe the March of the Swedes is very suddenly intended. Our last Letters from Lublin advise, That all things were dispos'd for the Election of a new King; and that it was thought the Choice would fall upon Prince Ragotzki. The Czar hath given direct and satisfactory Answers to the several Proposals made to him by the Republick. Monsieur Slundt having been generously pardon'd by the King of Sweden, expected his Enlargement on the Birth-day of his Prussian Majesty; but his Enemies have taken so effectual an Advantage of his Confinement and Disgrace, that, instead of being releas'd, he will be try'd by a Council of War upon a new Accusation, of having given an Account of the King's Stores to a Foreign Prince. Monsieur Dupuy, who was under an Arrest for indirect Practices in the Affair of Neufchatel, is set at Liberty, upon taking an Oath that he will no more concern himself in that Negociation. Monsieur Leyonstedt, the Swedish Minister, attended his Majesty Yesterday, by Order of the King his Master, to explain the Necessity there was that the Four Swedish Regiments of Horse should take their Quarters in Silesia. He represents them as a Body not exceed-

ing

From the days of Gutenberg, printers had required about one minute to set each line of type. Attempts had been made as early as the 1840s to develop a machine that could be used to set type faster, but none were found acceptable. The critical breakthrough finally came in 1886 when Ottmar Mergenthaler, a German immigrant living in Baltimore, demonstrated his invention—a machine that could sequentially cast whole lines of type as single units—to the *New York Tribune*. Using a keyboard similar to a typewriter, an operator could produce an amazing five lines per minute, or about 6,000 characters per hour.

Mergenthaler's linecasting machine revolutionized typesetting and spawned a company—Linotype—that would dominate the printing and publishing industries for many decades. By the end of the nineteenth century more than 3,000 machines were in use around the world. His invention, and those that followed, made it possible for innovative publishers to catch up with the growing demand for reading material and display advertising.

The period from 1890 to 1920 is often considered the golden age of print media. Publishing empires flourished, and many newspaper publishers, such as William Randolph Hearst, Joseph Pulitzer, and Lord Northcliffe, became as well known to their readers as the celebrities and world leaders their publications covered. Publishers' power and influence was so great in those years that they could easily make or break politicians and rally public support for foreign wars, as well as for their own personal causes.

## The end of print predominance

Newspapers in the early 1920s would be forced to redefine their role by the introduction of a new and far more powerful mass medium—broadcast radio. Like the Internet and cyber media today, the development of relatively low-cost, home radio receivers and electronic broadcast media created a great deal of anxiety as well as excitement. Some pundits argued, even then, that printed newspapers were doomed by electronic media.

Despite the obvious threat, enterprising newspaper companies were undeterred and did not hesitate to sponsor some of the world's first radio stations. But once the novelty wore off publishers soon became discouraged by the high cost of broadcasting and the absence of offsetting incomes. After just a few years, many publishers sold their radio stations and abandoned their sponsorships, believing that broadcast radio would not succeed as a commercial medium.

By the beginning of the 1930s, however, advertisers discovered broadcast radio's ability to deliver large national audiences and became eager sponsors for programs. Publishers now saw radio as a formidable competitor for advertising dollars and began to fight back. The majority attempted to boycott advertisers who placed radio ads, and refused to publish radio schedules and promotions. They also undertook a number of innovations, a prime example of the survival principle of mediamorphosis.

For example, in response to the threat of broadcast radio many publishers revamped content and formats to broaden their newspapers' appeal among more diverse audiences and advertisers. Newspaper publishers began experimenting with special sections, departments, and packages targeted at specific groups. Weekend magazines, women's sections, children's pages, features pages, and comics pages blossomed. Departmental journalism, as it was called, not only succeeded in attracting new readers and advertisers; it also led to the more orderly packaging of information. Multisection, departmentalized content now provides the underlying structure for most of today's newspapers.

Reporting styles also changed partially in response to competition with radio. Rather than just telling the traditional "who did what" in short takes, which is what radio did best, newspapers began expanding stories to provide the "why." The rise of interpretive reporting is considered one of the most significant developments of the 1930s and 1940s. In this period, newspapers also began providing more background information and analyses.

Soon after World War II, newspapers were confronted with yet another new and even more powerful electronic medium—television. In the United States, TV rapidly displaced radio, as well as many of the once prominent general circulation magazines, such as *Life, Look,* and *The Saturday Evening Post.*

Once again pundits predicted the death of print media, and by the end of the 1960s many publishers feared they might be right. The high costs associated with antiquated industrial age technologies and processes threatened the very existence of newspapers and magazines at a time when they were being forced to make expensive changes to compete with television for advertising revenue. However, much to the relief of publishers, new computer typesetting and printing technologies introduced in the late 1960s made it possible to dramatically reduce manufacturing costs as well as increase the use of color and graphics. By the beginning of the 1980s, most newspapers and magazines had once again undergone substantial changes in content, design, and technology.

While further improvements are still possible, it now appears that newspapers and magazines have finally pushed ink-on-paper publishing to its limit. Many print media professionals have conceded that no future redesign, content improvement, or advanced color press can be expected to displace electronic media or reverse the downward trends that began in the 1920s with the introduction of broadcast radio. But, as we will see in subsequent chapters, that does not mean that printed publications and the written word are necessarily doomed. The document domain continues to evolve to serve its original purpose—to provide structured mediated messages with maximum portability across time and space.

## Digital language and the third great mediamorphosis

In the past few decades, it has become obvious that we are now in the midst of a *third great mediamorphosis* that began with the application of electricity to communication early in the nineteenth century. Since the invention of the electric telegraph, there has been an unprecedented transformation and expansion of all three media domains.

Coincidentally, a new class of language has emerged as a powerful agent of change—*digital language*. This is a language unlike any other. The three classes of language discussed so far in this chapter—expressive, spoken, and written—were developed to facilitate communication between humans. Digital language, which uses numbers to encode and process information, was developed to facilitate communication between machines and their components. Only through a mathematically mediated translation process can digital language be used for communications with and between humans.

Today, this fourth class of language is typically associated with the relatively recent developments of electronic computing and telecommunications, but, as we will see in chapter 4, its origins can be found in the efforts of scientists and entrepreneurs to deal with a crisis brought about by the industrial revolution early in the nineteenth century.

The effect of digital language and technologies upon the media domains is so profound that an understanding of present and future transformations is not possible without at least a basic knowledge of the terminology and underlying concepts. Just a few years ago, terms like *digital, megabyte, modem,* and *cyberspace* were rarely seen or heard in mainstream media. They were considered too technical for most people to grasp. When they were used, they were almost always set off by quotation marks or accompanied by brief explanations. Today these terms have become almost commonplace in the news media and contemporary literature, yet they are still not well understood among those who are not intimately involved with digital technologies.

## The shift from analog to digital technologies

To comprehend the significance of digital language, we must first understand the distinction between digital and analog. The term *digital* refers to the fingers and toes, which have been used by humans for millennia to count and represent numerical data. Modern digital technologies are essentially just extremely fast counting systems that process all forms of information as numerical values.

Before the development of modern digital computers, nearly all systems for computing and communicating were analog. **Analog computers** are basically measuring devices. They respond to, or measure, continuously changing conditions. Household thermometers, clocks with hour and minute hands, and automobile gauges are examples of simple analog computers. From the beginning of the industrial age, analog computers were built into machinery to provide automatic feedback and control. The most complicated analog computer of all is the human brain, which has an enormous capacity for concurrently processing vast amounts of continuously changing inputs and coordinating complex responses in "real time."

However, despite their usefulness, all analog computers made by humans suffer from a serious flaw—they cannot measure with enough precision. The problem lies in their ability to consistently record continuous changes continuously. With all measurements, there is always room for ambiguity. In systems that require precise coordination of events, slight inaccuracies in their readings can be amplified many times over and result in very large errors.

Digital computers are capable of measuring with far greater precision because they do not tolerate any ambiguities. Instead of continuously recording signals as they are received from the smallest to the largest values, digital computers recognize only a discrete number of precise values.

Digital systems thus offer three distinct advantages over analog systems: (1) they can significantly reduce the amount of data required for processing, storing, displaying, and transmitting information; (2) they can indefinitely reproduce data with no apparent loss of quality; and (3) they can easily manipulate data with great precision.[20]

**Bits and bytes.** To store and process data, digital systems employ very large arrays of microscopic electrical switches that have only two states, or values. These **binary** switches can be interpreted as either on or off, one or zero, yes or no, black or white.

The data recorded by a single switch is called a **bit,** which is the smallest element of machine-readable information. Since a bit can only represent a one (on) or zero (off), digital language relies on a binary (base two) counting system, rather than the decimal (base ten) system commonly used in most modern societies. For example, in the binary system the decimal number two is represented as 10, four as 100, and eight as 1000 (see Exhibit 3.3).

In digital language, strings of bits are assembled according to defined rules, or standards, to form "words" called **bytes** that can be easily read by computers. Terms such as *kilobyte* (1,000 bytes) and *megabyte* (1 million bytes) are used to define the size of computer files or the amount of available storage.

**Commingling of bits.** All words, images, and sounds recognizable to humans can be reduced to computer bits that are basically indistinguishable from one another. As Nicholas Negroponte emphasizes in

---

[20]Charles Van Doren provides an excellent lay explanation of digital and analog technology in chapter 13, "The Twentieth Century: Science and Technology," in *A History of Knowledge,* pp. 345–350.

**Exhibit 3.3** Comparison of decimal and binary numbers.

| Decimal Number | Binary Number |
|:---:|:---:|
| 1 | 1 |
| 2 | 10 |
| 3 | 11 |
| 4 | 100 |
| 5 | 101 |
| 6 | 110 |
| 7 | 111 |
| 8 | 1000 |
| 9 | 1001 |
| 10 | 1010 |
| 100 | 1100100 |
| 1,000 | 1111101000 |
| 10,000 | 10011100010000 |
| 100,000 | 11000011010100000 |
| 1,000,000 | 11110100001001000000 |

his book *Being Digital,* "bits are bits."[21] His point is that within digital language, human distinctions among text, images, and sounds are irrelevant. The bits used to describe the textual elements of a newspaper story are identical to the bits that describe the audio and video elements of a radio or television program. They can coexist and commingle within any sort of digital communication system. There is, however, one important distinction. Many more bits are required to describe a photo than the text of a typical news story, and vastly more bits are required to describe a few seconds of audio or video.

## The development of digital technologies

Until the 1950s, telephone systems operated quite well providing analog voice communication using copper wires and mechanical switches. The relatively slow speed of human speech made it possible for multiple conversations to take place simultaneously on a single line. When a word or two was garbled or there was a little noise on the line, the consequences were insignificant.

---

[21]Nicholas Negroponte, *Being Digital.* New York: Knopf, 1995, pp. 11–20.

***The need for digital translators.*** The demands of the Cold War and digital computers changed all that. Fears of a surprise attack by Soviet bombers motivated the United States to begin developing a network of computers in the early 1950s that could track incoming aircraft and help coordinate military responses. However, before the network could be built, engineers had to find a way for computers to talk with each other on the telephone.

The exchange of information within and between digital computers relies on electrical signals, known as pulses, to create streams of ones and zeros. Unfortunately, old-fashioned rotary phones relied on similar pulses. After the connections were established, all subsequent pulses were filtered out. Also, because computers communicate at far greater speeds than humans, they could easily overload the phone system, which had been designed to take advantage of the numerous pauses that typically occur in human conversations. Computers' speed and reliance on exact sequences of ones and zeros also makes them far less tolerant of garbles and random noise on a line.

Engineers at AT&T solved the basic compatibility problems between computers and telephones by developing **modems** (modulators/demodulators). These devices translated (modulated) digital language into analog signals that the phone system could handle. At the other end, identical devices would translate (demodulate) the signals back into binary code.

The potential for transmission errors with these early modems was not a significant issue for the military because its computer centers used expensive, dedicated telephone lines to provide relatively "clean" communications and used redundant systems to verify data. But in the "real" world where people had to rely on ordinary telephone lines, modems alone were not enough to assure efficient, error-free communication between computers.

***Overcoming data loss and corruption.*** Further innovations came in the late 1960s from another U.S. military-funded project—ARPANET. Engineers from AT&T were again enlisted, this time to find a means of reliably transmitting digital data over long distances without requiring dedicated connections between each and every computer in the network. To accomplish this goal, they developed a method for segmenting computer data into small "packets" that would be more manageable within the existing telephone infrastructure. They appended a header to each packet that identified the segment and contained the instructions for reconnecting it with the other segments. They also incorporated a mathematical verification scheme to assure that no data were lost or corrupted during transmission. **Packet switching,** as this approach is called, provided the essential standards that made the Internet and consumer online services possible.

The growing popularity of personal computers and online networks since the early 1980s has created a steadily increasing demand for faster and more reliable digital communications. To deal with the emergence and anticipated growth of multimedia computer systems, telecommunication companies around the world have been racing to replace their old copper-wire infrastructure with vastly more efficient digital fiber-optic networks. These networks have, in turn, required the development of more advanced packet-switching standards and different devices for connecting computers to telephones.

*Avoiding traffic jams.* The popular notion that telecommunication networks are like highway systems may not be entirely accurate, but it does provide an easy way to visualize two important concepts— **bandwidth** and **compression.** As with highway systems, the Internet and consumer online services rely on networks of expressways and feeder roads to efficiently move vehicles (or bits in the case of digital networks) to and from points within the system. Almost every computer user who has spent time online has experienced periods when interactions suddenly slow to a snail's pace. Using the highway analogy, these delays are essentially caused by congestion and traffic jams.

When we are driving on real highways, we recognize that our speed is not always determined by the horsepower of our car. The more significant variables are the number of available traffic lanes and the number of cars trying to get to the same place at approximately the same time. As the number of cars begin to reach or exceed a highway's optimum capacity, drivers are compelled to slow down. The same is true of the information highway system.

*Country roads and expressways.* Within a telecommunication network, the measure of an information highway's optimum carrying capacity is its bandwidth, which can be measured in **bits per second**

(**Bps**) or cycles per second (hertz). For computer users who connect to networks through a modem and standard telephone line, the maximum bandwidth available typically varies between 2,400 and 28,800 Bps.[22] This is known as a **narrowband** channel. It is intended for routine voice communication and transmissions involving relatively small amounts of data, such as fax, e-mail, and typical computer text files. These channels can be thought of as the two-lane country roads of the information highway system.

Computer users who want to communicate from their homes at faster speeds usually have the option of switching to the equivalent of an eight-lane expressway by connecting through a high-capacity digital channel called an **Integrated Services Digital Network,** or simply **ISDN.**

Significantly faster communications are possible through so-called **broadband** channels. These information "superhighways," which use fiber-optic lines or coaxial cables, can carry millions of bits per second. The most common broadband connections in U.S. homes are those installed by satellite and cable-TV operators. These channels are intended for television and transmissions involving large amounts of data, such as video conferences, multimedia presentations, computer files that include video and audio clips, and interactive services such as multiuser games, home shopping, and video messaging.

*Condensed data.* Even with ISDN or faster channels, however, computer users can still experience occasional slowdowns and traffic jams. A telecommunications network comprises many phone lines feeding into higher capacity trunk lines. Other lines of varying capacities connect these trunk lines with World Wide Web data bases, bulletin boards, and consumer online services. A network therefore is only as fast as its slowest link.

When traffic increases to the point where it begins to regularly exceed the capacity of a highway, the usual solution is to add more lanes. But telecommunication networks have two options—increase the bandwidth or compress the transmitted data. Compression in

---

[22]These values are estimates of the maximum bandwidth possible with a specific modem on a typical phone line. The actual capacity is determined by the quality of the phone line, as well as by the type of modem.

the highway analogy is equivalent to eliminating all the empty spaces between cars. However, in digital communication systems, data compression goes much further. Using complex mathematical formulas, compression programs are able to identify nonessential data that can be edited out without causing ambiguity and can locate repeated patterns and redundancies that can be reduced through the use of less space-consuming codes. This is the digital equivalent of carpooling. Nearly all modems employ automatic compression programs to increase their capacity, but computer users and information providers also rely on a variety of additional compression programs designed for specific purposes, such as compressing photographs and full-motion video.

## The cyberspace frontier

The development of digital language is likely to have a profound transformational effect on human society, just as the development of expressive, spoken, and written language did. We are in the earliest stages of that transformation, but we can already see how computer networks using digital language are greatly extending human interactions throughout the world. And millions of people are now spending a significant portion of their time in an ethereal place known as **cyberspace.**

The term *cyberspace* was first used by William Gibson in his science fiction novel *Neuromancer,* published in 1984. Since then, it has been generally associated with the "conceptual space" where people interact using computer-mediated communication (CMC) technologies.[23] Various uses of **cyber** as a prefix or adjective, such as cyberculture and cyber cash, have become increasingly popular to describe practically anything related to CMC activities. For some, the explosion of CMC activity in the past few years is "looking more and more like a biological growth spurt."[24]

The Internet, consumer online services, and a myriad of public and private bulletin boards are providing the essential CMC infrastructures to support this universe of the mind. Media scholar

---

[23]Howard Rheingold, *The Virtual Community: Homesteading on the Electronic Frontier.* New York: HarperPerennial, 1993, p. 5.

[24]Derrick de Kerckhove, *Brainframes: Technology, Mind and Business.* Utrecht, Netherlands: Bosch & Keuning, 1991, p. 72.

Derrick de Kerckhove, director of the McLuhan Institute in Toronto, sees cyberspace as a three-level integration of technologies:

1. *Inner:* The rapid development of computer power.
2. *Outer:* The international standardization of technologies for linking computers in networks.
3. *Interactive:* The bionic interactivity between humans and machines in virtual reality.[25]

Ultimately, as chapter 7 describes, virtual reality machines connected to global networks are expected to give humans the capacity for sharing their thoughts and emotions directly, without the need for intermediate devices and interfaces. In the process, a whole new media domain may emerge.

## The mediamorphic role of language in perspective

We have seen in this chapter how the emergence of spoken language and then written language resulted in two great mediamorphoses within the human communication system. Each inspired countless transforming technologies that contributed to the branching and growth of the three media domains, as well as to the rapid advancement of human culture. In each case, development and diffusion spanned many human generations, and the media technologies were not uniformly adopted throughout the world. Numerous isolated, indigenous cultures, for example, did not acquire written language and document technologies until this century—more than 50 centuries after the widespread adoption of clay tablets and papyrus scrolls in the Middle East.

Since the application of electricity to communications and the emergence of digital language, however, the evolution and expansion of human communication have been accelerating at a breathtaking rate. Several major social and technological developments have occurred within individual lifetimes, and earlier distinctions in media forms appear to be progressively blurring.

From the previous two chapters, we acquired insights into the patterns of technological change and the dominant traits of the

_____
[25]Ibid., p. 73.

media domains. The next two chapters focus on the forces that are influencing the next critical stage of the third great mediamorphosis—the computerization of media and the conversion of all technology-mediated forms of communication to digital language. The remainder of this book explores the ways that this third great mediamorphosis will affect the three domains of communication media. Will each domain continue to evolve and expand along its historic path, or will one or more of the domains begin to die out, as some are predicting? Or will an entirely new cyber domain emerge from the convergence of media forms caused by the ascendance of digital language? It is far too early to know the answers, but it is exciting to contemplate the questions.

*chapter four*

# technologies of the
# third mediamorphosis

The emergence of digital language has led to immense changes in human communication and information processing within an amazingly brief period of time. These changes have become evident to nearly everyone in the past two decades. However, contrary to the many popularized views that associate the origins of our so-called information society with World War II and the development of electronic computers, the seminal events that initiated the present mediamorphosis actually occurred more than a century earlier. In this chapter, we focus on the transforming technologies that have emerged since the onset of the third mediamorphosis and the role that digital language is now playing in the development of new media and the transformation of established media enterprises.

## A crisis of control

By the beginning of the nineteenth century, the steady progression of commerce, science, and technology had reached a point where traditional communication systems were no longer adequate to deal with the rapidly increasing demands for faster exchanges of information. With the construction of the first railroads, "speed" emerged as a central parameter of social and economic development. And with speed, "instantaneous" communication, feedback, and synchronicity between distant points became vital requirements.

Sociologist James Beniger has hypothesized that the information society developed as a result of a crisis of control created by the railroads and other steam-powered transportation in the 1840s.[1]

---

[1]James R. Beniger, *The Control Revolution: Technological and Economic Origins of the Information Society.* Cambridge, MA: Harvard University Press, 1986, p. 25.

Suddenly, goods could be moved between cities and across continents and oceans at the full speed of industrial production. "Never
before," Beniger says, "had the processing of material flows threatened to exceed, in both volume and speed, the capacity of technology to contain them."[2]

Problems associated with attempts to maintain control at a distance, he notes, inspired a stream of innovations in information processing, bureaucratic control, and communications. Developments
progressed so rapidly that, in his opinion, "the basic societal transformation from Industrial to Information Society had been essentially completed by the late 1930s."[3]

To support this argument, Beniger has verified and extended the
pioneering efforts of economist Fritz Machlup. In the late 1950s,
Machlup measured the sector of the U.S. economy associated with
what he called "the production and distribution of knowledge"[4]
(see Exhibit 4.1). The results clearly show that the information
(knowledge workers) sector began to grow precipitously in the
1830s when the development of railroads created a "supervening
social necessity" for instantaneous communication and feedback
across distances. Between 1830 and 1840, those employed in this
sector grew from substantially less than 1 percent to more than 4
percent of the total U.S. labor force.[5] By 1930—more than a decade
prior to the development of electronic computers—the information
sector already employed a quarter of all U.S. civilian workers. By
1990, this sector had grown to about half of the civilian labor
force.[6]

The number of available media choices has also been growing at
an accelerated rate since the 1830s (see Exhibit 4.2). While no statistical comparisons are possible, it seems reasonable to suggest that
more new forms of communication media have emerged in the past
two centuries than in the whole of prior human history. And all have
had a profound influence, during this brief period, upon nearly
every facet of our social, political, and economic systems, as well as
our cultural identities and perspectives.

---

[2]Ibid., p. 12.
[3]Ibid., p. 293.
[4]Quoted by Beniger, *Control Revolution*, p. 21.
[5]Beniger, *Control Revolution*, p. 23.
[6]U.S. Bureau of Labor Statistics.

**Exhibit 4.1** The civilian labor force in the United States by four sectors, 1800–2000.

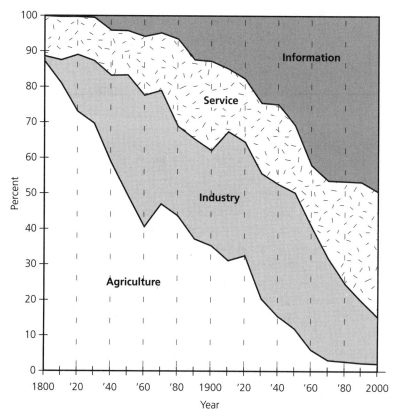

**Source:** From *The Control Revolution* (p. 23) by James Beniger, Cambridge, Mass.: Harvard University, © 1986. Reprinted by permission of the President and Fellows of Harvard College.

## The application of electricity and digital language

The key technological event in this societal and cultural transformation—without which solutions to the control crisis might not have been found—was the application of electricity to communication. The existence of electric charge had been known to humans for millennia through natural phenomena, such as lightning and static, but its basic properties and the methods for controlling its energy potential remained a mystery until the beginning of the nineteenth century.

**Exhibit 4.2** The relative expansion of media choices.

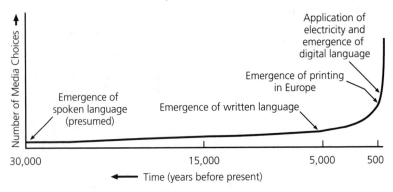

An **electric current** is essentially the orderly flow of elementary atomic particles (electrons) within a conductor, such as copper wire. The discovery that electric current could relay coherent messages through specially designed circuits led to the invention of the electric telegraph, which made instantaneous communications possible. "Instantaneous communications in turn meant a vast increase in the usefulness—and thus quantity—of information."[7] While there can be little doubt that electricity is the agent of technological change that sparked this *third great mediamorphosis,*[8] several other key developments early in the nineteenth century contributed as much to this transformation's defining agent—digital language.

Among the pioneering innovations that foreshadowed the development of digital language and modern computers was a pattern-weaving loom designed by the French entrepreneur Joseph-Marie Jacquard in 1804. His loom employed a set of wooden cards with holes punched in them that automated the repetitive task of weaving patterns into cloth. This is the earliest recorded use of punch-card programming—a system that would be widely adopted in later decades for calculating machines and early computers. Even though it triggered one of the first worker revolts against industrial age automation technologies, his invention was a great practical success.

---

[7]Steven Lubar, *InfoCulture: The Smithsonian Book of Information Age Inventions.* Boston: Houghton Mifflin, 1993, p. 5.

[8]The designation of this transition as the third great communication revolution reflects my hypothesis that the development of digital language is comparable to the development of spoken and written languages in its significance to the evolution of human communication.

## The prototype of modern computers

An initially less practical but ultimately more important development was provided in 1834 by the English mathematician and inventor Charles Babbage, who incorporated Jacquard's punch-card idea into the design of his mechanical "analytical engine"—the prototype of modern digital computers. Babbage's design also adapted another idea developed in France near the turn of the century.

Faced with the daunting task of creating a new set of mathematical tables vital to navigation, astronomy, and engineering, a team of French engineers and mathematicians devised a method for solving complicated problems that would furnish the fundamental concepts of computer programming. Their method involved using a set of rules (programs) for breaking down a problem into many small pieces that could be easily and quickly solved, and then reassembling the individual pieces to yield the solution. The people who did these calculations were called "computers."[9]

Even though a working version of the analytical engine was never built in Babbage's lifetime, he continued to work on the underlying mathematical principles of digital computing until his death in 1871. His collaborations with Ada Byron[10] laid the foundation for multipurpose computers that could communicate through the use of digital language. For her invaluable contributions, Byron is recognized as the world's first computer programmer.

The concepts of digital language and computing developed slowly after Babbage's and Byron's deaths and would have little direct effect on the media domains until the final decades of the twentieth century. But, in the meantime, other technologies energized by electricity would contribute to the development of several new forms of communication media.

## The first information highways

Long before Samuel Morse transmitted the message "What hath God wrought?" over Ezra Cornell's wire from Washington to Baltimore in 1844, the vision of a new medium that could provide

---

[9]Lubar, *InfoCulture*, p. 355.

[10]Ada Augusta Byron, also known as Countess of Lovelace or Ada Lovelace, was the only child of the famous English poet Lord Byron. The Ada computer programming language adopted by the U.S. Department of Defense in 1983 is named in her honor.

instantaneous communication across great distances stirred the imaginations of military and business leaders, as well as those of forward-thinking publishers. Morse was one of those publishers.

Driven by a sense of mission "to cleanse New York City of its moral impurities," he and two other like-minded moralists had founded the *Journal of Commerce* in 1827. The paper quickly gained a much envied reputation for its innovative systems for news gathering. One approach involved an early version of the "pony express." For decades, reporters had used rowboats to collect dispatches and cargo manifests from incoming ships anchored outside the New York harbor. By the 1830s, competition among newspapers had become fierce and occasionally violent. To gain a few hours and avoid confrontations, the *Journal of Commerce* began landing its "newsboats" south of Brooklyn and speeding the gathered information to Wall Street on horseback. The U.S. Postal Service eventually forced the paper to give up its stable of ponies, asserting that this approach competed with its government-mandated monopoly. But by then Morse's electromagnetic recording telegraph and his code devised of dots and dashes were about to render the ponies and the newsboats obsolete.

As impressive as the first transmissions were, the telegraph business, like most new media ventures, did not get off to a quick start. Many people initially questioned its value and wondered who would be willing to pay the high costs of sending a few words between cities. Contemplating the world from the shore of Walden Pond, philosopher and author Henry David Thoreau wrote: "Our inventions are wont to be pretty toys, which distract our attention from serious things. They are but improved means to an unimproved end. We are in great haste to construct a magnetic telegraph from Maine to Texas; but Maine and Texas, it may be, have nothing important to communicate."[11]

Nevertheless, the telegraph prevailed because the value of instantaneous, long-distance communication was recognized by the leaders of two major enterprises—railroads and newspapers. As wires were stretched across continents and finally the oceans, news reported from faraway places that most people had not heard of or cared

---

[11]Henry David Thoreau, *Walden* (1854; reprint 1951), pp. 66–67; quoted in Mitchell Stephens, *A History of News: From the Drum to the Satellite*. New York: Viking, 1988, p. 273.

about before became a popular staple. Telegraphic news soon created in readers an expectation of immediacy and a growing sense of closeness. More than a century before the phrase "global village" entered our vocabulary, pundits were predicting that electric media would make a "neighborhood among widely dissevered States" and blend together not just the people of the United States but the whole world "into one homogeneous mass."[12]

### What hath Bell wrought?

Electricity actually had its earliest and most direct influence on the interpersonal media domain. By collapsing the physical and psychological barriers of time and distance that had always limited human interactions, the telegraph, and later the telephone, greatly increased their users' power to maintain relationships and to control activities at a distance.

This was not immediately obvious, however, even to the inventors. When Alexander Graham Bell submitted his patent application for a telephone in 1876, he was no more certain than anyone else about how it would be used. That people could use telephones to communicate directly and instantly without the assistance of trained operators to technically mediate messages was not thought to be feasible. Nearly everyone saw the electric telegraph network with its legions of intermediary coders and decoders as the only possible model for long-distance person-to-person communication.

Some, including Bell, initially speculated that **telephony** might become a popular form of broadcast entertainment. Opening the lines at scheduled times would allow people to hear live concerts in distant cities or to participate in political debates. For a couple of years, Bell and his assistant, Thomas Watson, raised money to continue their telephone research and development by demonstrating a version of this concept. Using a prototype of his "audio-telegraph," Bell amused stage audiences with organ music played by Watson in an adjacent room or occasionally in a distant city. Contemporary newspapers reported that audiences were quite astonished and even filled with dread by the eerie sounds and voices that emerged from

---

[12]The "neighborhood" quote is attributed to Samuel Bowles, editor of the *Springfield* (MA) *Republican*, 1851, and "homogeneous mass" to James Gordon Bennett, editor of the *New York Herald*, 1844; quoted in Lubar, *InfoCulture*, pp. 84–85.

Bell's machine. But the dread, as well as the idea of using telephony for mass entertainment, quickly faded once people began to understand that a telephone was not a "talking" machine. The recognition that telephones could conveniently extend oral communication between individuals without delays or added complexity contributed significantly to the medium's rapid diffusion.

## Wireless communication

At the close of the last century, people were just beginning to sense how dramatically electricity was changing their lives and the world as they had known it. The electric light had transformed night into day and was altering the natural circadian rhythms of life. The electric telegraph and the telephone had collapsed distances and were redefining "God's" time. The phonograph and motion pictures had captured sounds and sights and were reshaping commonly held perceptions of the "real" world.

So, when a 25-year-old Italian inventor and entrepreneur by the name of Guglielmo Marconi brought his "wireless" telegraph to the United States in September 1899, people were quick to see it as yet another of the seemingly limitless possibilities afforded by the harnessing of the electron. The idea that people in rural America might one day be able to communicate instantaneously "through the air" with friends and neighbors, as well as with people in distant lands, was now exciting. And few cared that Marconi's transforming technology had harnessed yet another agent of technological change—**electromagnetic radiation,** or radio waves.

The British physicist James Maxwell laid the theoretic foundation for wireless communication in the mid-nineteenth century when he predicted that an oscillating electric charge would be surrounded by varying electric and magnetic fields, and that another electric circuit designed to resonate at a similar frequency could detect those electromagnetic fields. A short time later, Heinrich Hertz, a German physicist, confirmed Maxwell's theory and demonstrated that radio waves, as well as light waves, could be used as carriers for wireless communications.

The basic element of electromagnetic radiation is a unit of energy that Albert Einstein named a **photon.** At the beginning of the twentieth century, a group of physicists developed the theory of **quantum mechanics** to account for small-scale physical phenomena, such as photons, which could not be explained by the theories of classical physics. The development of quantum mechanics has provided the underlying foundation essential to modern electronics and communication.

## The electronic age

Although the age of electronic communication began with Marconi and the harnessing of electromagnetic radiation, much of the credit for transforming radio into the first electronic broadcast medium belongs to amateur radio operators. Throughout the first two decades of the century, these radio enthusiasts known as **hams** were mostly middle-class urban men and boys who looked on their activity as a hobby or sometimes as a public service. They took great pride in their technical skills, but, most of all, in their ability to make contact with other hams in faraway places. They often spent their evenings, when radio interference was likely to be at a minimum, listening for faint signals and exchanging brief bits of information, such as their location and station call letters.[13]

Most amateurs regarded two-way exchanges of information to be the natural and appropriate use for this new medium. There were even predictions that radio could ultimately replace wired telephones and become a popular, nearly free form of extended interpersonal communication. A few amateurs, however, began to explore a different vision. In the 1910s, they started occasionally broadcasting music and news without expecting a response from their listeners. By the early 1920s, there were some 15,000 transmitting stations in the United States, nearly all run by amateurs. Perhaps as many as a quarter million people listened to these broadcasts.[14]

"Serious" amateurs tended to look down on those who merely listened to radio and considered broadcasters a nuisance because their signals cluttered the air waves. They also complained that

---

[13]Susan Douglas provides vivid descriptions of the early amateur radio operators and their role in the development of national radio in her book *Inventing American Broadcasting, 1899–1922* (Baltimore: Johns Hopkins University Press, 1987) and in "Amateur Operators and American Broadcasting: Shaping the Future of Radio," in Joseph Corn, ed., *Imagining Tomorrow: History, Technology and the American Future* (Cambridge, MA: MIT Press, 1986).

[14]Lubar, *InfoCulture*, p. 214.

broadcasters didn't transmit their station call letters frequently enough. What mattered most to these hams was not the content of broadcasts but the locations of the transmitters.

## The development of commercial radio

One of the earliest amateur broadcasters was Frank Conrad, an engineer who began regularly transmitting news and Victrola[15] music from his Pittsburgh garage in 1916. His idea soon caught the attention of his employer, Westinghouse Electric, which was actively seeking new markets for its radio equipment.[16]

Prior to World War I, radio telephony research was primarily focused on developing a secure means for communicating between two points. Conrad's broadcasts helped to change the mindset of Westinghouse's executives and convinced them that radio's real potential was as a mass medium. In 1920, Westinghouse moved Conrad's "studio" and transmitter to its Pittsburgh factory, applied for a broadcasting license, and on November 2 put the first commercial radio station, KDKA, on the air.[17] It was an immediate success. As expected, the station's regular broadcasts created a strong demand for the company's new receivers, which had been greatly simplified for nontechnical users. Other radio manufacturers quickly followed Westinghouse's lead. A dozen years later about half of all stations in the United States were operated by radio manufacturers, and one-fifth by sellers.[18]

*Radio newspapers.* Newspaper publishers were among the first nonmanufacturers to launch independent stations. Some thought the medium might be used to economically distribute electronic editions and thereby reduce their dependence on mechanical presses and delivery trucks. Others regarded it simply as a means to promote the content of their printed editions to increase circulation. But publishers soon discovered that equipping and operating a radio station was an expensive and basically unrewarding endeavor. In an

---

[15]Victrola was an early brand name for a phonograph player.

[16]Susan Smulyan, *Selling Radio: The Commercialization of American Broadcasting 1920–1934*. Washington, DC: Smithsonian Institution Press, 1994, p. 14.

[17]Ibid.

[18]Lubar, *InfoCulture*, p. 215.

article written for *Radio Broadcasting* magazine in 1924, the managing editor of the *Minneapolis Tribune* asked, "What is the good of a newspaper running a radio?" Like many other publishers, the *Tribune* ultimately decided that "the return on good will was not worth the expense involved."[19]

Numerous methods for financing broadcast radio were proposed in the 1920s, from taxing radio sets and vacuum tubes to selling "air" time for advertisements. None were universally popular. But despite early resistance from politicians, citizens' groups, amateur radio operators, and newspaper publishers, radio advertising gradually took hold in the United States. By the beginning of the 1930s, intrusive commercials were already becoming a common and lucrative source of revenue for stations and the newly formed national radio networks.

***The need for national broadcast media.*** The development of broadcast radio as a national information and entertainment medium came about gradually, from the seeds planted by the amateur radio operators who sought to make contact with other hams in distant locations. Cultivation of those seeds, however, was left to those who saw the vision of broadcast radio as a unifying force for the nation as the railroads and telegraph had been in the previous century.

The need for new communications technologies that could draw the country together had become apparent to nearly everyone in the first two decades of the twentieth century. Many worried that the great influx of immigrants and the physical and psychological dislocations caused by industrialization were fragmenting the nation.[20] Broadcast radio thus emerged in a society that already recognized the social, political, and economic reasons for a new national communication medium to be developed.

Among the earliest attempts to demonstrate radio's national unifying potential was Major J. Andrew White's famous broadcast of the Dempsey–Carpentier championship boxing match in 1921. Although he was unable to cover the entire country, he managed to reach an estimated 300,000 listeners "scattered . . . from Maine to

---

[19]As quoted in Smulyan, *Selling Radio,* p. 40.
[20]Ibid., p. 31.

Washington [DC] and as far West as Pittsburgh."[21] The technology required to provide coast-to-coast broadcasting was still a decade away, but White had made his point—Americans were ready for national radio networks that could offer nearly immediate access to news, sports events, and entertainment of interest to people in all regions of the country.

***The emergence of national radio networks.*** By the mid-1920s, the novelty of listening to distant radio stations was wearing off and listeners were becoming more interested in the quality of reception and programming as well as in radio receivers that were easier to use. When the Radio Corporation of America (RCA) founded the National Broadcasting Company (NBC) in 1926, its executives promised that the foremost objective of this first U.S. radio network would be to provide improved reception and higher quality programs. But radio historian Susan Smulyan has shown that national radio networks were actually created to cut costs and provide large national audiences for advertisers.[22]

During the next two decades, the networks and companies marketing national brand products collaborated to make broadcast radio the dominant communication and advertising medium in the United States. The transformation of radio programming to serve the objectives of national networks and advertisers had an enormous impact on U.S. culture.

Where local radio stations had featured diverse programming that appealed to regional audiences as well as to ethnic and racial minorities, national networks and advertisers shaped program content to appeal primarily to what they believed were the interests of white middle-class men.[23] Their original motives had more to do with creating a national mass market and selling products than promoting a particular set of social values, but one of the unfortunate consequences of this transformation was an obvious reinforcement of ethnic, racial, and religious discrimination throughout the United States that would not be publicly confronted until the 1960s.

---

[21]Ibid., p. 28f.

[22]Ibid., pp. 38–39.

[23]Lubar, *InfoCulture*, p. 226.

As the networks consolidated their power, they became much more than a unifying force for the nation. They also became a powerful socioeconomic force that created our modern consumer society as well as many of the myths that would define the U.S. image around the world. The business model developed by the national radio networks in the 1930s would later provide the foundation for broadcast television networks and the rapid ascendance of TV after World War II.

Despite the dominance of commercial broadcast radio since the 1920s, interpersonal forms of radio and amateur operators did not disappear. After the schism that led to the development of one-way radio broadcasting, amateur **shortwave radio** became basically a hobbyist's medium. Today, hams continue to promote two-way, interpersonal applications for radio and still frequently play important roles when natural disasters and wars interrupt other forms of communication. Even though their numbers are dwindling, their spirit appears to be living on within the current generation of online computer enthusiasts.

## *The development of television*

When RCA unveiled "live" television at the 1939 New York World's Fair, visitors were amazed, although not entirely surprised by what they saw. Live broadcasts of sports and news events, entertainment, and political speeches that combined moving images with sound had been anticipated for decades. The development of television was, in fact, a much longer process than most people today realize. Its progenitors and dominant traits can be traced back to the 1830s and the nearly simultaneous inventions of photography and electric telegraphy. For nearly a half century, each evolved along distinctly different but gradually converging paths. As both technologies were improved and became more affordable, they spread quickly throughout nearly every facet of private and public life.

Photography's capacity for capturing and preserving realistic images of family members, homesteads, and exotic places did much more than provide a historical record or low-cost substitute for hand-painted portraits and landscape art. It contributed to a rapid change in the way people viewed the world and enjoyed their leisure time. People soon discovered that photographic images could reveal hidden truths, such as the horrors of war, as well as create grand illusions, such as the pristine views of a virgin, "uninhabited" western frontier ready for development.[24]

Equally significant were new sources of entertainment and amusement inspired by the medium. Stereoscopic devices that could create the illusion of three-dimensional images became wildly popular beginning in the 1850s. And by the 1870s, Eadweard Muybridge was already experimenting with a device that could create the illusion of motion using sequential images placed around the edge of a rapidly spinning disk. The seemingly miraculous ability of the telegraph to provide "instantaneous" communication between remote points similarly affected people's long-held notions about the world and inspired new ideas of leisure and entertainment as well.

When Bell made his first telephone call in 1876, electric telegraphy was already a major business enterprise and essential fixture in global commerce and politics, as well as in a great many people's lives. So, too, was photography, which like telegraphic news was also becoming a popular staple of newspapers and magazines.[25] Once Bell demonstrated that voices and sounds could be carried over wires almost as easily as Morse code, it didn't take long for inventors and entrepreneurs to begin speculating about the possibility of transmitting pictures.

***The early visions of television.*** Even though the telephone soon became established in people's minds as an extension of interpersonal communication, the notion that electric media might one day provide aural and visual news and entertainment seemed to be taken for granted. Some early predictions, particularly of television, were remarkably prescient. Cartoons and illustrations published as early as 1879 show families sitting in their living rooms watching "live"

---

[24]The U.S. railroads often used carefully composed scenic photos to entice people into settling the western states and territories or visiting places along their routes. See Lubar, p. 54.

[25]Until the 1870s, photographs had to be manually converted into woodcuts before they could be printed. And woodcuts could only reproduce black and white images without gray tones and required considerable skill and time to produce. The use of photography in newspapers and magazines didn't take off until the development of halftone and zinc engraving processes in the early 1880s. The first newspaper to publish a photograph using these processes was the *New York World* in 1883.

broadcast news reports from faraway places and interacting with other people via the equivalent of a modern video-conferencing system.[26] It actually took many years of painstaking effort by hundreds of scientists, engineers, and entrepreneurs before television, as envisioned in the late 1870s, became a practical form of electronic broadcast media.

The technological convergence of telegraphy and photography that ultimately led to the birth of both television and facsimile systems occurred in 1884 when Paul Nipkow devised a relatively simple mechanical method for converting images into electrical signals. His method involved a light sensor and a disk with tiny holes arranged in a spiral. When the disk was spun and placed between a picture and the sensor, the points of light that passed through the holes were converted into proportional amounts of electrical current. The data were then sent through a wire to an identically perforated, synchronized wheel that recreated the image when a modulated light was projected through the holes onto a screen. This primitive scanning device, which came to be known as the Nipkow disk, didn't work very well, but it provided the first small step on the long path to practical television and facsimile systems.

From that first point of convergence until the middle of the twentieth century, television would coevolve with telephony, wireless telegraphy, facsimile, radio, and motion pictures. All would benefit to some extent from each other's development and would assimilate a variety of shared traits, but as each technology matured it would diverge and fill a different niche in the ever expanding human communication system.

By the beginning of the twentieth century, the idea of television, as well as the name, was already widely known. All that seemed to remain was for someone to assemble a complete and functional system. But, as many would discover, the development of commercial television would prove to be far more difficult and expensive than anyone suspected.

**Mechanical-electrical television.** Despite its known weaknesses, the Nipkow disk continued to play a role in early television experiments. In the 1920s, Scottish inventor and entrepreneur John Baird

---

[26]Lubar, *InfoCulture*, p. 243.

incorporated a version of the mechanical scanning disk in his development for the British Broadcasting Corporation (BBC) of what became the world's first operational television system. Although it could only produce a coarse picture on a very small screen, some 2,000 Baird TV sets were sold in the years from 1929 to 1937 during which the BBC broadcast a limited number of TV programs.[27] While the Baird system stirred substantial public interest in the potential of television, it lacked the capacity for economically transmitting and receiving images at fast enough rates to produce larger, higher resolution images. That could only be achieved when the mechanical parts could be replaced with electronic components.

*Electronic television.* The invention of the **cathode-ray tube (CRT)** in 1897 was a first step. Ten years later, Russian scientist Boris Rosing devised a prototype of the modern TV set using a mirror drum scanner and a CRT to show the pictures. The suggestion of using a CRT on both ends—one as a camera and the other as a display—soon followed, but it wasn't developed until the late 1920s. And while Rosing was experimenting with CRTs, dozens of inventors in different parts of the world were struggling to develop more powerful devices for transmitting, capturing, and amplifying radio signals. Lee De Forest's development of the first triode **vacuum tube,** which he called an Audion, is generally credited with launching the modern electronic era.[28] Other equally important inventions, such as Howard Edwin Armstrong's **superheterodyne circuit,** greatly improved the quality of reception. All would be significant contributions to the development of practical home radio receivers and higher power transmitters, as well as to the development of electronic television.

Credit for making the key breakthroughs, however, is shared by Philo Farnsworth and Vladimir Zworykin. Farnsworth received a basic patent on electronic television in 1930 and some 50 other related patents in the following five years. Even though his system was not an overall commercial success, his patents covered the essential concepts (which earned him substantial royalties). Zworykin independently developed similar ideas while employed by

---

[27]Ibid., p. 244.

[28]Tom Lewis, *Empire of the Air: The Men Who Made Radio.* New York: HarperCollins, 1991, pp. 51–55.

Westinghouse and RCA. He had begun working on television with Rosing in Russia before emigrating to the United States in 1919. With limited funding and little encouragement from Westinghouse, he invented an electronic camera tube in 1928.

Two years later, when RCA hired Zworykin, he managed to convince the company's president, David Sarnoff, that it would only take four men and $100,000 to produce an operational television system. The actual development effort would, in fact, involve hundreds of engineers for nearly twenty years and cost RCA more than $13 million before it began yielding profits.[29] But Sarnoff never seemed to waver in his belief that TV would ultimately be enormously successful and vital to RCA's future.

By the end of 1930s, television seemed on the verge of commercial development, but controversies over technical standards, spectrum allocations, and the uses of this potent new medium, as well as the financial strains of the Great Depression, conspired to delay its commercial introduction. Hopes that RCA's World's Fair exhibit signaled the start of the television age were soon dashed by the United States' entry into World War II, which halted the manufacturing of TV sets and the anticipated development of TV broadcasting.

However, despite government restrictions, research continued and regulatory battles over standards and spectrum allocation raged on. And as soon as the war ended, TV was reintroduced and quickly became the principal driver of the consumer electronics industry and the postwar economy.

*Color television.* Less than a year after RCA introduced black-and-white television at the 1939 World's Fair, CBS demonstrated the first practical color television system. It produced beautiful color, but it had two major drawbacks. The additional color information would not fit into the **very high frequency** (**VHF**) channel space[30] assigned

---

[29]Lubar, *InfoCulture*, p. 247.

[30]The Federal Communications Commission (FCC) originally allocated space for television channels with a standard 6-MHz (megahertz, which is a million cycles per second) bandwidth below 300 MHz, which is known as the very high frequency (VHF) band of the radio spectrum. From 1940 to 1947 the FCC allowed FM radio to operate in the 44–50 MHz range. After a 1947 FCC ruling, FM was moved upward in the spectrum to between 88 and 108 MHz and VHF television was allocated 13 channels between 44 and 216 MHz.

to TV broadcasters without seriously compromising color quality. And even then, the existing black-and-white sets would not be able to receive the signals. The solution, from CBS's perspective, was to establish a new high-definition monochrome and color standard in the much larger **ultra high frequency (UHF)** band[31] and have people buy new TV sets.[32]

However, RCA saw this solution as a threat to its huge investments in black-and-white television and did all it could to block its rival's efforts. When CBS asked the FCC in 1947 to consider a new color television standard based on its technology, RCA used its political influence to delay a decision until it could develop its own color system, which its executives promised would be fully compatible with existing black-and-white TV.[33]

But after four years of disappointing results from RCA, the FCC finally approved CBS's system. However, by then the market had changed significantly. The number of standard black-and-white sets in U.S. homes had soared from about 150,000 to more than 12 million. Prices were falling and demand was increasing at phenomenal rates. In 1951, CBS tried broadcasting color programs for four months before conceding that few people were willing to buy new, more expensive TV sets just for color. Then, in December 1953, the FCC approved RCA's standard instead of CBS's. In 1954, RCA began selling color TV sets. However, the sets were expensive and difficult to tune and the rate of adoption was slow. Sales didn't surpass a million a year until 1965 when NBC began broadcasting the majority of its prime-time shows in color and the average price of color sets fell below $500.

### McLuhan's global village

One of the first media scholars to clearly discern the cultural significance of electronic media was Marshall McLuhan. This eccentric professor from the University of Toronto was quickly embraced as

---

[31]In 1941, the FCC allocated space for experimental television in the region of the radio spectrum above 300 MHz known as the ultra high frequency (UHF) band. The FCC anticipated that 82 channels could fit into the UHF band using the standard 6-MHz bandwidth. CBS's 16-MHz bandwidth requirement for color television would have allowed only 27 UHF channels.

[32]William Boddy, *Fifties Television: The Industry and Its Critics*. Urbana: University of Illinois Press, 1993, pp. 42–43.

[33]Lubar, *InfoCulture*, p. 251.

a celebrity and counterculture guru in the 1960s for his controversial perspectives on technology and modern life. He saw the "mosaic" images of television as the antithesis to the "typographic age." He believed that print media distanced humans from the world and each other while electronic media made us more interdependent and recreated the world in the image of a "global village."[34]

While most of McLuhan's musings are difficult to understand or take seriously, some of his insights into TV's influence on the messages the medium conveys have proven to be quite prescient. Nothing about the popularity of so-called reality TV programs or the interminable coverage of the O. J. Simpson trial, for instance, would have surprised him. Early in the 1960s he observed that: "Electric speed tends to abolish time and space in human awareness. There is no delay in the effect of one event upon another." Also: "When information moves at electric speed, the world of trends and rumors becomes the 'real' world."[35]

The Lisbon earthquake of 1755 provides a dramatic example of just how much the expectations of news and immediacy have been transformed by electricity and modern communications technologies. More than 60,000 people perished in what was one of the most violent earthquakes in historic time, yet it took several months for news of the event to spread across Europe and reach the American colonies. When the news finally did arrive in the ports of Boston and New York, the newspapers of the day gave it only a brief notice.

Had the Lisbon earthquake occurred today, news of this event would be flashed to media organizations throughout the world at almost the speed of light. Within minutes, bulletins would be heard on radios, and "live" video images would begin to appear on TV screens. A slew of rumors and constantly changing death tolls and property-damage estimates would justify a steady stream of news "updates." Interviews with survivors, rescuers, and untold experts would fill hundreds of news columns and hundreds of hours of broadcast air time, as well as hundreds of megabytes in computer databases and bulletin boards. In other words, just as McLuhan

---

[34]Marshall McLuhan, *The Gutenberg Galaxy: The Making of Typographic Man*. Toronto, Canada: University of Toronto Press, 1962, p. 31.

[35]As quoted in Derrick de Kerckhove, *Brainframes: Technology, Mind and Business*. Utrecht, Netherlands: Bosch & Keuning, 1991, pp. 140, 92.

prophesied, hardly anyone living today is capable of escaping this electric news blanket that now covers the globe.

## The computer age

A century after Charles Babbage designed his analytical engine, scientists began to expand on his ideas. Actually, the basic components proposed in the 1940s were not significantly different from those conceived by Babbage. However, instead of using gears and ratchets as Babbage had proposed, early computers contained thousands of vacuum tubes and miles of copper wires. Each tube acted as a switch. Punched cards similar to those used by Jacquard's looms determined which switches to turn on and in which sequence based on a set of preloaded instructions called **programs.**

The first large-scale electronic digital computer was funded by the U.S. Department of Defense at the end of World War II to quickly recompute artillery firing tables. This massive machine, known by its acronym ENIAC (Electronic Numerical Integrator And Calculator), was built at the University of Pennsylvania in 1946. It was incredible to behold—100 feet long, 10 feet high, weighing 30 tons. It drew more than 100,000 watts of electric power, used more than 18,000 vacuum tubes, required 500,000 hand-soldered connections, and cost nearly a half million dollars to build.

And the early generations of vacuum-tube computers were not only big and expensive, they were also generally unreliable and frustrating to use. A scientist could spend days punching data into thousands of cards, only to discover after the program had been run that an error in a single card or a "bug" in the system invalidated the results.[36] But this was not to be a serious problem for long.

### Computers on a chip

The miniaturization of computer components began in earnest by the end of the 1950s. The development of **transistors** and other so-

------

[36]With vacuum-tube computers, *real* bugs in the system were not an uncommon problem. Grace Hopper, one of the earliest and most revered programmers, is credited with documenting the first actual case of a bug being found—a moth stuck in a relay, which she dutifully taped onto a page in her log book. Since then, the term *bug* has been used by engineers and programmers to describe most system problems.

called **solid-state devices** (which exploit the strange electrical properties of silicon and related crystals) led to the eventual elimination of vacuum tubes and a dramatic reduction in copper wiring. Solid-state devices offered many advantages over earlier electronic technologies based on vacuum tubes. They were lighter in weight, cheaper and easier to manufacture, far more reliable, generated substantially less heat, required less power, and took up much less space.

Engineers soon discovered that all individual elements of an electrical circuit could be contained more economically on a single **chip** of silicon. In 1969, it occurred to a circuit designer at Intel Corporation that it might be possible to make general-purpose, programmable **integrated circuits** that could do whatever customers might want. Two years later, Intel announced "a new era of integrated electronics" when it introduced the first commercial **microprocessor**—a "computer on a chip." Since 1972, new generations of microprocessors several times more complex and powerful than their predecessors have been introduced every few years. Microprocessors are now found in automobiles, cameras, washing machines, and hundreds of other everyday objects. But their most important role has been in the development of personal computers and digital communication networks.

## The network of computer networks

Once the private domain of U.S. researchers and scientists, what we know as the Internet has become a vast global communication system that is used by millions of people around the world for academic and business purposes, as well as for personal correspondence and information retrieval. The Net is actually a loose-knit web of thousands of interconnected computer networks. No government or commercial entity owns the Net or directly profits from its operation. It has no president, chief executive officer, or central headquarters. And even though it was originally funded by the U.S. government, its development has been more organic than bureaucratic.

*The ARPANET experiment.* The Internet was born at the height of the Cold War, in 1969, as an experimental network called ARPANET. In its first year, ARPANET connected four university computer centers that were involved in military-related research for the U.S. Defense Department's Advanced Research Projects Agency. The focus of the research was to design an "internetwork" of computers that would continue functioning even if major segments were knocked out by nuclear bombs or saboteurs. Thus, the network itself was assumed to be inherently unreliable, with a high probability that any portion could fail at any moment.

To assure that messages could get through under these conditions, the designers chose to avoid the central control model historically used by the military to link its bases with command headquarters. Instead, they adopted a "headless" distributed network approach modeled after the postal system. In this model, communication always takes place between a source and a destination.[37]

*The postal system as a communication model.* The best way to understand how Internet messages are routed is to consider the postal system. When messages are sent by mail, they first go to the nearest postal substations where they are then routed to metropolitan or regional post offices. From there they are delivered by way of other regional distribution facilities to the local post offices and substations nearest to their destinations. It then becomes the responsibility of each neighborhood carrier to get the messages to their intended mailboxes. Only minimal information is needed at each stage to assure accurate routing. If any distribution point along the way is overloaded or "disappears," the messages can be rerouted through other distribution points. Neither the senders nor the postal workers need to know or care how the messages are routed to their intended receivers, so long as they arrive.

The process of sending electronic mail (e-mail) on the Net is an extension of the postal model. Every computer connected to the network is assigned a unique address. The sender's computer is given responsibility for putting each message into a digital "envelope" and addressing it correctly. The address is structured according to a set of rules called the **Internet protocol (IP)** that governs how mail will be routed. Actually, the IP functions much like a stamped envelope with a mailing address.

---

[37]Information about the Internet was gathered from two principal sources: Paul Gilster, *The New Internet Navigator* (New York: Wiley, 1995) and Ed Krol, *The Whole Internet User's Guide & Catalog,* 2nd ed. (Sebastopol, CA: O'Reilly & Associates, 1994). I have also used articles in newspapers and magazines.

**Cyber communities.** While the original purpose of the Internet was to facilitate the electronic exchange of research, programming, mail, and other information among educators and researchers, it evolved in ways no one planned or expected once the military relinquished Internet development and funding responsibilities to civilian organizations in the early 1980s. Important scientific data and scholarly thoughts have continued to account for much of the traffic, but it is the relationships among people that have shaped the medium. What has mattered most to Internet users is the free exchange of ideas and discussion of values. Over the years this rather anarchistic network of networks has become a haven for uncensored, free-wheeling discussions on everything from sexual fantasies to religious teachings.

**Accelerated growth of the Internet.** Throughout the 1980s, the Internet quietly spread to most major academic institutions and research centers in the United States, and to many other locations around the globe. When the decade began, the Internet connected about 10,000 people in the United States through 400 computer hubs. By the end of the decade, it connected several million users through more than 5,000 hubs in 26 countries. And however phenomenal the Internet's expansion may have seemed in that period, its growth in the following five years surprised nearly everyone. By 1995, an estimated 30 million people in more than 100 countries had gained computer access to news services, libraries, scientific and academic journals, bulletin boards and **databases,** as well as to each other, through more than three million Internet connection sites.

**Taming the Internet.** Two developments in the period between 1989 and 1994—**Mosaic** and the World Wide Web—are probably the most important factors in the sudden popularity of the Internet. Without these technologies, or their equivalents, widespread commercialization of the Net would not have been possible. The Internet protocols and cryptic command language provided experienced network engineers with a functional development environment, but they were definitely not "friendly" to nontechnical users.

In 1992, a small group of **software** developers and students led by Marc Andreessen at the University of Illinois's National Center for Supercomputing Applications (NCSA) in Champaign, Illinois, decided to tackle the problem. They proceeded to develop a dynamic graphical user interface (GUI) that greatly facilitated the browsing of certain Internet databases. About a year later, free copies of their first-generation **browser** program, which they called Mosaic, began circulating throughout the Internet. Within months, Mosaic-based pages seemed to sprout up everywhere on the Net. Mosaic's appeal has been its simplicity. It immediately gave nearly everyone who possessed basic computer skills the ability to create and use easy-to-follow visual road maps to the vast amounts of information stored on the World Wide Web (known as the Web or WWW).

The Web is actually an international string of computer databases connected by the Internet that use an information-retrieval **architecture** developed in 1989 by Tim Berners-Lee, a British computer specialist at the CERN physics laboratory in Geneva. Berners-Lee's system relies on the form of information linking known as hypertext or hypermedia. This standard, upon which the Mosaic technology depends, greatly simplified the managing and displaying of mixed-media content and opened the door to online **publishing** via the Net.

***Breaching the service walls.*** The Internet became so popular by 1995 as a result of the Mosaic and Web technologies that consumer online networks, such as America OnLine, **Prodigy**, and CompuServe, suddenly began offering Net access to their customers. Previously, subscribers to these services could only retrieve information or use e-mail within the confines of the service to which they subscribed. Once the proprietary walls came tumbling down, online customers were no longer obligated to subscribe to several services in order to gather the information they wanted or communicate with all of their online cohorts.

The explosive growth of Internet activity, which in 1995 was increasing at an estimated rate of 10 to 15 percent per month, has come to be viewed by pundits as the stirrings of mass appeal for some new form of information exchange. Many users firmly believe the Net is a much better vehicle for free speech and public debate than any of the other existing forms of communication media. Even though the Internet's collective audience is still relatively small and fragmented compared to the established forms of mainstream media, its potential power to influence opinion makers and young affluent voters has not been overlooked by politicians and special interest groups. As a sign of the times, nearly all candidates in the 1996 U.S. presidential campaign felt obligated to establish their presence on the Net.

Where the Internet and the other transforming digital technologies of the third great mediamorphosis are ultimately leading humankind is beyond anyone's capacity to accurately predict. But the end of their evolution and influence upon the human communication system and civilization appears nowhere in sight.

A torrent of transforming technologies from the electric telegraph to microprocessors and the Internet has tested and confirmed the enormous adaptive power of the human communication system. And, even with all of the many changes that have already occurred, a period of deceleration and calming is unlikely anytime soon. By taking a long view and comparing the past two centuries with those that went before, it is evident that we have, in fact, only been experiencing the initial stage of this great transformation.

## Mediamorphic principles and the future of cyber media

The rapid expansion of media choices and the growing popularity of "virtual universes" where information exchange exists on an ostensibly higher plane have definitely made the understanding of new media technologies and the future of established media enterprises even more crucial, as well as more complex. But, while it may seem that the old rules and dominant media traits might not be applicable to mediamorphosis in the next century, I don't believe that to be the case.

The evolution of human communication, which we have been following, provides substantial support for the principles of mediamorphosis and their continuing relevance. Several recent developments, however, suggest that two of the fundamental principles of mediamorphosis introduced in chapter 1—the survival principle and the delayed adoption principle—might need further clarification.

***The survival principle revisited.*** Although the survival principle seems to imply that all forms of media, as well as media enterprises, will always adapt and evolve in response to changing conditions, it should not be assumed that individual forms can successfully adapt and evolve forever. Eventually, most forms of communication, like living species, will be subsumed or die out. But the process usually takes some time and does not occur the instant a new form emerges.

The phonograph provides an instructive example of an older technology that was subsumed in the mid-1990s by a newer technology—digital compact disc (CD) systems. The evolution of electrical phonograph players and records spanned more than 70 years. During that period, the medium successfully adapted in response to competition from radio, player pianos, tape recorders, and audio cassette systems. After World War II, the development of high-fidelity and stereo recording and playback systems created a booming market for the phonograph business. But, by the 1990s, it could no longer adapt to the market pressures brought to bear by the emergence of digital CDs. Yet, phonographs and CDs coexisted for more than 10 years before manufacturers decided for economic reasons to phase out the production of electrical record players and vinyl records.

An example of a medium that died out entirely early in the 1990s is the commercial telegraph. After some 150 years of successful adaptations, the telephone and modern digital telecommunications networks finally appropriated the last remaining niches occupied by the relatively slow-speed telegraph. Yet, even after its passing as a commercial medium, the telegraph key and Morse code continue to be used by amateur radio operators around the world.

*The delayed adoption principle revisited.* The sudden rise of cyber media would seem to contradict the delayed adoption principle but, as we learned in chapter 1, our short human memories all too often confuse surprise with speed. Much of the apparent acceleration and chaos we are now encountering in the world of telecommunication is clearly the result of a great many convergences occurring simultaneously. While some might argue that the Mosaic browser technology and World Wide Web are exceptions to the rule, they are actually just enhancements to the Internet, which *has* required nearly three decades to move from proof of concept to widespread acceptance.

That's not to say that the aggregated pace of technological change has not been gaining momentum in the final years of this century. The linking of tens of millions of individual minds through the Internet and other telecommunication systems may, indeed, be accelerating the cross impacts of emerging technologies and the development of new media. Nevertheless, we can be quite certain that most lessons from our past are unlikely to be discarded in the future, regardless of the overall pace of change.

# Technologies of the third mediamorphosis in perspective

As we have seen in this chapter, all electronic communication technologies we now take for granted owe their existence to a crisis of control that arose early in the nineteenth century as the industrial revolution began spreading across the European and North American continents. The development of increasingly faster methods for producing and transporting goods, which drove industrialization, created a supervening social necessity for instantaneous feedback between distant locations, as well as for more expeditious ways to gather and process the increasing amounts of data that were becoming vital to the efficient operation of corporations and governments.

The application of electricity to communication and the spread of digital language have done more, however, than merely provide solutions to this crisis. In less than two centuries, they have contributed to a blindingly rapid transformation and expansion of the human communication system that is unprecedented in human history. Within this extraordinarily brief period of time, the third great mediamorphosis inaugurated by these powerful agents of technological change has had a profound influence upon nearly every individual, society, and culture. Human notions of distance, time, and reality itself have been radically altered by the new forms of media that have only recently emerged and diffused throughout the world.

Yet, despite the obvious importance of innovations and inventions to the mediamorphic process, they alone, as the opportunity and need principle states, are unable to assure the widespread adoption of new media. In the next chapter, we look beyond the emerging new media technologies to examine some of the contemporary social, political, and economic forces that are now influencing the development of new media and the transformation of established mainstream media and telecommunication businesses.

*chapter five*

# the cultural context of the third mediamorphosis

So much has been written about the profound cultural changes that have occurred in U.S. society since the end of World War II that a separate volume would be required just to provide an overview. I have therefore chosen to present in this chapter only the highlights of those contemporary forces—social, political, and economic—that I believe are the most relevant to the present situation and to the next stage of the third mediamorphosis.

While there are many diverse points of view, historians and sociologists generally agree that our culture has been shaped in the past five decades by the convergence of three momentous postwar developments: (1) The Cold War and the United States' emergence as the world's dominant economic, political, and military superpower; (2) the explosive rise in birth rates immediately following the war that produced a great "baby boom"; (3) the rapid diffusion of television and other electronic media throughout all social and economic strata of society. Let us now examine some of the cultural consequences of this convergence in an effort to better understand the motivating reasons for the apparent rush in the final years of this century to develop new media technologies, as well as to transform established media and telecommunication enterprises.

## Social forces

Because it did not suffer massive destruction during the war, the United States was well positioned to provide much of what the world needed to rebuild. The result for most Americans was a wealth-producing economy that permitted the rapid expansion of a working middle class. After suffering through the Great Depression and wartime rationing, the increasing affluence brought by global trade and domestic economic growth was a welcome change. Rising incomes and government assistance programs made it possible for vast numbers of people to buy new homes, appliances, and cars, to get a college education, and to have children. During the Depression and war years the birth rate in the United States had steadily declined, but once the war ended, couples quickly reversed the trend and created the greatest population explosion in U.S. history. More than 77 million children were born between 1946 and 1964—17 million more than if normal birth patterns had prevailed.

## The television generations

Those who were born in that period have the distinction of being members of the first television generation. During their school years, TV emerged as a new and amazing technological wonder. For the so-called baby boomers, the TV set quickly became their pacifier, their baby-sitter, their teacher, and their companion. Where radio had conveyed the sounds of the world instantaneously to the ears and imaginations of the previous generation, TV brought the homogenizing images that defined this generation's sense of reality and itself.

For them, the joy of entertaining oneself was quickly replaced by the joy and expectation of being entertained. A continuous stream of "live" news and entertainment poured into homes and filled the time that once was used for leisure reading, conversation, sharing meals, and imaginative play. To provide more time for watching the "tube," cooking steadily gave way to frozen TV dinners, and dining at a table was replaced by eating on folding TV trays. By the time this generation began to have children, the medium had penetrated nearly all social and economic strata, and had spread from the living room into dining rooms, kitchens, bedrooms, and even the bathrooms of some homes.

**The creation and destruction of myths.** During the past 50 years, the underlying television technology has hardly changed at all, but the world in which the second TV generation grew and matured was vastly different from the world their parents knew in their childhood, due in part to significant changes in the medium's content and cultural messages.

Throughout the 1950s, the national television networks and program sponsors jointly filtered and selected content to attract the largest possible audiences as well as to promote their image of a conservative, religiously devout, hard working, homogenous "middle American" way of life. Advertisers kept a close eye on potentially troublesome program content to avoid controversy and "association with political, artistic, or literary avant garde."[1]

Children, as well as adults, were led to believe in the early years of television that all was well in the world even though the threats of nuclear war and communism were always close at hand. Among the fictional TV families idealized by such programs as "I Love Lucy," "The Adventures of Ozzie and Harriet," and "Father Knows Best," there were no domestic problems that required more than a half hour to solve. In fact, no "real" domestic problems, such as divorce, teenage pregnancy, alcoholism, and the violent abuse of children and spouses, were even mentioned.

That all began to change in the early 1960s with the assassination of President John F. Kennedy, which suddenly brought the violent realities of the world directly into U.S. living rooms. The myths that had been carefully constructed and managed in the 1940s and 1950s were soon destroyed by the revelations of racial injustice and violence, the assassinations of other popular leaders, the Vietnam War and the U.S. defeat, and the Watergate scandal and President Nixon's resignation. All were seen and experienced through the medium of television with a shocking intimacy and vividness that had never been known before.

**The secret of adult censorship.** For young children, TV became a powerful "secret-exposing machine."[2] No longer were adults able to use literacy as a tool for control. With books and print media, adults could keep many of the harsh realities of life hidden from children or at least exercise some control over when they gained that knowledge. Television, especially after 1960, thoroughly undermined that system and contributed to the dilution of adult authority. Joshua

---

[1]William Boddy, *Fifties Television: The Industry and Its Critics.* Urbana: University of Illinois Press, 1993, p. 98.

[2]Joshua Meyrowitz, "Mediating Communication: What Happens?" in John Downing, Ali Mohammadi, and Annabelle Sreberny-Mohammadi, eds., *Questioning the Media: A Critical Introduction.* Thousand Oaks, CA: Sage Publications, 1995, p. 42.

Meyrowitz suggests that as television programs, especially talk shows, began openly discussing the topics that adults had been trying to keep from children, the medium exposed them to "the biggest secret of all: the secret of secrecy—the fact that adults conspire to censor children's knowledge."[3] In Meyrowitz's view, one of the reasons the current generation of children seems so much less childlike than previous generations is that they have been exposed from an early age to so many adult secrets through television.[4]

***Distrust of mainstream media.*** Although television has revealed many of the dark realities of life, it has also created many unrealistic expectations and perceptions, which have contributed to a general sense of national malaise and a lingering cynicism with regard to established institutions, mainstream news media, and nearly all authority figures. Television programs and commercials, for example, frequently show people enjoying the "American Dream"—owning homes, driving expensive cars, vacationing in exciting places, rearing healthy, intelligent children, and cavorting with their attractive spouses. Yet for most people these images are far from the reality they have experienced or are ever likely to experience. And, in the 1990s, programs based loosely on actual events have so thoroughly blurred the distinctions between fact and fantasy that the "made-for-TV" versions often become more real in people's minds than reality itself. Even television news coverage of political stories and regional conflicts has taken on the appearance of sports contests and John Wayne movies. This tendency to oversimplify and trivialize complex problems and significant events has made the job of critically evaluating the validity of information all the more difficult. An underlying distrust of mainstream news media and other traditional sources of information appears to be one of the contributing factors in the growing popularity of the Internet and other consumer online networks.

## The growth of media choices

For those born since the early 1960s, personal computers and global telecommunication networks are providing the means to bypass mainstream media, as well as to build and connect virtual communities in the ways that superhighways facilitated the rise of suburbs

---

[3]Ibid., p. 44.
[4]Ibid., p. 45.

and long-distance commuting in the 1950s and 1960s. This is a generation for whom mobile, interactive, mixed-media communications are taken for granted. Instead of relying on television, radio, newspapers, and magazines to define reality for them, many members of this generation seem determined to create their own more intimate and dynamic realities in cyberspace.

In fact, we have all grown so accustomed to having a broad range of choices for practically everything in our lives that few can even imagine a time, not so long ago, when newspapers and magazines were the only forms of information media routinely available, and immediate interpersonal communications was confined to face-to-face conversations. Until this century, the choices for entertainment were always limited and were always "live." No one expected to be continuously engaged by professional entertainers; people mostly entertained themselves or each other—when they had time. The rise of mass communications and the rapid growth of media choices in the twentieth century have profoundly altered expectations and daily routines in nearly all societies.

In the brief period since general circulation newspapers first reached more than half the U.S. population in the 1880s,[5] every generation has absorbed and been radically transformed by the emergence of at least one new form of mass media—phonographs and silent films at the beginning of this century, AM radio and "talking" films from the 1920s through 1940s, television and FM radio in the 1950s and 1960s, satellite and cable television in the 1970s and 1980s, and the Internet and consumer online networks so far in this decade. And instead of discarding the older forms, we have added to them and modified them.

Today, people routinely mix and blend many forms of media to suit their needs, and think little of it. A typical day for those who commute to work might begin with the bedside clock radio for weather and traffic conditions, followed by a morning television news or talk show while dressing, and a quick scan of the morning paper for interesting stories at breakfast. They might turn on the radio while driving to work for more news and traffic updates or listen to a cassette of a book or their favorite music. At the office, a

---

[5]Not all media scholars agree that newspapers were the first form of mass media. A common alternative view is that mass media began with commercial radio in the 1920s.

fax newsletter might be waiting along with a financial newspaper and a trade magazine. Throughout the day, they exchange bits of information with colleagues and clients by telephone, fax, express mail, memos, personal contact, and perhaps electronic mail and teleconference.

On their way home, they might try to reduce their stress by listening to an FM music station or by playing another cassette or CD. While preparing dinner, a broadcast or cable news program might provide information in the background and, if it's convenient, they might also try to peruse sections of the newspaper they didn't have a chance to read in the morning. Depending on their domestic situation and length of commute, they might relax after dinner with several hours of TV, a prerecorded movie, a video game, some CDs, a magazine or a book. Some might even use their personal computers to dial into a consumer online service to gather information or join a "chat" session.

None of this seems at all strange to us. And despite frequent complaints of media overload, our expectations of instantaneous communication and continuous entertainment continue to grow.

## Competition for time and attention

While the patterns of individual activity and media consumption differ between and within generations, one aspect of modern life that appears to be consistent for most people who are working, maintaining a household, and/or attending school is a *perceived* lack of time. This is not, of course, a new problem. Since the beginning of the industrial age, the constraints imposed by time have been a nearly inescapable fact of life. The distinction today, however, is not so much that current generations actually have less discretionary time than in the past—it is in the number of choices that now confront people each day and the number of activities they feel obligated to compress into their waking hours.

One of the most common ways people attempt to deal with their perceived shortage of time is to do several things at once, such as watching television or listening to radio while preparing a meal, doing household chores, talking on a telephone, or doing homework. The capacity to simultaneously process multiple media inputs appears to be expanding with each generation. Conversely, patience and attention spans appear to be shrinking.

This does not mean, however, that people are managing to fit everything they used to do into less time. One of the activities that appears to have suffered most in the past two decades is leisure reading. For publishers of mainstream newspapers and magazines, the most common and troubling reason given for canceling subscriptions is "no time to read." This excuse is often interpreted as a sign that editors are not providing readers with enough relevant and compelling information to justify their time and effort. While many professional journalists agree with this interpretation, their ability to solve the problem has been made more complicated by the shifts in cultural values and social priorities that have occurred since the end of World War II.

In past generations, publishers could count on people acquiring a regular newspaper reading habit in their early twenties when they began working and building a family. That has not been the case among the TV generations. Even more troubling is the realization that children today rarely, if ever, see a printed newspaper at home. The days when parents used to read the comics to their children on Sunday mornings and discuss the day's news events are clearly long gone.

Publishers have been trying to reestablish the reading habit among younger audiences and combat the common perception of dullness by adding more color and visual elements, but this has been an uphill battle in unfamiliar territory. Instead of competing based on the quality and quantity of information, newspapers are essentially competing against the compelling aural/visual qualities of electronic media for the time and attention of younger audiences. The steady growth of personal computers in homes has heightened concerns that people will have even less time for leisure reading in the future.

## The decline of literacy

The assimilation of electronic technologies into everyday lives has had profound social consequences. In the 1890s, a well-educated person living in an English-speaking country was one who could recite from memory several complete poems by Alfred Tennyson, Elizabeth Barrett Browning, and other popular poets of the time, as well as lengthy passages from the classic prose of Shakespeare and Chaucer. Most university graduates in that decade would also have committed to memory a great portion of Western civilization's accumulated knowledge of the sciences, arts, and classical music.

*Shifting priorities.* But as books, newspapers, magazines, and other printed documents became commonplace, and radio and TV expanded their hold on people's time, rote memorization steadily gave way to the development of new skills. Instead of acquiring specialized knowledge through intensive reading, students were expected to gain a generalized world view through extensive reading.[6] Emphasis also began to shift from deliberate information analysis and critical thinking to quick information accessing and processing. As this century draws to a close, most recent college graduates can no longer recite Tennyson's "Charge of the Light Brigade" from memory, but they have been exposed to considerably more "bits" of information from more diverse sources than were even imaginable in the 1890s.

*Increasing concerns about the future.* The social consequences of these shifts have become the subject of deep concern and considerable debate. Surveys and scholastic tests conducted in the past three decades have shown steady declines in reading and writing skills, as well as in basic knowledge of history, geography, and the sciences. Some have suggested that literacy, as it has been historically defined, may no longer matter; that emerging forms of computer-based aural/visual media would soon relegate written language and print media to an elite form of communication.

Many educators and politicians have responded by decrying this apparent decline of literacy and recommending a return to the basics, or so-called three Rs—reading, writing and arithmetic. Publishers are openly worrying that there may not be anyone interested in or, perhaps, even capable of reading their publications in the next century, and historians are wondering if the end of history is at hand. All of these concerns are indicative of the profound transformations taking place within modern civilization as this third great

---

[6]Sven Birkerts provides an excellent explanation of the fundamental shift from intensive, repetitive reading to extensive, superficial reading in the third chapter of *The Gutenberg Elegies: The Fate of Reading in an Electronic Age.* Boston: Faber and Faber, 1994.

mediamorphosis enters its next stage—the total conversion of electronic communication media to digital language.

### Image versus content

All of these concerns about declining literacy may be valid. The world view experienced by the TV generations has, from Marshall McLuhan's perspective, a great deal more in common with original oral traditions than with contemporary literate cultures. This experience appears to run counter to the path of increasing literacy and individualism Western cultures have followed since the Renaissance in Europe.

To say that television has been a powerful medium is as much an understatement as it is banal. Yet, even after a half century of exposure, we remain intellectually awed by its seemingly limitless capacity to absorb our time and alter our perceptions. No matter how many pundits accuse it of being a "vast wasteland"[7] or a mindless and corrupting influence, we are still drawn to its low-resolution, flickering images like moths to a flame.

Everywhere in the world, television is both revered and reviled. Debates about the "proper" content and uses for the medium tirelessly rage on. Even in countries where political and religious leaders have attempted to severely restrict the channels and programs available to viewers, the medium has defied control. Television's images are generally believed to have hastened the collapse of totalitarian communist governments in Eastern Europe and the former Soviet Union. They are also credited with precipitating and reinforcing the civil rights and women's movements in the United States.[8]

This immense power of the television image to influence human expectations, social systems, and cultures has been recognized by politicians and theologians, as well as by intellectuals, since even before the first live broadcasts in the late 1930s. Numerous articles and books published during the years of the Great Depression

---

[7]The phrase "vast wasteland" was first used by FCC Chairman Newton N. Minow in a speech before the annual meeting of the National Association of Broadcasters on May 9, 1961. Minow's complete NAB speech can be found in Newton Minow, *Equal Time* (New York: Atheneum, 1964), p. 52.

[8]Joshua Meyrowitz provides an explanation of how television has influenced social relationships in "Mediating Communication," pp. 39–53.

focused on TV's potential for public good through its presumed ability to educate and inform, stimulate the economy, and unify the nation.

But there were also those who quickly perceived the darker side of the medium and its potential for abuse. Some feared its power to instantly and insidiously spread enemy propaganda into the living rooms of millions of homes. Others expressed fears that TV's power might be used by governments to control people and rob them of their privacy and freedom.

***1984 or Brave New World?*** For the past five decades Western cultures have been preoccupied with the specter of a totalitarian "Big Brother" world as described by George Orwell in *1984*, but media critic Neil Postman argues that the Orwellian uses of television to stifle the flow of information and continuously spy on citizens were not the real threat. In his view, Aldous Huxley's vision of a *Brave New World,* in which citizens are overwhelmed with trivial information and amused into a perpetual state of boredom, was far closer to the reality we are now facing.

Postman has been especially critical of television news programs that determine the newsworthiness of events by their videogenic qualities and their potential to attract the largest possible number of viewers. He has pulled no punches in his criticisms of the "Now . . . this" style of TV news reporting, in which the day's news events have been steadily reduced to 30-minute packages of disconnected 45-second (or less) sound bites:

> In television's presentation of the "news of the day," we may see the "Now . . . this" mode of discourse in its boldest and most embarrassing form. For there, we are presented not only with fragmented news but news without context, without consequence, without value, and therefore without essential seriousness; that is to say, news as pure entertainment.[9]

While television is the most highly evolved form of broadcast media from a technological perspective, it has often been accused of being the most regressive form in terms of content. Before television

[9]Neil Postman, *Amusing Ourselves to Death: Public Discourse in the Age of Show Business.* New York: Viking Penguin, 1985, p. 100.

was introduced, there were genuine hopes that the medium could serve to educate and enlighten people as well as entertain them. Broadcast TV has had its occasional bright spots in the past five decades, but they have been too few to dispel the prevailing feelings of disappointment with the medium.

**The loss of meaningful content.** In *The Age of Missing Information*, writer Bill McKibben raises challenges to McLuhan's vision of a global village created in the image of television. McKibben acknowledges the emotional resonance of the idea contained in this phrase. In his view, it suggests that: "We can follow the modern, commercial, political impulse toward globalization, toward standardization—and in the process create the intimacy of a village, the kind of close and connected personal and cultural life we've been vaguely missing."[10]

The notion that we are becoming more like preliterate tribespeople gathered as we are around our TV sets that serve as campfires and also as jungle drums beating out the news is indeed popular and compelling. But, as McKibben argues, this is merely a romantic illusion or, worse, a delusion. "What aspects of a village," he asks, "can be usefully translated to an almost infinitely larger scale? What is a village? What is a tribe?"[11]

Shared experiences in preliterate villages have traditionally involved storytelling in relatively small groups. Ever since oral communication became possible, people have talked to each other about what they have in common. Anything else would have been meaningless. When hunters returned to their villages, stories about the hunt and encounters with other tribes were as eagerly anticipated as the carcasses they carried. They had much to share that was meaningful to everyone in the village. Content had real substance and an understandable context.

In the electronic global village, we also restrict our conversations to what we have in common, which is why McKibben finds our TV campfires less productive than the old tribal ones. "We can find subjects of interest to all," he says, "only by *erasing* content, paring away information."[12]

———
[10]Bill McKibben, *The Age of Missing Information*. New York: Plum Penguin Books, 1993, p. 45.
[11]Ibid., p. 47.
[12]Ibid., p. 48.

It is the pursuit of the global market, not the preliterate village, which he suggests is hastening the trend away from cultural diversity. Global marketers are typically more interested in how the nations of the world are alike rather than different. As a result, image, not substance, dominates. Instead of sharing meaningful information, global villagers today share the image of drinking Coca-Cola, eating a Big Mac, and wearing Levi jeans.

McKibben does not argue that the old ways are necessarily better than the new, or that television is inherently a pernicious medium. His point is that we cannot afford to ignore the vital fact that important information, upon which humankind has relied for millennia, is being lost in the headlong rush to develop new forms of electronic media. In his view:

> Our society is moving steadily from natural sources of information toward electronic ones, from the mountain and field toward the television; this great transition is very nearly complete. And so we need to understand the two extremes. One is the target of our drift. The other an anchor that might tug us gently back, a source of information that once spoke clearly to us and now hardly even whispers.[13]

## Future media environments

If today's television commercials are any indication, there seems to be little hope that the trend away from natural sources of information will abate anytime soon. Advertisements for future media technologies and environments frequently push natural as well as printed sources of information into a backseat role or, in some instances, out of the vehicles of modern life altogether. Automotive and consumer electronics companies, for example, are now promoting future cars and vans with practically every imaginable form of electronic communications media built in, from telephones, fax machines, and televisions to global satellite tracking and navigation systems. Commercials for these "mediamobiles" often depict families vacationing in remote, pristine regions. But, instead of enjoying the natural splendors that surround them, the children are shown watching TV sets mounted on each seatback while the parents fuss with a navigational display, talk on their cell phones, or receive faxes.

---

[13]Ibid., p. 10.

Early in the next century, even this vision of mobile media environments may seem passé. The explosive development of computer-mediated communications in this decade is already beginning to transform the way people expect to travel and experience the world. Communication and transportation appear to be rapidly converging toward a point where the physical automobile may no longer be a necessity. With virtual reality systems, the medium *is* the vehicle.

Cyber media have also begun transforming the way people socialize and define themselves. In cyberspace, individuals can be whoever they want to be. They can change personas as easily as changing their clothes. This notion has been well illustrated in a popular cartoon created by Peter Steiner that shows two dogs with a personal computer. The one who is using the computer explains to the other that "On the Internet, nobody knows you're a dog."

Clearly, reality is no longer as easy to define as it once was. Quite possibly, future generations may come to accept that reality is whatever they want it to be. Through advanced **neural networks,** all of humanity may one day share experiences beyond anything we can comprehend today. In recent decades, visions of future worlds where life and media are virtually indistinguishable from one another have become increasingly popular with science fiction writers and film-makers. Such visions of the future may seem troubling and even frightening to us today, but they are, in fact, no stranger or more frightening than our world would have seemed to people living before the application of electricity to communications and the third great mediamorphosis.

## Political forces

Nearly every American is at least somewhat familiar with the Bill of Rights and the First Amendment to the U.S. Constitution, although its significance to existing and emerging forms of media is generally not well understood. The text of this amendment is as follows:

> Congress shall make no law respecting an establishment of religion, or
> prohibiting the free exercise thereof; or abridging the freedom of
> speech, or of the press; or the right of the people peaceably to assem-
> ble, and to petition the government for redress of grievances.

When the framers of the Constitution agreed to provide guarantees for the freedom of speech and the press, they seemed to be clearly implying that the government should assume a hands-off policy with regard to all forms of communication media. That, however, is not the political interpretation that has prevailed. In the years since 1791, when the Bill of Rights was adopted, the government has managed to legitimize its influence and regulation of communication media by utilizing a variety of constitutional arguments.

Newspapers and magazines have enjoyed the greatest amount of freedom from government regulation, to a large extent, because the framers abhorred the strict controls imposed by the British on colonial printing presses and publications. But, after the application of electricity to communications, Congress saw itself increasingly in the role of regulating new media to protect "the public interest." Consequently, a three-part division of communication regulatory policies evolved in the United States: (1) *print media,* which is essentially unregulated; (2) *electronic broadcast media,* for which the government licenses private owners and directly regulates the technology and content; and (3) **common carriers,** for which the government assures nondiscriminatory access for all. But, as we will see, the spread of digital communication technologies has begun to upset this regulatory scheme.

## *The indirect control of print media*

Even though newspapers and magazines are essentially unregulated, the government has been able to exercise some influence over their content and growth through indirect means. For example, postal reforms in the 1840s and 1850s established a reduced rate, which amounted to a government subsidy, for print media—so long as they complied with certain rules pertaining to their content and frequency of publication. Postal rules have typically restricted content that was deemed obscene by the "public decency" standards of the time, advocated the violent overthrow of the government, or exposed secrets that might threaten national security. They have also served to indirectly regulate the maximum ratio of paid advertising to editorial content. Newspapers and magazines have relied heavily on the postal service for delivery, so compliance has been a vital economic necessity for publishers. In recent decades, the newspaper industry has actively lobbied Congress to protect its special second-class postal rate while, at the same time, pushing to have fourth-class postal rates increased for competing direct mail advertisers.

Another approach commonly used by the government to indirectly control, or censor, print media has been to restrict access to information through secrecy policies and contracts. Perhaps the most disturbing example in recent history was the Reagan administration's issuance in 1983 of National Security Decision Directive 84, which "required all federal employees with access to 'sensitive compartmented information' to sign nondisclosure agreements that included provisions for the pre-publication review of all writings that the signers might produce for the rest of their lives."[14] This agreement not only covered classified information but *potentially* classifiable information as well—"in other words, anything that the government might decide it wanted to keep secret."[15]

Except for declared periods of national emergency, such as the Civil War and World War II, the First Amendment is supposed to grant publishers the freedom to criticize government policies and public officials, as well as to publish unpopular or controversial points of view, without the official threat of censure or imprisonment. But that doesn't mean they are free to print anything they want to print without legal or financial consequences. If a publisher prints information that exposes someone to public ridicule, shame, or contempt, or otherwise damages a person's reputation, severe penalties can be imposed for libel.[16] However, U.S. libel law also provides some measure of protection for publishers against attempts to stifle legitimate criticism and dissent. To win a libel case, the prosecutor must prove that a publisher showed "reckless disregard" for the accuracy of the published statements or that there was an "intent of malice."

### The regulation of electronic broadcast media

While Congress has always steered clear of legislation that would require licenses for printing presses or would levy special taxes on newspapers and magazines, as other countries have done, it has not

---

[14]Donna A. Demac, *Liberty Denied: The Current Rise of Censorship in America.* New Brunswick, NJ: Rutgers University Press, 1990, pp. 101–102.
[15]Ibid.
[16]Ibid., pp. 23–24.

hesitated to license broadcasters or impose indirect taxes on radio and television stations in the form of "free" time for public service programs and messages.

Licensing of transmitters began in 1912 soon after the military complained that private radios were interfering with its ship-to-shore communications. The problems of signal interference and of so-called bandwidth scarcity have been used ever since as justification for regulating transmitters and radio frequencies. The government's two basic arguments are as follows:

1. Without licensing and the controlled assignment of frequencies, chaos would reign and broadcasters might take unfair competitive advantage by using high-powered transmitters or spurious signals to drown out and harass their rivals.

2. Bandwidth (the range of electromagnetic frequencies available for wireless communications) is a scarce commodity that belongs to all the people, so the government has a constitutional obligation to oversee its allocation and use in the public interest.

Passage of the comprehensive Communications Act of 1934 created the Federal Communications Commission (FCC) and consolidated the regulatory responsibilities of diverse government agencies under its auspices. The act also formally established radio, and subsequently television, as a national communication medium and a form of interstate commerce that could be regulated. All of this served to further legitimize the government's growing political and economic influence over electronic broadcast media.

Cable-TV technology, introduced as **community antenna television (CATV)** in 1948, eliminated the problems of signal interference and bandwidth scarcity. Nevertheless, the FCC interpreted its regulatory mandate to include companies providing these services. Except for a period between 1984 and 1992 when the Reagan and Bush administrations gave cable TV companies almost total freedom, the FCC has regulated their prices and services.

### The common carrier role of telephony

Since early in this century, the government has been influencing the development of telephony, but not in the same ways as either print or broadcast media. At the end of the nineteenth and beginning of the twentieth century, Alexander Bell's telephone and the company he spawned, American Telephone and Telegraph (AT&T), had spanned the continent and become a powerful commercial and political force. While many competing independent telephone companies had sprung up in those years, none could rival AT&T. The company was proud of its unabashedly monopolistic goal of "One system with a common policy, common purpose and common action; comprehensive, universal, interdependent, intercommunicating like the highway system of the country, extending from every door to every other door, affording electrical communication of every kind, from every one at every place to every one at every other place."[17]

Of course, not everyone was happy with AT&T's dominant position. Many people thought the telephone system should be taken over by the postal service, as it had been in most other countries. But after a long series of antitrust investigations that concluded in 1913, the U.S. attorney general finally agreed to a settlement with AT&T that would allow it to maintain its dominant position in the telephone business, and a virtual monopoly on long-distance communications, in exchange for certain concessions. These included allowing independent telephone companies to interconnect to the Bell system and accepting government regulation as a public utility. Fees that provided AT&T with a "fair rate of return" were to be set by state public service commissions. The government also defined AT&T, as well as the independent telephone companies, as "common carriers" and required them to provide "universal access" in each state they served. As common carriers they could not create or control the content that was sent through their lines.

### Regulatory policies and the new media

The spread of digital language and the resulting convergences of communication technologies in the past two decades have begun to confound the established three-part regulatory scheme. For example, it is now technically feasible for cable-TV companies, which are no longer considered common carriers, to provide competitive telephony services, and for telephone companies, which are not considered broadcasters, to provide pay-per-view TV services. Adding to the confusion are unregulated, low-cost voice telephone and video services on the Internet, which can be accessed through either telephone or cable-TV lines.

---

[17]Quoted by Steven Lubar in *InfoCulture: The Smithsonian Book of Information Age Inventions*. Boston: Houghton Mifflin, 1993, p. 127.

When President Clinton signed into law the Telecommunications Act of 1996, pundits claimed that this first major overhaul of U.S. communication regulatory policies since 1934 would radically change the communications business in the United States and speed the way for new media development. Although this law eliminates many of the regulatory barriers that had existed between different forms of communication and allows for somewhat more competition, a great many questions remain unanswered.

For instance: Are consumer online services common carriers or publishers? If they are common carriers, then they cannot legally restrict or exercise editorial control over any information posted to their networks; if they are publishers, they are vulnerable to libel suits even if they do not originate the libelous information. Several consumer online services have already been confronted by this legal dilemma.

The sudden explosion of Internet and consumer online services has also forced lawmakers to hastily reexamine existing copyright provisions because it is now so easy to reproduce, manipulate, and distribute anything that can be converted to digital language. And despite several copyright revisions introduced in the 1990s to address this issue, the situation is still murky at best.

Often even the best of intentions can lead to greater confusion or have an opposite effect, especially when politicians and judges have little or no understanding of the emerging new media technologies. Among the most controversial provisions of the Telecommunications Act of 1996 is one that would make it illegal to transmit, or in any way make available, indecent materials to minors via any telecommunication system. While the intent is to protect children from exposure to pornography, this restriction has been challenged by civil liberties and Internet groups on the grounds that the indecency standard is too vague and unconstitutional. Technically, this provision could even criminalize the posting of fine art that included nudes as well as open-forum discussions about AIDS and other subjects that might involve human reproduction and health.

The blurring of legal and regulatory distinctions is certain to increase in the next decade. Through digital engineering nearly all future forms of electronic media can be expected to blend traits from all three domains. Of particular concern is the position regulators might take with regard to digital print media. Publishers are already using the Internet and consumer online services to electronically distribute their products. In a few years, they should be able to deliver digital editions directly to a variety of portable information appliances that function more like electronic paper than personal computers using satellite and cable-TV channels as well as broadband telephone lines. These editions will certainly include audio and video clips and wireless transactional services in addition to traditional text and still images. This, of course, begs the question: If a newspaper is no longer mechanically printed on paper and is delivered via a cable-TV or direct broadcast satellite channel, should it be treated as a print medium, be regulated as an electronic broadcast medium, or possibly be required to function as a common carrier (if it simply aggregates content from many sources without applying editorial controls)?

Unfortunately, with so many digital technologies maturing simultaneously and affecting so many different aspects of the human communication system, changes in government regulatory policies run the great risk of stifling new media rather than encouraging it. However, stifling is often the intended purpose. The lobbyists and associations for media and telecommunication industries usually are not hesitant to evoke Brian Winston's law of suppression of radical potential when a new medium begins to threaten the business and financial interests of the established enterprises they are paid to represent.[18]

## Economic forces

The economic reality that must be understood is that new media do not develop in a vacuum. All emerge within a complex system and must immediately begin to compete with existing forms of communication for time, attention, and support if they are to survive and become financially successful. This is one of the essential messages contained in the principles of mediamorphosis. Even though emerging forms of communication will coexist with established forms (the coevolution and coexistence principle), they will also compel those

---

[18]Brian Winston, "How Are Media Born and Developed?" in John Downing, Ali Mohammadi and Annabelle Sreberny-Mohammadi, eds., *Questioning the Media: A Critical Introduction.* Thousand Oaks, CA: Sage Publications, 1995, p. 69.

forms with whom they must compete to adapt and evolve to survive (the survival principle). The development of radio provides an instructive example of the influence economic forces can have on the mediamorphic process.

For more than a decade after broadcast radio emerged as a new form of mass media, the principal economic beneficiaries were the manufacturers and sellers of radio receivers and transmitting equipment. In broadcast radio's first stage of development, owning stations and producing programs were expensive propositions for which the only possible return on investment was some measure of "good will." Newspaper publishers were among the first enterprises to own radio stations and provide regularly scheduled programs, but most soon quit the medium because good will alone was not enough to justify the expense. Other early station owners, such as auto dealerships and department stores, also quickly became discouraged by the high costs and limited tangible benefits.

Consequently, by the early 1930s, only about a quarter of all U.S. stations were owned and operated by companies that were not involved in the manufacturing or selling of radio equipment. However, the economics of radio broadcasting was already beginning to change as the medium entered its second stage. A source of income that would ultimately make broadcasting a highly profitable business had been identified—advertising. National radio networks and commercial sponsorships finally provided the market and financial resources that would shape the medium's future and provide lucrative opportunities beyond manufacturing and selling equipment. But this development had the adverse effect of putting broadcast radio into direct competition with the well-established and powerful newspaper industry, which also depended on large audiences and advertising revenue for its continuing survival.

Publishers fought hard throughout the 1930s to prevent commercial radio, particularly the emerging national networks, from broadcasting news and taking advertisers away from print media. They tried to restrict the medium's growing power by applying political pressure in Washington, as well as by applying economic pressure in their local markets. Newspapers in those days often shut out or penalized advertisers who appeared on radio. Until the 1970s, many U.S. newspapers even refused to publish the program listings of competing radio stations. In the end, broadcast radio prevailed and newspapers adapted. But, by the beginning of the 1950s, the process started all over again. This time radio stations, as well as newspapers and magazines, were put into the position of having to adapt to economic pressures brought to bear by the emergence of television.

The World Wide Web has been following a path similar to that of broadcast radio. In this first stage of its development, the principal economic beneficiaries are the technology companies selling essential software and computer equipment and the telecommunication companies providing Internet access for consumers and high-speed lines for information providers. So far, few individuals or companies publishing on the Web are benefiting financially. Although some cross between the broadcast and print advertising models appears to be the most likely future source of revenue, **Web sites** must first demonstrate their ability to attract and hold the customers that advertisers are seeking. No one, at this point, is certain how Web advertising will evolve or how established mass media companies will adapt to growing competition from this new medium.

### Competition for audiences and advertisers

While increasing, or at least maintaining, readers, listeners, and viewers is an important goal for all mass media companies, it represents only part of their marketing strategy. An essential part of that strategy is the medium's ability to attract advertisers. Without the continuing support of advertisers, mainstream media companies could not survive.

More than three-quarters of the U.S. newspaper industry's revenue comes from a combination of classified and retail advertising. Within the magazine business, advertising accounts for about half its total revenue. For commercial radio and television broadcasters, advertising is their only significant source of income.

Throughout most of this century, the media and advertisers had a mutually beneficial and interdependent relationship. But as the audiences for mass media have become more fragmented and enigmatic, the ability of newspapers, magazines, television, and radio to match advertisers with potential customers has eroded.

*Newspapers.* For most newspaper publishers, the financial consequences of competition with television and radio were masked by the overall growth of the U.S. population and economy, particularly during the 1950s and 1960s. But that changed abruptly in the

**Exhibit 5.1** Advertising market shares for U.S. media in 1995.

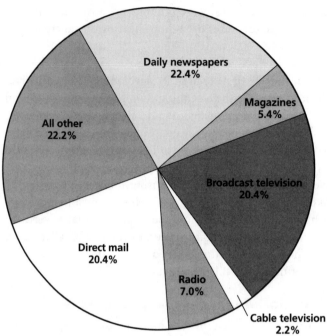

Daily newspapers
22.4%

Magazines
5.4%

All other
22.2%

Broadcast television
20.4%

Direct mail
20.4%

Radio
7.0%

Cable television
2.2%

**Sources:** Newspaper Association of America (newspapers); McCann-Erickson, Inc. (all other media).

early 1970s, when sharply rising costs for labor, energy, and paper began cutting deeply into their profits. Fortunately, new technologies came to the rescue just in time. Computer systems and phototypesetting machines made it possible to streamline the labor-intensive production processes and dramatically reduce costs. The combination of new technologies and a robust economy throughout most of the 1970s and 1980s made newspapers more profitable than they had been since the 1920s.

That period of prosperity, when 30 to 40 percent profit margins were not uncommon for newspapers, ended in the late 1980s. A prolonged recession combined with the economic fallout from a decade of leveraged buyouts and giant mergers took a toll on newspapers. More than 60 U.S. daily newspapers died in the first four years of the 1990s, and more are expected to die in coming years. However, as ominous as these closings may seem, they are not generally regarded as harbingers of failure for the newspaper business as a whole. These recent closings, for the most part, merely reflect the long-term trend in the United States toward consolidated, single newspaper markets. Overall, newspapers continue to have high consumer acceptance, reaching about two-thirds of U.S. households.

While television offers more glitz and attracts larger audiences, newspapers provide advertisers with a much greater percentage of the most desirable households—those with higher incomes and better education—than any other form of mass media.[19] Daily newspapers collectively remain the dominant player in the U.S. media industry, with annual revenues in 1995 of $46 billion and 22.4 percent share of total U.S. advertising dollars (see Exhibit 5.1).[20]

**Magazines.** The competition with electronic broadcast media for audiences and advertisers has had a far greater impact on the magazine business than it has had on newspapers. In the 1940s, mass circulation magazines, such as *Life, Look,* and the *Saturday Evening Post* could command the attention of large national audiences and receive high fees from advertisers. When television took over the roles of those magazines and eroded their advertising support, magazine publishers were relegated to serving niche audiences.

Since the early 1980s, there has been a virtual explosion of small specialty publications worldwide. In 1994, the Standard Rate and Data Service (SRDS) listed 14,000 U.S. consumer magazine titles. But 20 years earlier, there were only 4,500. And not included in these figures are the enormous numbers of smaller publications made possible by the introduction of low-cost desktop publishing systems and cheaper offset printing.

The rate of growth in new titles does not appear to be diminishing in the 1990s. Samir Husni's *Guide to New Consumer Magazines,* recorded 838 new launches in 1995, which was the largest number of entries since Husni began tracking premieres in 1985. The other side of the coin, however, is that most new launches will not survive more than three years. Some publishers even plan for

---

[19]*Facts About Newspapers.* Washington, DC: Newspaper Association of America, 1996.
[20]Ibid.

frequent revamping of content and format to conform to the shifting interests of audiences and advertisers.

While many new magazines are launched by entrepreneurs, six major corporations publish the majority of consumer magazine titles and account for a significant portion of the total circulation. About one-third of all U.S. magazine revenue and 40 percent of the profits are controlled by Time Warner alone. But, as impressive as the total number of magazines may be, the business collectively receives the smallest share of annual U.S. advertising expenditures—about 5.4 percent in 1995 (see Exhibit 5.1).

*Broadcast radio.* Radio has gone through much the same transformation as magazines in response to increasing competition. Media experts of the 1930s and 1940s predicted that AM radio would be the most important and profitable form of mass communication well into the next century. Even as television began gaining a mass audience in the late 1940s, experts saw no threat to radio. However, by the early 1950s the same experts declared radio a dying medium with little hope for survival. But radio didn't die. As we saw in chapter 1, it metamorphosed into what some scholars have defined as a new form of mass media—FM radio.

Instead of trying to hold onto the dwindling and fragmenting market of the large general-audience AM radio stations, many small, semiautomated FM stations were created. By **narrowcasting** specialized content for niche audiences, these owners discovered a market need not being fulfilled by other media forms. But the rapid growth of low-power FM stations further segmented the market for radio in the 1970s and 1980s and dealt a nearly fatal blow to AM radio. The once dominant AM radio stations have only recently begun to show signs of recovery.

Even though television usurped radio's position as the dominant mass medium, radio's mobility and variety of offerings have made it the most popular medium in history. In 1995, nearly 600 million sets were in use throughout the United States. Less than 1 percent of U.S. households have fewer than five radio receivers. The number of commercial radio stations has grown from 2,800 in 1950 to more than 11,000 in 1995. Radio's share of advertising revenue is still less than half of what it was at its peak in 1945, but in recent years it has been inching upward again. In 1995, radio accounted for about 7 percent of all advertising dollars (see Exhibit 5.1).

*Television.* The once seemingly invincible U.S. television networks have also been facing stiff competition, primarily from cable channels and movie rentals. In 1980, the combined audience share of the three original networks, ABC, CBS, and NBC, stood at about 98 percent. By the 1993–94 season their share had dropped to about 61 percent. The introduction of two new national networks in the early 1990s—Fox and United Paramount Network (UPN)—has taken another bite out of the Big Three's audience share. In 1991, all three networks lost money for the first time in their history.

Direct broadcast satellites (DBSs), cable services, and video-on-demand services through telephone lines, as well as a new generation of video games and interactive video services, are expected to further fragment TV audiences and erode the ability of the networks and commercial channels to match advertisers with potential customers.

Some media analysts are predicting that television will soon go the route of radio. Even the concept of discrete channels appears to be on the verge of becoming obsolete. Within a few years, viewers should be able to easily aggregate the programs they want to see, at the times they want to see them, without having to surf channels or learn how to program their VCRs.

Yet, despite the growing competition and a lengthy recession, television broadcasters and cable operators have been steadily increasing their combined share of advertising dollars, which in 1995 surpassed newspapers for the first time in history. But some media analysts believe television advertising revenue may be headed for a steep and irreversible decline. The expanding ability of audiences to **zap** commercials or switch to commercial-free alternatives, such as HBO, Cinemax, and pay-per-view, is already raising serious concerns about future growth in broadcast television's advertising revenue. And the battle for TV audience time has only just begun.

### New media and the relative constant

Since the 1980s, the apparent inevitability of yet another new form of mainstream media emerging and diffusing into the marketplace has served to heighten competitive tensions within established mass media companies. All are concerned that their shares of the market will be eroded even further and that the value of their particular forms of communication media will be greatly diminished by new technologies.

These concerns are not without foundation. Throughout this century, media companies have found that the ebb and flow of their fortunes are closely tied to the state of the economy and the number of competitors in their markets. When the overall economy is growing, their wealth usually grows; but when a new media competitor enters their market, their wealth generally suffers, especially in periods of economic stability or decline.

If audiences and advertisers were willing to increase the total amount of time and money they spent on mass media as each new form emerged, media companies would have little to fear. But that is not a choice either has historically shown a willingness to make. Instead of increasing spending, audiences and advertisers have tended to reallocate the time and resources that they have already committed to mass media in order to support new forms. This reslicing of the media pie means that each existing form of mass media gets a proportionally smaller share of the market if all else remains equal.

Newspaper publisher Charles E. Scripps is credited with being the first to elaborate on this economic constraint. He described the apparent relationship between mass media and the economy and relationships among the various forms of media as the "relative constant."

**Evidence and anomaly.** Research conducted in the early 1980s by Maxwell E. McCombs, professor of communications at the University of Texas at Austin, verified that between 1929 and 1975 total consumer spending for mass media relative to several key economic indicators did, indeed, remain constant, even after television emerged in the late 1940s.[21] This would seem to explain the rapid decline in audience and advertising spending for general circulation magazines and AM radio during the 1950s in spite of an expanding and robust U.S. economy. While McCombs's study was based solely on U.S. data, these economic constraints imposed upon mass media by consumers are believed to be consistent within nearly all market-oriented societies.

––––––
[21]Maxwell McCombs and Chaim Eyal, "Spending on Mass Media," *Journal of Communication* (Winter 1980), 30 (1): pp. 153–158. This is an update of McCombs's original independent research in "Mass Media in the Marketplace," *Journalism Monograph* (August 1972), 24.

A 1992 follow-up study conducted by McCombs and Jinok Son, however, discovered what appears to be an anomaly in the relative constancy principle for the years between 1975 and 1987. For the first time, consumers seemed willing to significantly increase the portions of their income that they devoted to both existing and new forms of media.[22]

***Special conditions.*** Several factors may provide a plausible explanation for the 1975–1987 anomaly in the principle of relative constancy. For one thing, that period saw a veritable explosion of major electronic innovations, such as cable TV, VCRs, videodisc players, personal computers, and videotex, enter the U.S. marketplace. Since 1975, cable TV has become a formidable competitor for audience and advertiser support. Today, nearly two-thirds of all U.S. households subscribe to one of about 8,500 cable systems.[23] Video rentals and VCRs have also successfully competed in the mass media marketplace. By the early 1990s, more than half of all U.S. households had a VCR, and Americans were spending more than half a billion dollars per month on rentals and purchases of tapes for VCRs.[24] Personal computers and online services had not yet become significant competitors for consumer time and money in 1992 when Son and McCombs compiled their data, but obviously they, too, have become forces to be dealt with in the 1990s. Videodisc players and the early videotex services, on the other hand, languished and failed to attract more than a minute share of the market.

Another factor may have been the accelerated growth of the U.S. economy and personal income in the early 1980s. Americans, who were at least partially influenced by the "feel-good" philosophies of the Reagan era, generally seemed more willing in that period to spend money to acquire new possessions and services, even if it meant also acquiring greater debt. The so-called yuppies (young upwardly mobile people) were particularly enamored with new electronic forms of media.

Whether the surge of media spending that Son and McCombs discovered in the 1975–1987 period represents a new general trend

[22]Jinok Son and Maxwell McCombs, "A Look at the Constancy Principle under Changing Market Conditions," *Journal of Media Economics* (Summer 1993), 6(2) pp. 23–36.

[23]Ibid.

[24]Ibid.

or is simply a statistical blip is not yet known, though the economic realities of the 1990s do appear to have had a moderating effect on spending for all forms of media. Anomalies aside, the general premise of relative constancy cannot be ignored. For entrepreneurs who intend to invest in new media, significant audience and advertising support are still essential for financial success. And, to gain that support, new media must be able to take the majority of it from existing forms of mass media.

## Cultural context of the third mediamorphosis in perspective

The social, political, and economic forces discussed in this chapter have clearly influenced and been influenced by the development and spread of an extraordinary array of new media technologies in the twentieth century. There has been no other century in history when humans have assimilated and had access to so many forms of media. This stage of the third great mediamorphosis has obviously contributed to a steadily increasing expectation of continuous entertainment and emotional stimulation as well as a growing human capacity for simultaneously processing multiple media inputs.

Although newspaper and magazine publishers have tended to attribute their declining readership to the growth in media choices and a perceived lack of time for reading, their problems stem more from the profound changes in social values brought about by the TV generations. Among the consequences of these changes have been a significant societal shift away from literacy and mediated content toward images and interaction. The implications of these changes for the future of mass media are discussed in the subsequent chapters.

We have also seen in this chapter how the convergence of media technologies stimulated by the spread of digital language has upset the U.S. three-part division of communication regulatory policies. Until the 1970s, the distinctions among print media, electronic broadcast media, and common carriers (telephone systems) were relatively clear. But in recent decades many forms of communication have begun to overlap and create legal and regulatory dilemmas. While the Telecommunications Act of 1996 has been touted as a major overhaul of U.S. policies that will encourage greater competition, many critical issues arising from this transformation remain unresolved.

In the next stage of this third great mediamorphosis, the battles for audiences and advertising dollars are certain to be waged with even greater determination and effort. All media companies now see themselves struggling not just against each other, but also against a changing economic order, new and potentially formidable competitors, growing social, economic, and racial diversity, a struggling educational system and declining literacy, and a public that seems to increasingly distrust and disregard mass media.

Taken as a whole, the current level of audience and advertising fragmentation, even without the threat of a popular new medium, would seem to present a nearly insurmountable obstacle to future growth for all existing mass media companies. Quite a few pundits have concluded that the continuing growth of cyber media will ultimately fragment audiences and advertising to a point where mass media will cease to exist. But a close examination of each established form of media reveals that total fragmentation may not be the inevitable outcome.

Still, established media will face stiff competition from a new generation of entrepreneurs who are embracing digital media. Although the growing popularity of the World Wide Web and consumer online services has stimulated established enterprises to experiment with digital systems, most have not taken advantage of lessons learned in the early 1980s from the first wave of electronic publishing ventures. In chapter 6, we study Viewtron—the first U.S. trial of a consumer online service—to identify some of the lessons from its failure that may be relevant to the next stage of the third great mediamorphosis.

# lessons from failure

The suddenness with which the Internet and World Wide Web burst into the limelight in 1994 caught most people in mainstream media businesses by surprise. For many, consumer cyber media appeared to arise from nowhere without the slightest warning. Yet, for some, the recent stampede to online publishing evoked strong feelings of déjà vu. These are the surviving media pioneers who participated in the first attempts to develop and commercialize cyberspace in the 1970s and 1980s.

The Internet was still an embryonic, military-funded project when the initial market trials began for consumer videotex services, as online networks were originally known. By 1979, market researchers and pundits were already predicting the death of mass media—particularly newspapers and magazines—and their eventual replacement by personal interactive media accessed through home information and entertainment centers. Between 1977 and 1986, dozens of media and telecommunication companies, as well as governments around the world, collectively poured hundreds of millions of dollars into the development and marketing of videotex services only to be frustrated by a persistent lack of enthusiasm from consumers.

Convinced that electronic publishing would not be commercially viable in this century, most media and telecommunication companies shut down their videotex services in 1986. However, not everyone lost hope. A few entrepreneurial enterprises continued, believing it was only a matter of time before consumer online networks caught on. They may have been right. But, unfortunately for them, online technology as it was defined in the 1970s would prove to be the Neanderthals of the 1990s.

While many experts now believe that computer-mediated communications have finally come of age, the lessons of the recent past should not be too quickly forgotten. It is unfortunate that the stories of the first-generation online services have not been fully told. The lessons from their failures are perhaps even more instructive than those that would have been gained had they succeeded, particularly as they apply to the principles of mediamorphosis.

In this chapter, I provide a brief case study of a service in which I was intimately involved—Knight-Ridder's **Viewtron**. This was the first and most ambitious of the early consumer online services launched in the United States. My reasons for including this story are to provide a historic context for evaluating contemporary visions of electronic publishing and cyber media as well as to reinforce some of the points that have been made in preceding chapters about technological change and the mediamorphic process. To broaden and balance the lessons learned from the Viewtron experience, we also examine another variation of consumer online services that emerged from the technological convergences of the 1970s—interactive TV.

## The troubled birth of consumer online services

The British post office, which until the late 1980s controlled all telephone and television networks in the United Kingdom, didn't plan to threaten or transform established media companies when it initiated a series of research projects in the late 1960s and 1970s. Its principal objective was to develop new services that would stimulate usage of telephones and TV sets. Originally, the post office's telecommunication research labs (now known as British Telecom or BT) were charged with developing a videophone that could display text on ordinary TV screens for the hearing impaired. Somewhat later, the initiative was expanded to provide interactive transaction and information services to hotels, offices, and homes via the telephone and TV set.

### The development of teletext

The first efforts focused on a low-cost, interactive broadcast technology known as teletext. The system that emerged was deceptively simple. Between each frame of a TV broadcast is a separator known as the **vertical blanking interval** or VBI. The only time viewers normally see these separators, which appear as thick black lines, is when the controls on their TV sets need adjustment. Teletext technology took advantage of these usually empty spaces to sequentially broadcast several hundred frames, or "pages," of textual information in a continuous loop.

With a special decoder and a numeric keypad, viewers could request specific information by entering the appropriate page number, much like changing channels with a remote control. As soon as the requested page ran past the decoder, it was "grabbed" and displayed on the television screen. The page would stay on the screen until the viewer requested another page or switched back to regular television programming. This approach was relatively inexpensive and easy to implement as well as uncomplicated and simple to use. But to achieve this level of simplicity and efficiency, content and presentation had to be severely restricted.

That is, the number of teletext pages that could be broadcast within a single TV channel was constrained by practical considerations. At the standard broadcast rate of 30 frames per second, the cycling of more than a few hundred pages would result in intolerably long delays. If, for instance, 500 pages were broadcast sequentially, a viewer could wait more than 15 seconds for a requested page to be displayed. This problem was partially overcome by broadcasting the most popular pages more often, but this only served to extend the response time for less frequently requested pages.

Also, the text and graphic elements that could be displayed on a teletext page were limited by the space available within the VBIs and the resolution of standard TV screens. A page could contain only about 100 words in one standardized type size and style. Small colored squares, called tiles, were used to construct primitive graphics that were generally more decorative than functional. The coarse, stair-step effect created by the tiles tended to give pages that contained graphics the appearance of needlepoint homilies.

Nevertheless, teletext met the original objectives of the British post office. Even with its practical and aesthetic limitations, it seemed to have obvious practical applications. By the mid-1970s, teletext was already well on its way to becoming a commercial service in the UK.

## The development of videotex

Once teletext technology passed the research phase, attention shifted to a much more complex and challenging problem—how to simplify the process of interactively accessing much larger stores of information. In the early 1970s, only a few databases could be accessed remotely by computers, and those were far too expensive and complex for nontechnical people to use.

The proposed solution was to create a new hierarchical database system based loosely on the teletext model. Instead of scrolling unformatted text, which continues to be standard on most contemporary databases, researchers adopted the more graphical teletext page format defined by the shape of the standard TV screen.

The underlying technology, which was originally called viewdata in the UK and later also came to be known as videotex (without a final *t*), was designed to easily connect subscribers to large central databases via a telephone and a special decoder box. Like the teletext services, a numeric keypad would be used to request and display specific information on a standard television screen. Videotex was to be the "user-friendly" computer database service for people who were not computer literate, which in the late 1970s was practically everyone.

Videotex pages were linked to menus that formed so-called decision trees. Beginning with a main menu, subscribers could work their way through a series of branches and submenus by pressing the appropriate numbers on their keypads until they eventually arrived at the information they were seeking. With this approach, videotex services could provide subscribers with a far greater range and depth of information than teletext or any other existing form of mainstream media.

To turn videotex technology into a commercial service, the British post office established an enterprise called **Prestel**. Beginning in 1978, newspaper, magazine, book, and catalog publishers as well as advertising agencies and educational institutions throughout the UK were actively recruited by Prestel to serve as "information providers."

## Technologies looking for markets

From their start, teletext and videotex were new technologies looking for new markets. They were elegant solutions to problems that had not yet been defined, least of all by typical consumers. In the United Kingdom, where people leased their TV sets and telephones from the government, introducing new information services and TV sets with built-in decoder boxes was considerably easier than in the United States. But getting people to use these early forms of cyber media proved to be equally difficult in every country in which they were introduced.

Broadcast teletext services did find a reasonably successful niche in several European and Asian countries by the beginning of the 1990s, largely because their governments convinced TV set manufacturers to build in low-cost teletext decoders and the services were provided free of charge to television viewers. Such was not the case for videotex. Nearly all of the pioneering videotex services launched by media companies in the early 1980s survived for only a few years. One of those services was Viewtron, which the Knight-Ridder newspaper group began developing in 1979 and commercially operated until 1986.

## The Viewtron experience

Executives at several large U.S. newspaper companies had become aware of the work being done by the British post office in 1978 and decided to take a closer look. Few who visited Prestel's information providers in those heady days could decide if videotex was an extension of television, newspapers, or the telephone, but its potential threat to established media companies seemed clear.

Knight-Ridder and Times Mirror were among the first newspaper groups in the United States to take defensive action. Instead of waiting for other companies to pursue this technology and use it to attack their markets, they decided to preempt its development. Both companies would invest tens of millions of dollars in the early 1980s attempting to understand and control the videotex market.

As a member of the original Knight-Ridder videotex development team, and later as Viewtron's first director of design, I had the privilege of sharing in the excitement and travails of midwifing this new medium. For those of us who participated, the experience provided many important lessons about human nature and electronic publishing. One of the critical lessons it taught us was to treat market research for emerging media technologies with caution, because in the "real" world people do not always want what they say they want, or do what they say they will do.

### *The secret mission*

Mystery and intrigue seem part of the English mist in February, so it was fitting that Knight-Ridder would choose that month for a secret mission to London and Norwich. The year was 1979, and publishers were deeply anxious about the emerging information technologies that some people believed would challenge and possibly even replace printed newspapers.

A four-person development team, of which I was a member, had been selected covertly from staff of newspapers and subsidiaries within the Knight-Ridder group. James K. Batten, the vice president for news who later became the company's chairman and chief executive officer, asked each of us in private meetings to volunteer for a venture that he believed was of the utmost importance to the future of the company. Our objective, Batten told us, would be to learn everything we could about Prestel and then help to develop a similar service in the United States.

He explained that Norman Morrison, Knight-Ridder's director of information systems, had alerted the company to the potential threat posed by videotex technology. After executive visits to England, he and most of the other officers had become convinced that the threat was real and believed that Knight-Ridder must act quickly.

I had only the vaguest idea what Prestel and videotex were, but the opportunity to spend several weeks in England investigating new media technologies was impossible to refuse. The secrecy surrounding our mission was so tight that only Batten, a few other senior Knight-Ridder executives, and our designated team leader, John Woolley, knew all our identities before we assembled for the first time at the Portman Hotel in London. The Portman had been chosen because it was one of the first hotels in England to provide its guests with access to Prestel. This was to be our introduction to the world of videotex before moving on to Norwich, where we were to receive hands-on training. However, much to our disappointment, the service was "down" for maintenance throughout our entire stay. Prestel was not yet a commercial service and formal public trials were not scheduled to begin until March or April, so no one at the hotel was particularly concerned. But not all was lost.

In our rooms, we discovered that the TV sets had been recently adapted to access two broadcast teletext services called Ceefax and Oracle. Like children with a new toy, we spent a significant portion of our time in London playing with these services to learn all we could about their content and design. Of the nearly 300 pages that were available, most provided basic information, such as weather forecasts, sports scores, movie and restaurant guides, and brief news items. Horoscopes and soap opera summaries also seemed to be popular. Looking back, it was probably fortunate that Prestel was unavailable. If it had been functioning, our secret mission would not have been secret for long—at that time, the Portman had only one TV set with access to Prestel, and it was located in the main lobby.

As we journeyed by train through the rolling English countryside to Norwich, we were constantly watching over our shoulders, suspicious of everyone. England in those days was crawling with agents from competing U.S. media companies, or so we had been told.

The Eastern Counties Newspapers Group in Norwich was actively developing content for the Prestel trials, and its executives had generously offered to show us how pages were created and organized. As the designer on the team, my assignment was to master the computer tools and page creation techniques developed for Prestel.

As with teletext pages, graphics were built with small colored tiles and text was limited to one size and one style (see Exhibit 6.1). Creating recognizable images and editing information to fit within the pages proved to be our greatest challenge, but by the end of the second day we were already turning out acceptable pages.

**Exhibit 6.1** A typical Prestel page in 1979.

## The market trial at Coral Gables

Soon after our return from England, Knight-Ridder and AT&T quietly formed a joint-venture relationship. Bell Laboratories were to develop the computer tools needed for creating the videotex pages as well as the customer terminals. Knight-Ridder was to be responsible for all content, the host computers, and the overall management and marketing of the service. To fulfill its obligations, Knight-Ridder created a wholly owned subsidiary called Viewdata Corporation of America (VCA).

Within a year, VCA launched the first U.S. videotex service, which later would be given the name Viewtron, in the affluent Miami suburb of Coral Gables. The 15-month market trial was designed to evaluate customer acceptance of the Prestel technology and service model in the United States. Throughout the trial, VCA only had about 30 employees.

The 35 families who participated in the Coral Gables trial were selected by researchers according to a predetermined set of criteria. Executives of VCA wanted only those families who were most likely to become early adopters of new technologies. They reasoned that if the people who were already predisposed to buying and using new technologies disliked the videotex service, it would have little or no chance of succeeding in the broad consumer market. If the opposite was true, they believed the service at least had a fair chance of becoming a profitable business.

Out of necessity, the content developed for the Coral Gables trial was limited in its breadth, but the staff managed to offer a great deal of depth in some specific areas. In addition to providing generous amounts of general and local news, community events listings, and reference information, the VCA content staff also gathered and manually created videotex versions of menus from local restaurants, organized contests, and even helped make deliveries of products ordered by the trial subscribers (see Exhibits 6.2 and 6.3).

Staff researchers collected volumes of usage data and conducted extensive personal interviews in an attempt to understand how the selected families used the service and to determine how much they would be willing to pay if it were to become commercially available. Throughout the trial, feedback from the families was encouraging. They seemed to like the service and were genuinely upset when they had to give up their videotex terminals and free access.

**Exhibit 6.2**  A sample menu page from the Viewtron trial.

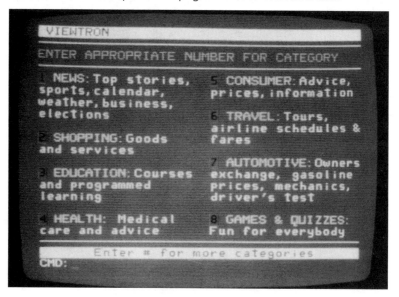

**Exhibit 6.3**
An early Viewtron page with mosaic-style graphic.

By plan, none of the families had the service for the full 15 months of the trial. The researchers' objective was to observe and evaluate as many families as possible with VCA's limited number of customer terminals. Consequently, only 10 to 12 families participated in each of the trial segments, which averaged three to six months in duration.

The research results convinced executives of both companies that the public was ready to accept this new medium, but obvious hints of problems to come were missed. In retrospect, the interviews and usage data clearly revealed that access to databases of general news, information, and advertising was less exciting to subscribers than the ability to easily communicate with other subscribers. But that was not what anyone was prepared to hear at that time. Nearly everyone involved in the trial saw Viewtron as an advertiser-supported electronic newspaper. Its potential role as an interpersonal communication medium was considered secondary.

### What you want—when you want it

During the retooling phase between the market trial and the official start of commercial service, Knight-Ridder and AT&T decided to adopt a new, more advanced display standard, known by the acronym NAPLPS (**North American presentation level protocol standard**). This standard eliminated the coarse appearance of Prestel pages. Instead of constructing pages with tiles, artists could create more sophisticated graphics using a variety of geometric shapes.

The rapidly expanding VCA staff worked night and day for nearly two years to develop the system software and create the thousands of pages needed to form the Viewtron information base to which "live" news and advertising would be added later. As might be expected, not all went smoothly.

When AT&T delivered the first frame creation terminal (FCT) early in 1982, there was much excitement about its capabilities. It was a truly remarkable machine for its time. Engineers from AT&T's Bell Labs were justly proud of its sophisticated drawing tools, but most of all they were excited by its color palette that allowed artists to choose from some 64 million combinations of hues, shades, and intensities. No one seemed concerned that standard home TV sets could not distinguish more than about 100 colors or that, unlike the precision monitors used in the FCTs, color quality on home TV sets could not be controlled by our central computers.

***The Scepter crisis.*** Bell Labs would require nearly 15 more months to complete the design of the customer terminal, so we had no way of knowing how the pages we were creating would appear in the homes of subscribers. Because they were available, we used all the tools and colors at our disposal to create spectacular graphics and well-designed pages. As slides for presentations they were great, but as videotex pages they would prove to be a disaster.

We discovered just how blinded we had been by our great expectations the day we finally received the first shipment of customer terminals, which AT&T called the Scepter. In anticipation, we had set up about a dozen TV sets of different brands and sizes in a small conference room. We had expected some problems, but none of us was quite prepared for what we saw when the pages were finally displayed.

Those first few moments as we stared at the pages were deadly silent. The reality we faced that day was that many of the pages could not be easily read on standard TV sets because the colors we had chosen for text and backgrounds often blended together. All our efforts to select pleasing colors, and to match those in corporate logos, sports insignias, and the like had been for naught. A blue logo on the FCT might appear green on some home TV sets, and purple on others. Textures, which we had used extensively, were also inconsistent between the FCTs and the customer terminals.

Even more troubling were the graphics. On the FCTs they had displayed quickly, so no one had given much thought to how they would be displayed in the home. Had we known how long the customer terminals would take to display the graphics (some required more than 10 minutes!), we could have saved ourselves many thousands of hours. As a result, most of the pages had to be redesigned several times before the start of service to accommodate the limitations of the customer terminal as well as the changing tastes of nervous executives (see Exhibit 6.4). Bell Labs did somewhat improve the display speed for later versions of the Scepter, but its slowness remained a serious problem throughout the Viewtron trial.

Our disappointments with the customer terminals, however, were not confined to color and graphics. All business planning with AT&T prior to this time had assumed that home terminals would cost about $100. But in July 1983, just three months before the commercial launch, AT&T casually revealed that the actual introductory price for each Scepter would be closer to a thousand dollars. After

**Exhibit 6.4** A typical page from Viewtron commercial service.

some negotiation, AT&T finally agreed to sell the Scepter for $600, which was significantly below its cost. Despite serious misgivings, Knight-Ridder's senior executives felt that the company was too deeply committed by this time to do anything other than proceed as planned.

*Almost touching the future.* When the service finally went public in October 1983, both companies moved quickly with much fanfare to make Viewtron a household name in south Florida. Advertising and brochures proclaimed "The Waiting Is Over" and "What You Want—When You Want It." Kiosks in department stores and malls invited shoppers to "Touch the Future." Research firms predicted anywhere from 10 to 50 million homes would have videotex information centers by the early 1990s. And media pundits declared that printed newspapers would become extinct in the near future. The VCA staff, which had grown to nearly 250 people, were exuberant, certain they were embarking on twenty-first-century careers.

But, as with so many grand prophecies, the future took a different path. After nearly two and a half years of disappointing performance, Knight-Ridder declared Viewtron a failure and shut it down in March 1986. **Gateway,** the other major videotex service (launched by the Times Mirror group in southern California), met the same fate in the same month. With their closing, more than a few newspaper executives breathed a sigh of relief. For many, it was a confirmation that electronic publishing would not present a serious threat to traditional print media anytime soon, or at least not until well after they had retired. But that would soon prove to be another example of what Paul Saffo describes as "technomyopia" (see chapter 1).

## What went wrong?

The single reason most often given for the failure of these early consumer videotex services is that the technologies and the markets for electronic delivery of information just were not ready. Saffo's 30-year rule certainly supports this hypothesis. With the benefit of hindsight, we can now see that consumer cyber media from the 1970s to the end of the 1980s were clearly in their first stage of development—"lots of excitement, lots of puzzlement, not a lot of penetration."[1]

However, as popular and accurate as that view may be, there was much more to the failure than simply being ahead of their time. Everyone who was associated with the Viewtron experience has a different personal perspective and set of opinions, but most of the reasons given by former executives and staff members for Viewtron's demise are contained below. Unfortunately, without the knowledge of what went before, many of these same mistakes are being repeated today by the present generation of cyber media pioneers.

***Unrealistic expectations.*** From their inception, U.S. videotex services were viewed as logical extensions of traditional printed newspapers. The benefits of these services were perceived to be their ability to provide news and information that was more timely, more thorough, and more personal. A favorite assumption within Knight-Ridder was that Viewtron would become an up-to-the-minute "micro-news" newspaper providing a wealth of items not typically found in mainstream media. This proved to be wishful thinking. Viewtron was never able to meet the expectations of its senior executives or its subscribers. Despite the great effort and expense put

---

[1]"Paul Saffo and the 30-Year Rule," *Design World* (1992: 24), 23.

into covering neighborhood events, subscribers frequently discovered that the desired information at the end of the decision tree was either out of date or nonexistent.

Particularly disappointing for sports enthusiasts was the service's inability to maintain current scores and statistics for local high school and community teams. Volunteers enlisted to provide coverage of local games were generally unreliable. All too often, subscribers could get the information they wanted more easily and more quickly from other sources. Promising to provide subscribers with anything they wanted, whenever they wanted it, proved to be a serious marketing error.

***Fears of competitive exposure.*** While stories from the Associated Press and other **wire services** were generally made available to customers almost as soon as they were received, that was not the case with stories from the local newspaper. Even though Viewtron maintained a close working relationship with the *Miami Herald,* which is a Knight-Ridder newspaper, many important stories did not appear first on Viewtron as originally promised. The *Herald's* senior editors worried that stories—particularly their exclusives—would fall into the hands of competing news media before they were published. That fear was not entirely without basis since editors at the Fort Lauderdale *Sun-Sentinel* and the now defunct *Miami News,* as well as several south Florida TV stations, were known to have active subscriptions.

The Herald's concern about exclusivity and competitive exposure created a frustrating impediment, but it may not have mattered all that much to Viewtron's subscribers. Except for major breaking news events, such as the approach of a powerful hurricane, subscribers spent a remarkably small portion of their time retrieving news. The lesson in this seems to be that online news services are viewed by most subscribers as information faucets, only to be turned on when there is a thirst or need not being satisfied by other readily available sources.

***A misunderstood technology.*** Nearly everyone within Knight-Ridder in the early 1980s saw Viewtron as an interactive, TV-based technology rather than an online computer service. Even after it became evident that TV screens were not well suited to reading large amounts of text, and that personal computers were gaining acceptance for home use, Al Gillen, VCA's chairman, had a great reluctance to position Viewtron as an information and communications service for PC users. Having come from a successful career in broadcast television, he tended to see videotex as an extension of TV technology and wished to avoid references to computers.

Not until Reid Ashe took over as chairman in 1985 was a serious effort made to adapt the service for PC users, but by that time it was too late to make a difference. The enthusiasm of Knight-Ridder's executives for Viewtron was already drowning in accumulated losses that would ultimately total nearly $50 million.[2]

***The wrong customer image.*** Another set of assumptions held by those involved in the early development of videotex concerned how people would use the medium. Before development began, Knight-Ridder commissioned a video to explain the concept to its board of directors and prospective partners. It is a telling presentation. The video shows a mythical U.S. family consisting of a father, mother, two young children, and a dog happily gathered around the living room TV set leisurely "watching" a videotex service. Each member of the family is seen patiently taking his or her turn calling up news items and topics of interest that are then discussed by everyone.

That image served to shape much of the thinking about how Viewtron would fit into people's lives, but it could not have been further from the truth. Rather than a "family" information and entertainment center, it was used much more as a reference library, or as an interpersonal message center. Subscribers almost always worked with it alone and usually for only a few minutes at a time.

Moreover, unlike the British model, which was designed to stimulate usage of telephones and TV sets, U.S. videotex services had to deal with the opposite situation—too much contention for telephone and television time. Many subscribers found they either had to install a second telephone line, and in some cases another TV set, or resort to using the services late at night or early in the morning.

***The waiting had just begun.*** Subscribers who were originally sold on the idea that Viewtron would save time were among the most disappointed by the service. Despite efforts to optimize graphic elements and strip out those that were nonessential, the data transmission

---

[2]AT&T is believed to have lost at least twice that amount.

speed, which averaged less than 1,200 bits per second, often made accessing information painfully slow.

The Viewtron customer service staff quickly learned that subscribers had little patience for delays. Even two- and three-second waits for a page to display were not good enough. What customers wanted was nothing less than nearly *instantaneous* response times. Some subscribers made jokes out of the company's slogan "The Waiting Is Over." Copies of Viewtron ads would occasionally show up with the slogan crossed out and replaced by "The Waiting Has Just Begun."

Efforts to provide compelling presentations and new features for advertisers consistently ran head-on into the time problem. Advertisers usually insisted on an abundance of graphics and sophisticated product logos on their pages, even when they were told that customers might be angered and turned away by the amount of time their ads took to be displayed.

*The dirty little secret.* Throughout Viewtron's existence, research continued to show high satisfaction ratings from customers, but that was of little consolation to Knight-Ridder's executives. No matter what Viewtron did, most customers followed the same predictable pattern—they would "play" with it for a short while and then quit.

Whether customers bought the Scepter terminal or leased it seemed to make little difference. Customers kept telling researchers they loved the service, even though they were not using it. Only four out of 10 customers who rented terminals continued to subscribe after six months. Even when Viewtron finally adapted its service for PC users who paid by the minute, more than 80 percent of the subscribers would become nonusers within 13 weeks. Of those who remained, the majority became relatively steady, hour-a-week customers.[3] This is what Reid Ashe has called "our dirty little secret." In his words:

> What we sold them was Information on Demand—a Mighty Wurlitzer of knowledge. Want to know what's happening in Uruguay today? Just pull this stop. What does the encyclopedia say about Archimedes? How's the weather in Dar es Salaam? It's all at your fingertips. We sold it. People bought it. We delivered. They were satisfied. But they quit using it, because they really didn't want it.[4]

---

[3]Reid Ashe, "The Human Element: Electronic Networks Succeed with Relationships, not Information," *The Quill* (September 1991), pp. 13–14.

***What customers wanted wasn't more information.*** When Viewtron's researchers analyzed the accumulated usage data in their effort to understand what went wrong, they found a rather surprising pattern among the minority who remained active subscribers. The research results, Ashe says, clearly show that it wasn't "more news" and "more information" they apparently wanted. "It was communication—interaction not with a machine, but with each other."[5]

The services that consistently had the most loyal followers were the electronic mail and CB sections, which like citizen band radio made it possible for users to interact anonymously with each other in real time. (By the mid-1980s, the popularity of citizen band radio had waned and online CB sections became known as chat rooms.) Because subscribers who participated in the CB sections used "handles," or aliases, there was no way of knowing who they were. But, judging from the content of the public messages and the assumed identities, most of the participants were probably teenagers.

More than a year before Viewtron and Gateway were shut down, Michael Noll,[6] an AT&T executive involved in the market trial, began publicly challenging the fundamental hypothesis underlying the videotex movement—that large, centralized databases of general interest information would satisfy the information needs of consumers. Noll argued that "the specific information needs of most people and their ways of satisfying these needs are not well understood."[7] He raised concerns that computerized databases might be too time consuming, difficult to use, and inadequate for most people. His suggestion that transaction and interpersonal message services might be more important than information retrieval to online customers has since proven to be quite prescient.[8]

***It wasn't a newspaper.*** While Viewtron was promoted as an electronic newspaper, there was little about the service that resembled

---

[4]Ibid.

[5]Ibid.

[6]A. Michael Noll left the AT&T Consumer Products division in 1984 to become a professor of communications at the Annenberg School for Communication at the University of Southern California. At AT&T he performed technical evaluations and identified opportunities for new products and services. He also performed pioneering basic research in a wide variety of media-related areas at Bell Labs in Murray Hill, New Jersey.

[7]A. Michael Noll, "Videotex: Anatomy of a Failure," *Information & Management* (1985: 9), 105.

[8]Ibid., p. 104.

the printed product. Unlike a newspaper, it lacked an obvious structure that could be easily browsed. Everything seemed to have the same relative importance and, despite frequent updating, the service appeared static.

Instead of a familiar, manageable package of information with a definite beginning and end, subscribers were confronted with a strange, seemingly endless labyrinth of information. For most, the notion of a newspaper containing hundreds of thousands of pages was beyond their ability to visualize. Even Viewtron's corporate champion James Batten frequently admitted to having great difficulty comprehending how information was organized within the service. He would constantly admonish the staff to simplify procedures and make the technology invisible. But, despite their best efforts, the process was never as easy as Batten and most of Viewtron's customers would have preferred.

The hierarchical menu system, which was originally conceived to simplify searches and reduce access time, more often than not only succeeded in confusing subscribers and extending their time online. The decision tree was so large that navigating from the main menu to an item of interest could require working through seven or eight layers of menus. With as many as a dozen options to choose from on each menu, the process was more like taking a multiple-choice quiz than reading a newspaper. If a wrong path were taken, customers generally had to back out through the menus until they found another branch that looked promising.

In hindsight, we can now see that the attempt to position Viewtron as an electronic newspaper was a mistake. The key error was not recognizing quickly enough that videotex derived most of its dominant attributes from the interpersonal domain rather than the document or broadcast domains.

***The cost was too high.*** Whether Viewtron would have succeeded had it been positioned differently or supported longer is still a matter of some debate. Most agree, however, that the amount of money customers and advertisers were willing to pay for videotex services in the 1980s was inadequate to cover the unexpectedly high production and marketing costs. The original Viewtron revenue projections were based on public utility and telephone billing models. They assumed customers would be willing to pay variable usage fees that would average about $30 per month. But it soon became evident that subscribers disliked variable charges determined by the amount of time they spent online. The $30 per month average per customer proved to be unrealistic as well. Even when Viewtron switched to a fixed rate of $12 per month, many indicated that the price was too high.

The marketing staff also discovered that people were much more resistant than expected to buying or even leasing the Scepter terminal, although the reasons were painfully obvious. The device was not only expensive and functionally limited, it was poorly designed. Nothing about the terminal's appearance attracted potential early adopters. The bulky white box with its black faceplate looked dull and old fashioned rather than high-tech and futuristic. Moreover, the small remote keypad had such tiny keys that people often had difficulty pressing the correct characters. The rubber keys also had the frustrating tendency to stick or break off.

Even with these problems, Viewtron might have succeeded if advertisers had been convinced of the service's potential value. But Viewtron never achieved a large enough critical mass of subscribers to attract substantial advertising revenue. By the time Knight-Ridder shut it down, the service had less than 20,000 subscribers scattered around the country.

***The medium was uncompelling.*** Videotex pages generally appeared dull and uninviting on TV screens. No matter how much effort the design staff put into visually enhancing the videotex pages, the medium could not compete with the compelling moving images of television or the ease of reading newspapers and magazines.

Once the initial excitement and novelty of Viewtron wore off, subscribers often complained that the stylized graphics got in the way and were of little value. Even the addition of small photographic images for real estate and retail advertising did not generate much enthusiasm, largely because they took a significant amount of time to display.

In retrospect, Viewtron might have had a better chance of succeeding if it had adopted the simpler approach taken by the French **Minitel**. Instead of employing an expensive, TV-based system with color graphics, the French opted to develop a relatively low-cost display phone with a small, built-in black-and-white monitor and keyboard. By associating the medium more with the telephone than the TV set, its subscribers, as well as its information providers and advertisers, did not expect Minitel's content to compete with commercial television or print media.

## The second stage of consumer online services

By the beginning of the 1990s, the U.S. market for consumer online technology had changed radically. Demand for personal computers to use at home was surging, and higher speed, lower cost communications were making online information and electronic mail more appealing. The three major U.S. services that survived the difficult transition years—Prodigy, CompuServe, and America Online—had managed to attract a modest base of subscribers and were actively aggregating a broad range of content. This was clearly the start of consumer online technology's second stage—"lots of flux, penetration of the product into society is beginning."[9]

*Content providers.* Partially driven by a new optimism, but mostly motivated by a fear of being left behind, newspaper and magazine publishers began again in 1993 to experiment with electronic publishing. This time, however, they decided not to develop and operate their own full-service networks, opting instead to assume the lesser role of content providers. Because each of the existing online services employed its own proprietary technology, publishers had to make a choice. The decision wasn't easy, but the majority decided to go with America Online because it was considered the easiest of the services to use and the most likely to succeed over the long haul.

While publishers initially planned to take a cautious, low-budget approach, they quickly discovered that online publishing was much more labor intensive than they had anticipated. Even though online services in this period were essentially text-based and only offered a limited capacity for custom design, graphics, and typography, the reformatting of content and managing of interactive services, such as chat rooms and electronic mail, proved to be quite time consuming and costly. There was also a high rate of subscriber turnover, called churn, which required publishers and service providers to devote significant amounts of money to marketing and actively soliciting new subscribers to replace those who canceled. The extent of the problem was revealed in October 1995 by Inteco, a Connecticut research firm, when it reported that many online users

---

[9]"Paul Saffo," p. 23.

were simply signing up for free promotional trials and then canceling. The study, based on interviews with 10,000 home users of online services, found "a significant amount of dissatisfaction" with all of the proprietary services, and estimated that more than 6.2 million Americans had tried and canceled subscriptions to the top online services.

*A new challenge.* Early in 1995, yet another electronic publishing opportunity or potential threat (depending on one's perspective) burst onto the scene—the Internet. Suddenly, publishers were faced with having to significantly expand their online operations to create new products for the Internet's World Wide Web, which required mastering procedures and technologies that differed substantially from the proprietary services.

The rising popularity of the newly commercialized Internet has posed an even more serious problem for established publishers. Because new technologies developed for the Internet have dramatically reduced the financial and operational barriers to entry for electronic publishing, practically anyone with a personal computer and a modem can readily become a publisher with a global audience. Who wins and who loses in this second stage of cyber media development is likely to be determined by how quickly individual publishers can secure significant and reliable sources of revenue. But even without a clear idea of how profits would ultimately be made from placing content on the Internet, hundreds of mainstream publishers, as well as broadcasters and entrepreneurs, seemed to instinctively sense that this was the beginning of something potentially very lucrative.

## The trials of interactive TV

The development of interactive media was not limited to teletext and videotex in the 1970s. Cable-TV operators in that decade of early telecommunication convergences were also beginning to explore the two-way potential of their networks. After 20 years of wiring homes in rural communities just to receive one-way retransmissions of broadcast TV programs, a few visionaries recognized that cable systems held the keys to much greater opportunities. Communication satellites and premium pay channels developed specifically for satellite and cable delivery, such as Home Box Office (HBO), provided the initial technology and content for a metamorphosis within this fledgling business.

The idea of including two-way feedback loops within cable networks had been around for some time, but even though the technology was simple, implementation was relatively expensive. It involved the installation of two lines into each cable-TV subscriber's home, one for sending and another for receiving transmissions, as well as complex processing systems at the cable operator's head-end facilities. As with broadcast teletext, decoder boxes and keypads were required to interact with the system.

### Warner-Amex's Qube system

Warner Communications and Amex Cable, an affiliate of American Express, jointly installed the first U.S. two-way service, called **Qube,** in Columbus, Ohio, in 1977. Compared with contemporary interactive media, the services offered by Qube during the market trial were not very sophisticated. Other than letting subscribers select pay-per-view movies, stations were limited to conducting simple polls and initiating requests for feedback.

Warner produced a variety of programs designed to take greater advantage of Qube's two-way capability. Some programs involved staged football games that allowed viewers to call the plays for local teams and quiz shows that gave viewers the opportunity to compete for prizes. Warner also experimented with a form of "electronic democracy."[10] Viewers could use their keypads to comment on issues presented during telecast city council and school board meetings, pick the individuals they thought were the winners in public debates, and cast their votes in mock elections. The results were quickly tallied by the system's central computers and displayed on the subscribers' TV screens.

These services were widely touted in the late 1970s as a preview of future television and interactive entertainment. But for all the fanfare, they produced little excitement among subscribers. Former Warner employees have reported that most interactive programs were usually watched by no more than 20 percent of the sub-

---

[10]W. Russell Neuman, *The Future of the Mass Audience.* New York: Cambridge University Press, 1991, pp. 110–111.

scribers.[11] One explanation for nonparticipation may have been the limited nature of what they could say.[12] The technology restricted viewers to simple yes/no or numeric responses. Consequently, queries were generally posed like multiple-choice test questions.

Ultimately, Qube met the same fate as Viewtron and Gateway. Like the newspaper-based videotex services, it failed to generate significant revenue for the joint-venture partners. After losing about $30 million,[13] Warner-Amex finally abandoned its interactive programming experiments in 1985 and allowed the Columbus Qube system to revert to a standard cable-TV operation. The only surviving vestige of the two-way market trial was its pay-per-view service.

However, despite its commercial failure, the Qube experiment succeeded in raising concerns about a potentially darker side of interactive media. When Warner and Amex began developing the system, they had much more in mind than interactive entertainment. They recognized that two-way communication also made it possible for them to continuously monitor the activities of Qube customers to determine what programs they were watching and to gather information about their interests and habits. The only way viewers could avoid monitoring was by turning off their TV sets. Even though Warner-Amex assured customers that it would protect their privacy, it reserved the right to sell aggregated information to advertisers and to use its databases as marketing tools.[14]

The specter of business enterprises, religious organizations, and government agencies covertly gathering personal information that people might want to keep private continues to haunt the development of interactive media. Contemporary arguments that feedback mechanisms are potentially more beneficial than harmful to customers of interactive TV and online computer services have not fully alleviated the concerns of critics that this technology might be employed to watch and manipulate private citizens.[15]

---

[11]Ibid.

[12]Melvin L. DeFleur and Sandra Ball-Rokeach, *Theories of Mass Communication* (5th ed.). New York: Longman, 1989, p. 344.

[13]Ibid.

[14]Wilson Dizard, Jr., *Old Media New Media: Mass Communication in the Information Age.* New York: Longman, 1994, p. 47.

[15]DeFleur and Ball-Rokeach, p. 345.

## The Cerritos experience

Prompted by their ever more fragmented audiences, the success of video games and other computer-based media, and the proposed capabilities of digital **high-definition television** (**HDTV**) technology, broadcasters and satellite/cable-TV operators once again jumped on the interactive bandwagon at the end of the 1980s. Since then dozens of market trials have been, and continue to be, conducted throughout the world in anticipation of a huge future payoff. Even though nearly all these trials, like the earlier Qube experiment, have so far produced disappointing results, this has not significantly deterred telecommunication businesses from continuing to invest tens of millions of dollars into the development of increasingly more advanced interactive TV technologies and market trials.

Among the more ambitious trials in recent years was a venture coordinated and financed by General Telephone Enterprises (GTE). In 1989, the company installed what was probably the world's most sophisticated cable system in Cerritos, California, to serve as a proving ground for as many as 19 experiments in advanced telecommunication services and interactive TV. Residents in this Los Angeles suburb of 53,000 were offered an array of high-tech services that was billed as the "wave of the future."[16]

Although GTE has closely guarded the results, news reports suggest that the response from customers was hardly enthusiastic. After four years, only a few hundred of the city's more than 7,000 cable subscribers had become regular users of GTE's most ambitious service called "Main Street," which let families use their TV sets for home shopping, news, sports, education, and entertainment options.[17]

The most popular offering was "Center Screen," which let customers view a movie within 30 minutes of ordering. While that service attracted about 4,000 subscribers, it did not draw customers away from video stores and supermarket video rental services in significant numbers, as GTE's executives had hoped. Also, instead of paying a premium for the convenience of not having to make trips to the video store, subscribers indicated they expected to pay less.

What GTE discovered in Cerritos is that interactive TV may actually emerge as "a collection of niches [that is, small markets]

---

[16]"'TV of Tomorrow' Is a Flop Today," *Washington Post* (September 1, 1993), p. F1.
   [17]Ibid.

rather than a single mass market. Everyone subscribes for different reasons, much like cable TV. Some subscribers prefer movies; others enjoy the play-along sports."[18] This suggests that interactive TV might not be as big a business as some have claimed. The greatest obstacles to interactive TV may be convincing customers that they really need these services and that the services are worth the price.

Nevertheless, most major broadcast and telecommunication companies are still moving ahead with their own versions of the Cerritos experiment, still believing that the home TV set is destined to become a dynamic, multidimensional window on the world. Time Warner's Orlando, Florida, experiment, for example, offers subscribers an even larger array of sophisticated services that, unlike GTE's trial, includes full-motion video and animation. But even with more advanced technologies, the gap between the vision and the reality of interactive TV within the general consumer market appears far from closing anytime soon.

## Lessons from failure in perspective

With the benefit of hindsight, we can see how the companies that launched the first U.S. videotex and interactive TV services were misled into believing that a new media technology alone would be enough to instantly create a strong market demand. The mistakes they made once again point out important principles of mediamorphosis—the principle of opportunity and need and the principle of delayed adoption—as well as the importance of recognizing the media domain in which a technology is developing.

### Opportunity and need

While there may have been an opportunity provided by the accelerating perfusion of digital language and the resultant convergences of media and communication technologies, no motivating social, political, or economic reasons had been established in the 1970s and 1980s to justify the development and widespread adoption of consumer cyber media. This is, as we learned in chapter 1, the essential admonition of the opportunity and need principle.

---

[18]Iris Cohen Selinger, "Cerritos Test Shows There's More to Learn about Interactive Television," *Advertising Age* (October 25, 1993), p. 25.

No matter how we look at their efforts, it is obvious that the development of consumer cyber media was in its first stage during that period, which means that no amount of additional money or market promotion would have made any difference in the outcome. In fact, it may have been that too much money and too much promotion contributed directly to their failure. By making large financial investments in upfront development, each of these publicly owned companies created an internal need to show positive results quickly. In their labors to achieve those results, they heavily promoted their embryonic services and thereby stimulated unrealistic expectations among consumers, as well as among their corporate officers and shareholders. In other words, they set themselves up to fail.

## *Delayed adoption*

Had they been cognizant of the delayed adoption principle and kept their initial financial commitments and expectations relatively small, they might have been able to sustain a long-term research and development effort that would have carried them into the potentially more opportune second and third stages. But that, however, is not an option that most large U.S. corporations have been typically willing to pursue. If we examine the most successful consumer online services today—America Online and the World Wide Web—we see that they grew out of entrepreneurial efforts with relatively limited financial resources.

America Online began in the mid-1980s as a small startup venture with a modest plan to develop and operate an easy-to-use bulletin board and electronic mail service for owners of Commodore and Apple II computers, which at that time were the most common PCs used in schools and homes. As the consumer market for PCs grew, America Online gradually expanded to provide similar services for users of IBM PCs and Apple Macintosh systems. By the mid-1990s, America Online had become the largest and most successful proprietary online service with more than seven million U.S. subscribers.

The World Wide Web, as we saw in chapter 4, developed out of an academic research need to simplify and standardize the process of retrieving information stored in databases linked by the Internet, which had been quietly expanding and evolving since the end of the 1960s. With the emergence of Mosaic browser technology in the mid-1990s, the Web became more accessible to nontechnical users and suddenly turned into the predominant global cyber medium for electronic publishing. By this time, the development of consumer cyber media was clearly in its second stage and the motivating reasons for using online services and electronic mail were becoming much more obvious.

These examples demonstrate that in the first stage of a new media development, it is often the tortoises rather than the hares that ultimately lead in the race. In the second stage, however, companies developing new media technologies must be ready to sprint to the finish line, as America Online and Netscape Communication Corporation, the developer of the most popular Mosaic Web browsers, have shown.

## The true nature of cyber media

Another significant factor in the initial failures of videotex and interactive TV services stems from the mixing of traits from different media domains, which often caused confusion about the true nature of cyber media. In the case of Viewtron, most of those involved came from the newspaper business and naturally saw videotex in the context of the document domain—structured, textual/visual, page-based, and mediated by human editors for readers who were primarily information seekers. Others at Viewtron, in particular the VCA chairman who came from a career in television, saw the medium as an extension of the broadcast domain—one-way, structured, aural/visual, TV-screen image-based, fixed location, and mediated by producers for viewers who primarily wanted to be entertained. (Although Viewtron was unable to provide audio or full-motion video, the assumption of an aural/visual presentation refers to the radio/TV style of writing, which is meant to be read aloud, as opposed to the newspaper/magazine style.)

Generally overlooked were the traits of the interpersonal domain—two-way, participatory, unscheduled, and unmediated—that were, in fact, the attributes that defined the medium for most early subscribers to online services. Also overlooked were the missing document and broadcast traits that prevented subscribers from accepting the medium as either an electronic newspaper or an interactive television. To be considered a newspaper, it needed to be portable, portrait oriented, and easy to browse. And, to be viewed as an extension of television, it needed audio and full-motion video. None of these traits could be incorporated into cyber media in the first stage.

## Hypotheses for the next mediamorphosis stage

These lessons bring us up to date on the third great mediamorphosis. Although it has been in progress for over a century, the critical cyber media technologies are only crossing from their first stage (as Paul Saffo defines it) to their second, when they are beginning to penetrate society. His model suggests that within the next decade or so we will enter the third stage, when cyber media will have become common and well integrated into daily life.

In the next three chapters, we leap into the future to consider several new forms of media that may emerge within the primary media domains. Following are some general hypotheses about the next stage of the third great mediamorphosis that derive from the lessons learned in this chapter and those lessons from our past discussed in the preceding chapters.

- Digital technologies will make all electronic forms of communication media more intimate and interactive.

- A variety of standardized teleputers—devices that combine telephone, television, and computer technologies—will be developed to display and interact with digital media.

- Global broadband networks will provide relatively low-cost access to mixed-media content.

- Two-way wireless communication, for at least voice and simple data, will be seamless and pervasive.

- Electronic mail services that combine text, graphics, voice, and video will be integral to nearly all emerging forms of digital media.

- Flat-screen display technologies suitable for reading electronic documents on portable devices as well as for viewing movies and TV programs in commercial or intimate home theaters will become commonplace.

# mediamorphosis within the interpersonal domain

Although we may be unable to clearly visualize the new forms of communication media that will emerge and become commonplace early in the next century, we can construct *reasonable* future scenarios by applying the principles of mediamorphosis and extending the dominant, propagated traits of the media domains. I have emphasized reasonable because that, I believe, is the best we can hope for. Even with an extensive knowledge of media technologies and trends across time, the vagaries of chaos and complexity, as we learned in chapter 1, assure that many aspects of the future will be quite different from what we may expect.

The future scenarios presented in this and the following two chapters describe a hypothetical September morning in the lives of three different households. These scenarios are intended to show how several existing and emerging forms of communication media within the interpersonal, broadcast, and document domains might adapt and be used by average, middle-class consumers in the year 2010. I've selected the year 2010 because it is near enough to make reasonable predictions, yet far enough to keep our minds open to the possibilities. Rather than provide an extensive view, I have chosen to focus more intensely on just one or two technologies within each media domain.

The "Cyber Dwellers" scenario in this chapter presents a retired couple using a virtual reality system to communicate with friends and family around the world as well as to gather essential information and to remain actively involved politically and socially within their local and virtual communities. In chapter 8, the "Interactive Video Family" scenario describes how a young couple and their teenage daughter might use various features of an interactive, digital television system. A single career woman who travels frequently uses a portable teleputer, called a tablet, in chapter 9's "Mobile Digital Document Reader" scenario to read and interact with electronic editions of newspapers and other documents.

These scenarios are designed to open our minds to probable futures for contemporary forms of communication media and to stimulate discussions about the mediamorphic process. The media that I have described in the different scenarios should not be viewed as mutually exclusive or disconnected—all are equally possible and capable of coexisting with one another. Nor should they be seen as definitive or all inclusive. I have incorporated only a selection of those emerging technologies that seem to extend the dominant traits within each media domain and conform to the principles of mediamorphosis. There can be little doubt that some aspects of these scenarios will appear dated, or even foolish, to readers in the next two decades. That, of course, is the risk taken by all who dare to predict directions the future might take.

Exhibit 7.1 shows the chronology of major technological innovations that have influenced the development of telephony and computer-mediated communications in the past two centuries and that are likely to influence the adoption and diffusion of interpersonal cyber media early in the twenty-first century.

### Scenario for 2010. *The cyber dwellers*

For Max and Emily, the decision to buy a renovated farm house on a few acres of land in eastern Oregon was made without hesitation. At age 67, Max is still healthy and vigorous. Retirement was never a consideration. In his mind, this move is merely a relocation and an opportunity to pursue other interests. Emily, who is a dozen years younger, has always wanted to raise exotic animals, so she hardly gave a second thought to quitting her teaching post in Denver. Emily is already in the corral feeding and caring for her pair of llamas as the sun rises over the Blue Mountains and Max starts his daily routine in the room he calls the holosuite.[1] The holosuite is actually their home theater and fitness room, which is equipped with the latest immersive virtual reality system.

After putting on his sensor-laden body suit and lightweight VR headset, Max climbs onto the exercycle for a physical workout while he takes

---

[1]*Holosuite* is a term created for the "Star Trek" television series to describe a room where individuals can act out their fantasies in a near lifelike setting. The assumption is that holographic imagery will ultimately evolve to a point

**Exhibit 7.1** Time line of interpersonal media developments, 1800–2010.

| Year | |
|---|---|
| **1800** – | – First experiments with electric current; punch-card programming |
| **1825** – | |
| | – Faraday discovers electromagnetic induction |
| | – Babbage designs first digital computer; Byron creates first digital program |
| | – Morse patents electric telegraph; Morse code developed |
| | – Commercial telegraph service; Bain patents facsimile transmission |
| **1850** – | |
| | – Transatlantic telegraph cable |
| **1875** – | – Bell patents telephone and forms Bell Company (AT&T's predecessor) |
| | – Police call boxes |
| | – Marconi demonstrates wireless telegraph; automatic switchboard |
| **1900** – | – First transatlantic wireless transmission; 1 million phones in U.S. |
| | – Vacuum tubes |
| | – Transcontinental long-distance telephone service established in U.S. |
| | – Amateur short-wave radio (ham); portable radiotelephones |
| | – Broadcast radio |
| **1925** – | – Commercial radio-facsimile systems |
| | – Picture telephone demonstrated; transatlantic radiophone service |
| | – Personal facsimile news services |
| | – Coaxial cable |
| | – First electronic computer (ENIAC) |
| **1950** – | – Commercial computer (UNIVAC); transistor; microwave systems |
| | – Transatlantic telephone cable; high-level programming languages |
| | – Communication satellites; commercial digital phone system; modems |
| | – Electronic telephone switching; digital computer games; hypertext |
| | – Microprocessors; digital computer network (ARPANET); fiber-optic cable |
| **1975** – | – Personal computers; local area networks; commercial video game systems |
| | – Digital fax machines; cellular phones; consumer online services |
| | – Breakup of AT&T; digital multimedia systems; portable computers |
| | – Virtual reality systems; World Wide Web; intelligent agents |
| | – Commercial Internet; net browsers; avatars; video-capable PCs; cyber cash |
| **2000** – | – Merger of public telephone and Internet systems worldwide |
| | – Global satellite networks for wireless telephony; commercial VR telephony |
| | – Copper-wire infrastructure totally replaced by fiber-optic networks in U.S. |

*(Continued)*

where images will also appear to be solid objects. In the context of this scenario, though, it is only the name given to a room that contains a virtual reality system.

a mental spin in cyberspace. The headset combines earphones, a microphone, and a visor that looks like a pair of trendy wraparound sunglasses. Tiny projectors mounted in the visor focus images directly onto the retina. With an eye tracking device also mounted in the visor, the microphone, and touch pads on the handlebars, Max is able to effortlessly navigate through a dynamic, three-dimensional virtual environment called a **metaverse**. The exercycle is fully integrated into the VR system, so he can monitor his speed, distance, heart rate, blood pressure, and calorie burn as he peruses his morning news-mail and interacts with his cohorts.

As soon as Max jacks into the global VR Web, he is instantly "beamed" to a teleport hovering over what appears to be a small town complete with shops, a bank, library, school, medical clinic, entertainment center, government buildings, and private dwellings. All of the town's 1,024 denizens are represented by lifelike 3-D simulations called **avatars**. In the metaverse, people can be whoever they want to be. Max has adopted the persona of a barnstorming pilot from the early 1920s, so his avatar always appears with a long flowing purple scarf and a brown leather flight jacket emblazoned with a Flying-M insignia. He knows people who appear as Japanese ninja, race car drivers, astronauts, Vikings, medieval damsels, and even as animals or mythical beings. There are other barnstorming pilots, too, but they are clearly differentiated by the color of their scarves and the insignias on their jackets.

Since the metaverse is not restricted by physical laws, such as gravity and aerodynamics, avatars can quickly **fly** to any location within their cyber communities. From the teleport, Max first navigates to his dwelling, which is located in the northwest quadrant of the residential ring surrounding the town center. Dwellings are private areas that only their owners and invited guests can enter. When he opens the front door of his dwelling, he finds a "newspaper" waiting for him. This is not a newspaper in the traditional sense. It's actually a one-of-a-kind cyber medium compiled by a team of personal agents from dozens of news sources, as well as the contents of his own mailbox and calendar. Emily has her own "newspaper" that she calls *Delphi,* after the famous oracle in ancient Greece. Max has chosen a more flamboyant name to match his personality—*Mad Max Monitor.*

Nearly all the items in each "newspaper" have been selected to conform with the individual's personal interests and tastes. In addition to manually entering and deleting specific subjects in their profiles, Max and Emily rely on "watcher" agents that track what they view and automatically fine tune the filters in their "search" agents to gather more of what they seem to like and fewer of the items they tend to skip over. Also included are a number of general interest items flagged by their trusted friends and news services as "top stories." Like so many of their cohorts, Max and Emily still refer to their VR communication and information service as a newspaper even though it is not mediated by professional editors.

This is not their only source of information and entertainment, however. They also subscribe to the electronic editions of several "real" newspapers and magazines, which they now read on portable tablets instead of paper. They have a large, wall-mounted, flat-screen display in their holosuite for watching movies and TV programs and occasionally for participating in distance-learning courses.

The lead priority item in the *Mad Max Monitor* for 7:14 A.M., Tuesday, September 21, 2010, is a **video-mail** message from Max's 4-year-old granddaughter Melissa, who lives in Singapore. His youngest daughter and son-in-law were transferred there last year. Delayed video messaging has become their primary means of staying in touch. Max activates Melissa's message by looking at her image and then pointing to the play button. She instantly appears in front of him as if she were actually in the room. Melissa reminds him that her birthday is Saturday and tells him that she wishes he could be there. Before she signs off, she makes a funny face and blows him a kiss. He hadn't forgotten. But despite his wish to be with her in person, a v-mail birthday greeting will have to suffice this year. With Emily's help, he is creating an interactive video of the farm and the llamas to send with their greeting.

Below Melissa's message is another priority item about a countywide water conservation meeting scheduled for 8 A.M. today. The region has been experiencing a serious drought for several years and now the county government is proposing strict water rationing and additional tax assessments to construct a new aqueduct from the Columbia River. This is a meeting that Max and Emily are planning to attend.

After scanning the other priority mail and news items in the *Mad Max Monitor,* Max opens the financial department to see how their investments are doing. He can instantly display their portfolio against current market trends, access up-to-the-minute information on any public company or market worldwide, and execute buy and sell orders at any time.

Next he opens the automotive department. Max has been watching for tire sales. Actually, it's one of his **agents** that for the past week has been scanning tire stores within a 25-mile radius of their farm. This morning the agent has finally found a store that has the tires Max prefers on sale at a price below his indicated upper limit.

Max hasn't dealt with this company before, so he queries Myles, a friend who lives in the neighboring town where the company is located, and then checks the local Better Business Bureau's files in the virtual library. By the time he completes his search, which failed to turn up any customer complaints, Myles has replied. As luck would have it, his friend bought a set of tires from the company last year and enthusiastically recommends the place. He says the service was great and the price he paid was competitive with other shops. That's good enough for Max.

Since this store is not one of the permanent facilities in Max's cyber community, he needs to temporarily locate it in a part of town that is zoned for user-defined facilities and activities. This is a simple procedure that involves moving the store's identifier logo into a vacant lot. Once there, the store's virtual image instantly appears to all denizens of the community. Others can now visit the store and take advantage of the sale. Unless a majority of the residents decides to make the store a permanent facility, it will disappear in five days.

Upon entering the store, a friendly customer service avatar greets Max with a brochure and price list. Max needs only a few seconds to make his selection and set up an appointment. Since he already has several errands to run on Friday, he chooses 11 A.M. on that day to have the tires installed. The avatar instantly confirms the appointment, calculates the cost, and puts the information into Max's personal calendar.

With that task taken care of, Max flies to the teleconferencing center in the town. He belongs to a private discussion group that has 14 participants, including himself, in five countries. While Max has met only four members in person, they have all become trusted cyber friends through their daily chats. Each has specialized knowledge about different businesses. Curt, for example, lives in Kent, Ohio, and maintains close contacts with people employed by several dozen companies in the state's so-called crystal corridor— one of the leading R&D centers for **liquid crystal display (LCD)** technologies. Curt is considered to be one of the most reliable sources of information about these LCD enterprises. Like several other members of the group, Curt derives a significant portion of his income from people who buy items from his knowledge "store."

Instead of transmitting their images each time they meet in cyberspace, they also use personal avatars, which are stored locally in their VR systems. When a member of the group speaks, the other participants see his or her avatar move forward and lip sync the message. At first, Max found the illusion to be rather disconcerting, but he has grown used to it now and accepts the avatars as if they were real people. He has also come to appreciate their benefits, aside from faster and more natural interactions. With avatars, he never has to worry about how he looks, especially when he uses the system just after getting out of bed.

This morning six members are already interacting in **real time** when he joins the group. Three other members have provided delayed responses to earlier discussions (these appear in his peripheral vision). Each discussion is automatically stored and indexed so that it can be selectively reviewed at any time by the members.

Raymond is speaking from Jakarta about an Indonesian venture that is preparing to go public next week. He has been following the company's activities for about six months and shows the group some of the charts he has prepared. Each of the participants can independently examine and manipulate the underlying data using their touch pads. Max injects a few oral comments about the venture's marketing strategy and inquires about another Indonesian company that was discussed several weeks earlier. Raymond replies that he has had lunch with the company's vice president of sales today and was assured that the company's projections are on track. Max still has difficulty dealing with international date line quirks in their real-time discussions. The fact that Raymond's today is Max's tomorrow always throws him.

As Max leaves the teleconferencing center, he is alerted that Emily has arrived and is now in her dwelling, which is adjacent to his. She has finished her chores and is working out on the treadmill. Both can use the VR system at the same time and share experiences if they choose to do so in the metaverse. But at this moment, *Delphi* has presented Emily with an urgent video message from her daughter Stacy, along with about a dozen other priority items. Stacy is a junior at Columbia University and has access to most of the latest communication technologies through the school's media center.

Emily plays the message and is not surprised to discover that Stacy is asking for "a little more" money. She tells her mother that she has a unique opportunity to participate in a global village seminar. The virtual conferencing costs are covered by the school, she says, but she will need another $800 for seminar materials and some miscellaneous items, which she doesn't elaborate upon. Emily is tempted to forward the message to her ex-husband with a recommendation that he should cover the cost since he is obligated to pay most of Stacy's college expenses, but she has second thoughts. Emily puts *Delphi* aside and flies into the town's virtual bank to draft a wire transfer from her account to Stacy's bank account in New York. The whole process takes only a few moments to complete. She then leaves Stacy a message telling her the money is available.

When Max bought the VR system, Emily was initially skeptical and hesitant to use it, but no longer. She has come to appreciate the opportunities provided by the system and the ease with which she can pursue her interests. In her virtual world, there are no crowds to contend with and everything is open 24 hours seven days a week, so she can enjoy the experience of doing things at her own pace, on her own schedule, without any annoying distractions or delays.

On her way back to her cyber home, she greets Max, who is again reading his "newspaper" in his dwelling, and tells him that she thinks Ariana, their female llama, is finally pregnant. They have been eagerly anticipating this event for several months. To show his pleasure, Max has his avatar present her avatar with flowers. This is one of the ways they can express emotions in the metaverse. She knows they will share warmer human emotions as soon as they are together again in the real world.

Emily now flies to the virtual veterinary clinic to set up an appointment for a local vet to examine Ariana and confirm the pregnancy. She then enters the teleconferencing center to talk with members of the International Llama Owners Association. Emily joined the club just after she and Max bought their breeding pair and has found it to be a great help. There are no other people she knows of who are raising llamas within a hundred miles of their farm. When their male was suffering from a gastrointestinal problem last summer that baffled the local vet, Emily turned to the association's members. Within an hour, she received dozens of responses to her plea. Among those who responded was Abelardo, a university professor who raises llamas in Cuzco, Peru. It was his simple dietary treatment that soon restored the health of Emily's llama. Since then, Emily and the Peruvian professor have become close cyber friends. Much to her pleasure, Abelardo is one of the first to answer her query today about prenatal care. After briefly discussing Ariana's condition, he congratulates her and points her to several useful documents on the subject. She can't help wondering how closely Abelardo resembles his avatar, which appears as a portly, round-faced man with golden skin, large brown eyes, and a black bowler hat. Someday she hopes to visit Cuzco and meet him in person.

Max joins her in the teleconferencing center to remind her of the water conservation meeting that is scheduled to start in about a minute. To attend the meeting, they fly into the cyber town hall where they are joined by several dozen other residents who are jacked into the Web and several dozen more who are physically present at the meeting. Through a live video link, the virtual attendees can observe the proceedings as well as participate in the discussions and voting.

Without the VR system, Max and Emily's ability to take an active role in government policy making would be seriously limited. Most of the meetings that directly involve them take place in their county seat, which is about 40 miles from where they live, or in Salem, the state capitol. If they wanted to physically attend a state meeting, they would have to drive for more than eight hours each way. Now they can devote more time to understanding the issues and fulfilling their civic responsibilities from home. The number of people using VR systems to get involved in issues of governance has grown substantially in recent years. Max often speculates with his cohorts that in the next decade, governments run for the people, by the people may become a virtual reality in the real world.

## Living in virtual worlds

In this scenario, I have projected the view that computer-mediated communication (CMC) networks will ultimately become intimate extensions of one's self. It also suggests that the boundaries between the "real" world and "virtual" world will dissolve and that advanced forms of interpersonal cyber media will become an integral part of a great many people's daily lives early in the next century.

Although the term *virtual reality* has only recently entered our vocabulary, the underlying concept actually dates back to the invention of the telephone. When people began using this technologically mediated system to communicate in real time across great distances, they were unknowingly opening the door to the virtual world. In the real world, person-to-person oral communication can only take place within the range of human voice and hearing. The telephone overcame that limitation by creating an illusion that the speakers were present in the same physical space and time.

While the telephone emerged gradually, as we saw in chapter 4, from the metamorphosis of the electric telegraph, these two technologies did not act on people's minds in the same way. With the telegraph, the speed of human communication between distant points was greatly accelerated, but it still functioned basically as a *delayed* form of interpersonal communication similar to the postal system for written correspondence. Consequently, it did not create a strong sense of spontaneity or copresence among the actual message senders and receivers. Only the telegraph operators may have had a heightened perception of copresence. But because the telephone functions as an *immediate* form of interpersonal communication similar to ordinary face-to-face interactions, the illusion of collapsed distance is much greater than it was with the telegraph. Like the development of the automobile, Alexander Bell's system provided a more efficient means of personal transportation. But in the case of the telephone, it is the mind rather than the body that is transported.

The development of radio and television contributed significantly to the concept of virtual reality by bringing a greater variety of immediate aural and visual experiences directly into people's homes from distant and often strange places. But these broadcast forms of communication have lacked the essential interpersonal traits necessary to creating a participatory virtual world. Only since the emergence of CMC networks, which have blended telephony and digital language, has it become possible to begin constructing the virtual environments and tools described in the scenario.

### Star Trek technologies

However fantastic the scenario may seem, we can be reasonably certain that by the year 2010 some of the mentioned communication technologies will be taken for granted and others will pale in comparison to the actual technologies that will have emerged "unexpectedly." We can also be certain that most emerging technologies will not be used exactly as envisioned by their developers. This has been the pattern throughout the twentieth century and will undoubtedly be the pattern for the twenty-first and beyond.

A recent public television program illustrated this point quite well. In this program about the next century, creators of the popular "Star Trek" series explained that their greatest difficulty has been coming up with technological wonders for their imaginary twenty-fifth-century universe that won't suddenly appear on the market within a decade or two. Back in the late 1960s, when they were creating the original "Star Trek" episodes, their conceptions of personal communicators, "comm" badges, voice-activated computers, and interactive video displays seemed far enough in the future to satisfy most viewers' imaginations. Yet all these devices have already become commonplace. Many contemporary cell phones, for instance, closely resemble the "Star Trek" personal communicators. Clip-on comm badges have been used for years by security-conscious companies to track people's movements within buildings. The latest models of two-way personal pagers are also not too far removed from the original concept for comm badges. And voice-activated computers with interactive-video capabilities are now routinely sold in electronics stores as well as in discount and department stores. Many of the next-generation "Star Trek" devices are also certain to become commonplace by the next decade, especially if Bill Gates, the chairman of Microsoft Corporation, has anything to do with it.

### Bill Gates's vision

In his book *The Road Ahead*,[2] Gates describes his vision of the virtual world we may experience in the next two decades. This is a world in which nearly all TV sets and computers are plugged into a global intelligent network and respond easily to our commands. He emphasizes that in the near future we won't be confronted by new media technologies; instead they will gradually blend into our surroundings and become nearly invisible. For Gates, who is a billionaire many times over, the future is now. His new home on the shore of Lake Washington near Microsoft's Seattle headquarters already incorporates many of his ideas. More than 100 microcomputers have been built into the home in such a way that the technologies can be readily experienced by everyone without having to master or even notice the complex operations behind them.

Just as on the starship *Enterprise,* residents and guests will be expected to wear special pins that identify them to the house. As each occupant moves from room to room, the lighting and heating will automatically adjust. Easily changeable digital images will be displayed on high-resolution, flat-screen displays mounted on walls. Movies and television shows can follow viewers and appear on displays located in different rooms. Gates can also "tell" the house what guests like so that when they arrive, the house will automatically greet them with their favorite music. Sensors and data recorders scattered around the house will gather statistics on the operation of all systems, which will be continuously analyzed by a central computer system to presumably assure that everything works as it should.[3] Obviously, few of us have the resources of a Bill

---

[2]New York: Viking, 1995.

[3]A full explanation of the technologies incorporated into Bill Gates's home can be found in "Plugged in at Home," *The Road Ahead*. New York: Viking, 1995, pp. 205–226.

Gates to enable wholesale installation of virtual, interactive systems in our homes today, but some of these technologies may very well become available within just a few years.

## Building virtual communities

The development of CMC networks and virtual reality systems, however, is not just about creating markets for new electronic gadgets or making our homes more "intelligent." It's primarily about building communities and facilitating human interactions. Since the widespread development of superhighways and suburbs in the 1950s, people have tended to become increasing detached from their local communities as well as from their relatives and cohorts. While some have considered this a liberating experience, many more have been left with a lingering sense of personal loss and growing isolation.

Although there are numerous explanations for the explosive growth of the Internet and consumer online services in the 1990s, the most widely accepted belief is that people are seeking to construct new communities based on shared interests and needs rather than entirely on locality and family relationships. This process of virtual community building through CMC networks has been going on for nearly two decades, but only recently has it begun to include people who are nontechnical and live their lives outside the world of academia and scientific research.

Living in a virtual world is not a substitute for life in the physical world, but it does offer opportunities for people to expand their horizons and to share experiences that might not otherwise be accessible to them. For example, in cyberspace, communities based on shared interests can involve people who live in out-of-the-way places, are confined for physical reasons to their homes or hospitals, travel frequently, and are too busy or possibly too shy to attend scheduled meetings or events in real-life venues. As mentioned in the scenario, the capacity for individuals to take an active role in their governance and to participate in policy making is also likely to be greatly enhanced by the spread of cyber media.

Like the real world, however, virtual communities are not without problems, and not everyone can be expected to function as a responsible and trustworthy citizen. Cyberspace is often likened to a new frontier filled with dangers as well as opportunities. Until we learn how to manage human interactions and transactions in the virtual world without stifling the freedoms and qualities that have attracted so many people around the world, most denizens of cyber communities will continue to have a great deal in common with the pioneers who settled in untamed frontier towns.

## Next-generation cyber technologies

As we contemplate the next generation of interpersonal cyber technologies, we need to keep in mind the principle of opportunity and need, which states that consumers do not adopt new innovations and inventions on the merits of technology alone. In today's media-rich world, an abundance of information is readily accessible without the need for computer-mediated communication technologies.

Despite the many references to "information overload," humans possess an inherent capacity for not only assimilating vast amounts of information but effectively filtering it as well. People are continuously making information choices in their daily lives, without necessarily feeling overloaded. There are, of course, frustrations caused by time conflicts and the inability of existing media to conveniently or economically meet specific needs and interests. But until the great majority of consumers perceive clear, compelling reasons to adopt new forms of cyber media, they are likely to remain reasonably contented with the array of media and telecommunication technologies currently available to them.

The supervening social necessity for more advanced CMC systems within academic, research, technology, business, and government communities, however, is already quite clear. Members of these communities have vital needs for reliable, timely information and interpersonal communication that relate directly to their specific areas of involvement, no matter where in the world the information or communication may originate or what they might cost. Systems that continue to rely on printed documents and face-to-face exchanges of information are no longer capable of meeting those needs. The torrent of new information added each day to the world's databases has simply overwhelmed the capacity of humans to effectively mediate without the assistance of CMC technologies. As these databanks expand to include graphics, photos, full-motion video, and audio, along with basic computer-readable text files, the process of harvesting useful and relevant information will become exponentially more complex.

Undoubtedly, versions of advanced CMC systems developed to deal with these problems will eventually find their way into the general consumer market. How they will be used and how deeply they will ultimately penetrate into our daily lives is a subject that strikes directly at the heart of established mainstream media companies.

## Personal agents and databases

In 1988, Apple Computer produced a video, called "The Knowledge Navigator," to illustrate its vision of the future. In this staged presentation, a portable flat-panel device that merged voice, full-motion video, text, communications, and computing was used by two college professors to exchange and interact with information in a completely intuitive and seemingly natural way. An intelligent agent represented as a lifelike "talking head" assumed the roles of a secretary and research assistant: screening incoming phone calls, searching databases, scheduling meetings, compiling news and information, and instantly creating multimedia graphics. Voice commands and touch were used for all interactions.

Since then, this notion that computer programs called agents might one day take on the role of surrogate humans and interact with people in a natural, interpersonal way has become increasingly popular. It is often assumed that person-to-computer communication in the next stage of the third great mediamorphosis will be nearly indistinguishable from person-to-person communication. But, while this may be the desired goal, there are a number of major obstacles that will need to be overcome before silicon-based agents can begin to match humans in their ability to evaluate and respond to information or to make humanlike intuitive connections between disparate and seemingly unrelated items. One of the greatest obstacles lies within the arrays of databases upon which agents are expected to apply their intelligence.

Contemporary computer databases may appear to be technological marvels, but they are, in fact, nothing more than electronic landfills—the digital refuse heaps of late twentieth-century civilization. That is, nearly all of the world's accumulated data files that have been converted into digital language and stored on computer disks and magnetic tapes exist in an unstructured form.

**Search engines.** To dig through these immense heaps of bits, computer engineers have had to devise tools called **search engines.** These tools essentially translate the words in an individual's search request into strings of bits that are then compared with the bits contained in a database until all possible matches are found. More advanced search engines have been designed to not just gather data but to also infer their relative importance. These search engines usually do this by counting the number of times certain requested terms appear in all the foraged files and then ranking them according to their probability of satisfying the individual's query.

Searching one database is difficult enough, but the problem becomes exponentially more difficult when it is necessary to search through many databases. As with humans, computers speak many different dialects and have great difficulty communicating with each other. Even though the World Wide Web and Mosaic browsers have provided an efficient way to provide visual, hypermedia doorways to information stored in some databases, this approach is unsuited to broad database searches. **Surfing** the Web in search of specific data can be frustrating and exceedingly time comsuming.

A possible solution that has been pursued for several years is the development of **neural networks.** This concept involves the creation of network structures for storing and processing information that resemble the pathways and synaptic connections found in the human brain and nervous system. Instead of the mindless "brute force" approach taken by contemporary search engines, neural networks would presumably learn from experience and become more intelligent over time. Such networks, however, are still in a very embryonic stage of development.

**Wandering agents.** Even though the widespread application of neural networks may not occur for several decades, silicon agents with limited intelligence are already being used to "roam" computer databases. One of the first primitive agents was developed in the mid-1980s by Vinton Cerf and Robert Kahn at the Corporation for National Research Initiatives (CNRI). They called their agent a **knowbot,** a contraction of knowledge robot. An early prototype was designed to continuously wander through databases at the

National Library of Medicine in search of interesting facts on people listed in publicly available databases. Agents similar to the CNRI knowbots, now called **spiders,** are routinely used today by Internet indexing services to locate and link computer files stored in the Web's databases.

In many ways, the models for these agents are the helpful librarians and research assistants who always seem to know exactly where to find just what we're looking for. Because agents can be tailored to meet individual requirements and are designed to deal with diverse data formats, they are considered ideal for personal information services, as described in the scenario. But they still have a number of drawbacks that remain to be solved.

As agents are required to act with greater intelligence and intuit connections, they become increasingly complex to build. The problem is roughly analogous to designing a metal detector capable of pinpointing every coin with a specific silver content buried in landfills scattered around the world. And that's not all. Once this amazing detector has located the coins, its on-board processor would also have to grade the quality of the coins and sort them by country, mint, year, and denomination.

Even neural networks and more advanced agents will have great difficulty solving some of the most frustrating human problems associated with broad database searches. These problems include knowing exactly what it is we want to know and then knowing how to phrase the search questions so that we don't end up with too many files or none at all. An equally troublesome enigma is how to know when *the* answer to a question has actually been found. Nearly all queries will yield answers, but not every answer will be the "right" answer. From the perspective of computers, all information is neutral. Right and wrong answers can only be determined in a mathematical context. With database searches, such judgments are generally subjective and are not easily made. And this problem is not getting any easier to solve. As the amount of data grows, the amount of "bad" data also expands. Some researchers have argued that "bad" data—erroneous, unsubstantiated, misleading, useless—are growing at a far greater rate in the world than are "good" data.

*Access, time, and cost.* Three other problems loom large on the horizon—access, time, and cost. As the number of roaming agents grows, database owners are likely to become increasingly concerned that intentional or accidental **viruses** contained in these agents could corrupt their data files. Antivirus programs and standardized codes may offer some measure of protection, but they may serve to limit accesses as well.

The proliferation of agents is also likely to result in frequent traffic jams. The impact of spiders and other personal agents upon the Internet is already being felt. But as databases are expanded and greater amounts of multimedia content, such as audio and video clips, are added, the time required for searches could expand significantly. When thousands, or perhaps millions, of agents begin competing for access, networks and databases are certain to clog and become painfully slow. Faster computers and communication networks may overcome some of the problem, but, as with highway systems in the real world, the traffic will always grow to exceed whatever capacity engineers have anticipated.

And while some database owners will undoubtedly continue to provide free public access, most can be expected to charge for access and items retrieved. Because prices are likely to vary from database to database, even when the bits of information are identical, agents will have to keep track of costs as they roam and know when a budget limit has been reached. When private, for-profit databases are involved, the results of searches are unlikely to be cheap.

### Immersive virtual reality systems

Another alternative for searching large databases or clusters of databases now under development involves the use of immersive virtual reality systems. Instead of externally navigating through cyberspace in search of information, as computer users are required to do today, immersive VR systems can actually project users into cyberspace by creating the illusion of being inside a three-dimensional database or more familiar environment, such as a library. A version of this idea was portrayed in *Disclosure*, a 1995 Hollywood movie. The lead characters in the film were shown using an immersive VR system to "walk" through a database, which was given the appearance of the New York Public Library. Data were clustered along the virtual walls in file drawers that could be opened just by pointing. An avatar, portrayed as an angel, was always on call to answer questions and provide help. While VR database search tools might not be quite so literal in the near future, they can be expected to provide users with an array of familiar visual, aural, and tactile clues.

Immersive VR systems are bound to be widely adopted in the next decade for interpersonal communication as well. As the cost and the size and weight of the VR headgear and sensors are reduced, the appeal of these systems will grow. With this form of cyber media, space, time, and reality itself can be transcended. The implications are mind-boggling. Humans have spent the past two centuries devising steadily faster and more efficient vehicles for physically traveling to distant locations. Everything from local commutes and cross-country flights to proposed human explorations of space are measured by the distance and time required to get from one point to another. Virtual reality radically changes all that. Instead of transporting our physical bodies to Mars, for example, immersive systems can bring Mars to us at the speed of light (after a robotic vehicle has been landed on the planet) without having to move a single human atom. These systems can also alter our concepts of physical size. With VR, doctors can travel into patients' hearts without penetrating their bodies, and molecular biologists can "shrink" themselves to a point where they can rearrange the atoms in molecules. In this sense, VR can be defined as a personal transportation system for the mind.

Immersive VR systems are just beginning to move from research laboratories into the consumer marketplace. As is the case with so many new media technologies, one of the first applications has been for entertainment systems. But the concept of immersive VR actually began to take shape in the 1960s with the development of computerized flight simulators to train military pilots and astronauts. By the beginning of the 1980s, this technology had come to be known as "artificial reality." The news media and general public seemed to take little notice, however, until the end of that decade when Jaron Lanier began promoting an immersive system called RB-2 (reality built for two). With a special headset and "data glove" connected to a powerful personal computer, he was able to convincingly demonstrate the commercial potential of the medium, which he began referring to as virtual reality.

Since then, immersive VR systems have been developed for a wide variety of real-world applications. In addition to pilot training, they are now being used by military units to simulate and prepare for combat situations, by companies and research institutions to monitor and handle hazardous materials, by chemists and biologists to examine molecular structures, and by psychologist to help patients overcome their phobias. A team of researchers at the University of North Carolina has demonstrated a VR system for architects that may one day make it possible for people to routinely "walk through" a home or office building and easily make design changes before it is constructed. Other systems are being developed for collaborative medical examinations and surgeries that may soon allow specialists at large metropolitan hospitals to assist doctors in rural clinics.

### Virtual environments and avatars

Neal Stephenson's *Snow Crash,* published in 1992, is credited with introducing people who had not been aware of the online fantasy worlds known as multiuser dungeons (MUDs) to the concepts of virtual reality metaverses and avatars. Stephenson's future vision of an immersive virtual environment with a complete community infrastructure that includes homes, offices, stores, transportation systems, and organizations as well as its own social, political, and economic "laws" has given shape to many ongoing development efforts and to the scenario in this chapter.

The appeal of these metaverses appears to be in their blend of the familiar and the fantastic. They can be both practical and fun at the same time, without being technologically intimidating. Unlike most contemporary CMC systems, they require only a minimum amount of time and instructions to learn how to use and navigate them.

By representing users as animated avatars, VR systems extend two essential attributes of voice telephony and the Internet—spontaneity and the potential for anonymity. In this universe of the mind, people can assume practically any fantasy role they choose, from samurai warrior to alien species, or simply adopt a persona and appearance that closely resemble their actual character and image. They need not be self-conscience about their real-world appearance, so their interactions and involvements can be significantly less inhibited.

The failure to acknowledge this common desire for visual anonymity is, I believe, one of the fundamental reasons why video telephones have not been successful in our society. There are, of course, situations where a person's image can be important, but one of the greatest strengths of interpersonal communication via the telephone and CMC systems has been the ability to not be seen. In a very real sense, telephony, online networks, and immersive VR systems create a more level playing field on which people can be judged by their minds and contributions rather than their stature and conformity to some physical ideal.

Avatars may also provide a convenient solution for companies, institutions, and government agencies that frequently deal with the public through the telephone. With generic avatars that display the preferred persona of an organization, automated communications can be made more efficient, personal, and natural. They can also extend one-to-one marketing and customer support without requiring companies to maintain large staffs 24 hours a day, seven days a week.

Although the images produced by today's immersive VR systems are still somewhat crude and cartoonlike, more powerful microprocessors are expected to offer the potential for nearly lifelike movements, tactile sensations, and far more realistic virtual environments in the next decade. As these systems evolve, they may quickly find their way into homes and offices. History has shown, as we have seen in the previous chapters, that once a new media technology is perceived to be entertaining or useful and to fit comfortably into people's daily lives at an affordable price, it can diffuse rapidly in the general consumer market.

### Light-wave communication

The widespread adoption of virtual reality systems and other advanced forms of cyber media within the general consumer market hinges on the ability of telecommunication companies to provide nearly universal access to broadband channels at an affordable price. Given the current pace of development, there seems little reason to doubt that by the year 2010 most U.S. homes and offices will be plugged into an entirely digital broadband communication network. Some people are so optimistic that they are convinced bandwidth will become a cheap and practically limitless commodity within the next two decades.

The reason for their optimism is **light-wave communication** technology. Even though scientists had long suspected that visible light could be used for more efficient communications, they didn't succeed until the late 1960s in demonstrating its enormous capacity for conveying and storing digital data. By the year 2010, light-wave communications are likely to be more pervasive than any other system, including satellite and copper-wire networks.

***Lasers and fiber-optic cables.*** Two inventions have made the greatest contributions to the development of light-wave communications—the laser and fiber-optic cables. Laser is an acronym for light amplification by stimulated emission of radiation. These devices produce intense beams of parallel light at precisely defined wavelengths. With ordinary light, the emitted photons scatter in all directions from the source. The photons that emerge from a laser source are highly focused, or coherent, so they can remain confined to a tight beam over great distances.

Powerful lasers have successfully bounced coherent light beams off the moon and have been under development by the U.S. military to intercept and destroy incoming missiles. Less powerful laser "torches" now routinely sweep the skies at festivals and rock concerts. Today, lasers are commonly used in warehouses, checkout counters, and handheld scanners to quickly read the bar codes on packaged goods and merchandise; in surveying equipment and gun sights to accurately fix locations; in construction and research tools to ensure precise alignments; in hospitals as scalpels for delicate surgeries; in compact disc players and laser printers to read and write data.

***Wires of glass.*** Like radio waves, laser light waves can be used to efficiently convey information through wires, as well as "through the air." But the wires required for transmitting light signals are not ordinary wires. They must be made of exceptionally pure and transparent silica (the principal ingredient of glass). These glass wires, or optical fibers, are as thin as human hairs, yet a single strand has the capacity to carry more information than a thick bundle of copper wires.

The first commercial fiber-optic cable was produced in 1970 by Corning Glass Works. Since then, optical fiber has been steadily replacing the old copper-wire communication infrastructures in nearly all countries. Millions of miles of fiber-optic cables have been laid under the oceans and are providing a clarity of communication for intercontinental telephony unmatched by copper. The transmission capacity of light-wave communication systems using lasers and optical fiber seems practically limitless. Since 1975, the transmission capacity of fiber optics has increased tenfold every four years.[4] The most difficult problem to be overcome appears to be the development of increasingly faster and more intelligent optical switches to direct the packets of information traveling at the speed of light.

**Fiber optics in the home.** Most telephone companies propose stringing optical fibers only as far as the curb to reduce cost. From there, coaxial cables or copper wires would be used to connect home computers, TV sets, and other electronic appliances. Direct access to fiber-optic telephone services from homes is not expected to be widely available in the United States much before the year 2010. The phone companies are not, however, the only source of optical fiber. Cable-TV operators are also rewiring their systems with optical fiber and expect to offer a range of interactive multimedia services directly into homes within just a few years. Utility companies may be potential suppliers of fiber-optic services as well. Many public utilities in the United States have installed optical fibers into homes to monitor the use of electricity and natural gas and are now exploring new opportunities to profit from this technology.

When the vision of a global information superhighway network is finally realized, it is certain to be built out of silica. And the vehicles that will cruise these glass tollways will be composed of light. Light-wave communications will provide the routes that lead to and accelerate the development of new forms of digital media in the twenty-first century.

## Future control and social issues

Even though the concepts of personal computer-mediated news services and virtual worlds seem to have widespread appeal, like all

---

[4]Emmanuel Desurvire, "Lightwave Communications: The Fifth Generation." *Scientific American* (January 1992), pp. 114–121.

new media technologies, their influence on individuals and society will not be neutral. The growing ability to filter and focus information to meet increasingly narrower sets of interests combined with the opportunity to "live" in virtual communities of one's own creation—and to thereby avoid real-world community involvements and responsibilities—presents genuine reasons for concern.

Those who see the positive aspects of cyber media suggest that greater individual control over the selection and flow of information will yield more informed and involved citizens. And that virtual environments and avatars will help to stimulate public discourse on issues and government policies. On the opposite side are those who see cyber media accelerating social fragmentation rather than unity. The Internet has already made it possible for people with anarchistic, sociopathic, or conspiratorial attitudes to reinforce their often paranoid and narrow views of the world through online associations with others who share the same beliefs. While the freedoms of speech and association are integral to democratic societies, many fear that fringe groups will use CMC networks to spread divisiveness and intolerance that could incite racial, ethnic, and religious confrontations.

These concerns deserve serious attention and will need to be addressed by practically everyone at some point; however, they are unlikely to be resolved easily or anytime soon. And a deeper discussion of these issues is outside the scope of this book. I have therefore chosen to focus on some of the future control and social issues that relate directly to the next stage in the mediamorphosis of interpersonal communication technologies.

## Trust and privacy in cyberspace

When William Gibson wrote about cyberspace in his 1984 science fiction novel *Neuromancer*, few people understood then that many of the CMC technologies and activities he described were already well on their way to becoming a reality. His Orwellian vision of a future underworld, where people would routinely "jack" into a global computer network to participate in various unsavory businesses, commit crimes, and act out their fantasies, may have been excessively harsh but it is not entirely implausible.

The story of cyber-criminal Kevin Mitnick's activities and ultimate capture, as told by Tsutomu Shimomura and John Markoff in *Takedown*,[5] illustrates that the antisocial potential of CMC technologies is not a fanciful notion. Just as in the real world, the sense of trust and community once shared by the developers of the Internet is all but a fading memory. "The electronic walls going up everywhere on the Net," Shimomura says, "are the clearest proof of the loss of that trust and community."[6]

The maintenance of trust and privacy in cyberspace is becoming more of an issue as CMC networks rapidly expand throughout the world and become increasingly commercialized. Although there have been repeated assurances by telecommunication companies and Internet service providers that data gathered about the activities of individual online subscribers won't be made public or abused, the potential application of these data for marketing purposes has been one of the great attractions for advertisers, commercial entities, and even politicians.

Another issue relating to trust and privacy is the obvious need for secure financial transactions. Until people feel confident that their credit cards and bank accounts won't be broken into by computer hackers, cyber commerce will develop slowly. People have also tended to be distrustful of technologically mediated transactions out of a not unreasonable fear that a computer error or failure in the system will result in a significant financial loss or frustrating problem to resolve. This is one of the reasons why the banking automated teller (ATM) and bank-by-phone networks have taken so long to become widely accepted. Even today, many people are still reluctant to use these electronic systems and prefer to do all of their transactions with banks in person.

Two technological developments that may help to overcome these problems are **encryption** and physical identification systems. With encryption, data can be encoded in such a way that only the sender and the recipient can decode the information. However, while encryption has been seen as vital to cyber commerce, it has presented a number of policy problems for governments. In the

---

[5]Tsutomu Shimomura with John Markoff, *Takedown: The Pursuit and Capture of Kevin Mitnick, America's Most Wanted Computer Outlaw—By the Man Who Did It.* New York: Hyperion, 1996.
[6]Ibid., p. 314.

United States, for example, encryption technologies have been classified as military weapons because they are used for coding military and other secret communications. With this classification, it has been technically illegal to export files or programs that contain encryption routines without a special permit. For users of the Internet, however, the definition of "export" is legally vague.

If a user posts an encryption program on a bulletin board or Web server located in the United States, the user is not actually exporting the file even though it can be retrieved by individuals who live outside of the United States. While this particular restriction may be relaxed in the near future, the availability of sophisticated encryption technologies for public use has been a major concern of police and intelligence agencies. If there is no practical way to unlock encrypted documents, these agencies have argued that they will be unable to intercept messages and transactions made by criminal organizations and terrorist groups. They also fear that people might use encryption to hide international fund transfers in order to avoid taxes. The underlying issue, therefore, is the control of information. Whatever additional control that individuals may gain from the spread of CMC networks and encryption technologies is seen as coming at the expense of governments and the established information gatekeepers.

Physical identification systems provide another level of security for digital transactions. These systems are several steps beyond the personal identification number (PIN) codes used by ATM and credit card customers. Instead of relying on passwords based on letter or number codes that can be forgotten or easily garnered by hackers, physical systems use unique human identifiers, such as fingerprints, retina scans, and voice prints. While the development of commercial physical identification technologies is still at an early stage, the supervening social necessity for secure transactions is so great that they are certain to be quickly adopted once their reliability has been proven and they become widely available.

## Censorship versus the free flow of information

Even though we seem to be moving steadily closer to Marshall McLuhan's vision of a global village, uniform international standards and policies to govern communication technology, as well as the flow of information, may well require several more decades to sort out. The political, cultural, and economic motivations for regulating media vary quite substantially from society to society. While many countries have adopted into their constitutions protections of speech and the press similar to those found in the U.S. Bill of Rights, their interpretations of free speech and a free press can be quite different from the U.S. view.

Some countries, for example, have passed into law guarantees that the media shall be able to publish the truth, but then declare that the government shall reserve the right to determine what is the truth. Consider for a moment how this law would have influenced the editors of the *Washington Post* when they learned of the Watergate break-in and its connections to President Nixon. Other countries have regulated the distribution of newsprint to put subtle but highly effective economic pressure on newspaper and magazine publishers.

As the Internet spreads its digital web across the globe, the contemporary vision of "universal access" is certain to encounter resistance in many countries where leaders see the free flow of information as a threat to their beliefs and power. Already China and several Southeast Asian countries have taken steps to control Internet access and limit the content that can be locally posted and accessed. While political and religious leaders in these countries publicly argue that their principal concerns are with material they consider pornographic, such as *Playboy* and *Penthouse* magazines, or potentially divisive, they are actually much more concerned with the prospect of having their power as the traditional information gatekeepers diminished.

Even in the United States, politicians and religious groups are pushing for more stringent controls on the flow of information through the Internet. Here, too, the public justifications have been based largely on efforts to prevent children from being exposed to pornography and pedophiles. But the real underlying issue is also about who will control information within the society. While many users of the Internet argue that all information should be allowed to flow freely, the historic trends have generally been for established governments and institutions to limit information access through direct or subtle forms of censorship.

Ultimately, however, attempts to stifle the free flow of information have failed. An important lesson can be taken from the rapid spread of printing presses and books throughout Europe in the fif-teenth and sixteenth centuries. Despite great efforts by the Catholic Church to control and suppress printed material it considered objec-tionable, this new media technology eventually led to the major social and religious upheaval called the Reformation.

## Mediamorphosis within the interpersonal domain in perspective

The vision of interpersonal cyber media presented in this chapter has been built upon a number of assumptions regarding the medi-amorphosis of interpersonal communications in the next decade. The safest of these premises is that computer-mediated communica-tion technologies will become more powerful, more essential, more pervasive, and more integrated. Contemporary computer applica-tions, such as word processing, spread sheets, telecommunication, and audio/video editing tools, will be highly integrated and stan-dardized within future systems. There would be no discernible dis-tinctions, from the perspective of consumers, between content and applications.

The Internet and consumer online networks will meld with tele-phone and satellite/cable-TV systems to form a seamless, global CMC service. Homes and offices in all but the most remote loca-tions will be plugged into fiber-optic networks, and direct satellite services will become commonplace. Computer-mediated forms of interpersonal communication can be expected to blend voice, video, text, and graphics. To ensure privacy, nearly all digital interactions and transactions will be encrypted (automatically coded).

Next-generation cyber media will routinely employ personal "intelligent" agents to gather, sort, and filter information and enter-tainment to match individual requirements and tastes. Agents will learn from experience and adapt to each person's changing prefer-ences. In addition to acting as personal librarians and researchers, they will monitor incoming messages, calendars, and finances as well as home and auto security systems.

And although agents may prove to be useful tools for gathering and processing information and managing electronic forms of inter-personal communication, they are unlikely to replace mainstream newspapers and other packaged information products or eliminate the need for human content mediators, such as journalists, information managers, and producers. As we will see in chapter 9, print media can continue to evolve and thrive in digital form. And despite the many negative assumptions, television broadcasting can also be expected to adapt and evolve, as we will see in chapter 8.

Most advanced CMC systems can be expected to incorporate immersive virtual reality technologies in the next decade. The market for networked VR systems may initially be driven by games and interactive 3-D movies, but it is certain to include a great many practical applications by the year 2010, such as remote but "real-time" conferencing and collaborating, shopping, and continuing education. Interpersonal VR interactions within cyber media are likely to involve avatars—lifelike or fantasy computer simulations of people—rather than live video images. These digital personas will be used to preserve individual privacy and anonymity when dealing with strangers and casual acquaintances and will provide faster and more efficient communication at a lower cost.

# mediamorphosis within the broadcast domain

In the world today, there are few places where people are not aware of Princess Di's divorce from Prince Charles, or O. J. Simpson's trial, or the most recent plight of children in war-torn regions. News of revolts, catastrophes, and discoveries, as well as fashion trends, movies, and recordings, are now aurally and visually shared by almost everyone everywhere at nearly the same instant. No one seems surprised these days to discover that teenagers in Indonesia, Peru, Turkey, and Russia listen to the same music and dress and act in much the same manner as their counterparts in the United States, England, Germany, and France.

This phenomenon has been attributed by Marshall McLuhan and others to the rapid diffusion of television and the nearly insatiable human hunger for information and entertainment. Despite the many criticisms and proposed changes in the technology, television remains a universally popular broadcast medium. Even in some of the world's poorest regions, TV antennas can be seen sprouting like metallic weeds from the roofs of shanties. All around the globe, television sets connected to high-tech satellite-TV dishes are now being installed in formerly isolated communities—a great many of which still lack indoor plumbing and other basic modern amenities. Because television is undeniably the most pervasive, most popular, most controversial medium within the broadcast domain today, I have made it the focus of this chapter. Moreover, as with telephony and the other forms of mainstream media, digital technologies are expected to radically transform television in the next stage of the third great mediamorphosis.

Nearly everyone, it seems, has an opinion about TV's future. At one extreme is the belief that it is doomed and will not survive much beyond the end of this decade. At the other extreme are those who argue that "high-definition" and "interactive" technologies will completely revitalize the medium and lead it to a new golden age. The scenario that follows takes the position expounded by the principles of mediamorphosis that TV will adapt and continue to evolve. A chronology of the major technological innovations that have influenced the development of television in the past two centuries and that are likely to affect its ultimate transition to a digital form of broadcast media early in the twenty-first century is found in Exhibit 8.1.

### *Scenario for 2010.* *The interactive video family*

The sound of crashing waves grows louder as the image of a magnificent pink sunrise with seagulls feeding in the surf magically appears in the window. But this is no ordinary window. It's a high-resolution, digital TV screen mounted on the bedroom wall. For Carol and Curt, however, the distinction is irrelevant; their sensation of awaking at the beach is quite real.

As always, Carol is the first to get out of bed. With her remote control, she signals their central home **server** that she won't be needing a more strident wake-up call this morning. Curt prefers, as always, to linger for several more precious minutes in the warmth of this "dreamscape." This is their favorite wake-up program because it brings back romantic memories of their honeymoon in Maui. In the five years they have lived in Kent, Ohio, this is the only ocean beach they have seen.

A variety of wake-up programs, as well as live video "windows," are provided by the local ITV (interactive television) service. Most incorporate scenes from nature, but there are also a number of fantasy scenes that are popular with teenagers. For example, Chloe's (their 14-year-old daughter) wake-up program looks and sounds like something from a Klingon[1] mating ritual.

In the kitchen, Carol starts the coffee maker as she watches and listens to the latest news on the flat-screen portable. After a summary of top stories, Carol's video agent displays a menu of other items that are likely to match her specific interests. At the top of her menu are the local weather and traffic reports. A tractor-trailer has spilled its load of produce on

---

[1]The Klingons are a fictitious warrior race created for the "Star Trek" television series.

**Exhibit 8.1** Time line of electronic broadcast media developments, 1800–2010.

| Year | |
|------|--|
| **1800** – | – First experiments with electric current |
| | – |
| | – |
| | – |
| | – |
| **1825** – | – |
| | – Faraday discovers electromagnetic induction |
| | – Electric telegraph demonstrated |
| | – First practical photographic system (daguerreotypes) |
| | – First commercial electric telegraph service |
| **1850** – | – |
| | – |
| | – |
| | – |
| | – |
| **1875** – | – Maxwell elucidates theory of electromagnetism |
| | – Motion picture system demonstrated |
| | – Images converted into electric signals; Hertz detects electric waves in air |
| | – Commercial kinetoscope systems introduced; motion picture camera |
| | – Marconi demonstrates wireless telegraph; cathode-ray tube; cinemas |
| **1900** – | – Continuous-wave transmitter developed; newsreels |
| | – Vacuum tube invented; first audio broadcast (Christmas Eve 1906) |
| | – De Forest patents Audion (first triode) |
| | – Conrad begins regular radio broadcasts from his Pittsburgh home |
| | – Radio Corporation of America founded; commercial radio stations |
| **1925** – | – Radio networks; first commercials; talkies; first TV system |
| | – FM radio invented; car radios installed; electronic camera tube |
| | – Communications Act of 1934 regulates broadcasting in U.S. |
| | – RCA unveils live TV at 1939 World's Fair; color TV demonstrated |
| | – Commercial TV inaugurated in U.S. |
| **1950** – | – Cable-TV system; wide-screen movies introduced; 3-D movies |
| | – Color TV sets; video recorders; movies on TV |
| | – TV in 90% of U.S. homes; TV characterized as a "vast wasteland" |
| | – McLuhan declares "the medium is the message" |
| | – Video cassette recorder; video games; HBO introduced |
| **1975** – | – TV satellites; VHS system introduced; two-way cable service |
| | – CNN founded; videodisk systems; digital sound synthesizers |
| | – Camcorders introduced; operational analog HDTV system, CD-ROMs |
| | – Digital HDTV demonstrated; interactive TV trials; digital radio |
| | – Digital Direct Broadcast Satellite (DBS) services; PC television and radio |
| **2000** – | – Operational digital HDTV system; intimate home theaters |
| | – Large high-definition, flat-screen displays; commercial VR movies |
| | – Commercial holographic projection systems; holographic movies |
| | – |
| | – |

the freeway she usually takes to her office. According to the report, cleanup could take an hour or two, and traffic is already backed up several miles. By using the display's voice-recognition feature, she selects the animated detour map. The program calculates that the detour will add about 15 minutes to her morning commute.

Back in the master bedroom, Curt is watching a morning talk show. The show was automatically recorded when it started about 45 minutes earlier, so he hasn't missed anything. Scheduling the programs they want to watch has been made much easier with the ITV service's on-screen guide. Their personal video agents are instructed to filter the programs and movies that are most likely to interest them from the thousands broadcast each day. Then Carol and Curt use their remote to select the programs they like from the customized guide and place them into their personal calendars, which are also shown on the display. They can easily rearrange the sequence and viewing times to suit their schedules. With so many local, national, and even international programs to choose from, they are, in a very real sense, able to create their own individual channels.

The scent of coffee and a toasting bagel catches Curt's attention, so he pauses the show and steps into the shower. Several minutes later he returns to the bedroom to dress and restarts the talk show where he left off. The system functions much like their old VCR, but without the frustration of recalling confusing programming commands. He doesn't even have to set clocks. Their central server regularly receives time signals from the ITV service and automatically resets the digital clocks in their house.

Chloe has finally been awakened from deep REM sleep. She had set her program to wake her earlier than usual since she has a report due today comparing the present multinational Mars expedition with the U.S. *Apollo* program some four decades earlier. Predictably, she has waited until the last minute to complete the assignment. Instead of working on the project this weekend, she spent most of her time watching old "Star Trek Voyager" episodes from the ITV archives and participating in a VR adventure with her buddies in more than a dozen cities across the country. Now after a quick dash to the refrigerator for a glass of orange juice and a nutribar, she goes to her desk to finish her multimedia presentation.

Curt drifts into the kitchen as Carol finishes her breakfast. She has moved the portable to the table so she can continue reviewing the video highlights of her personal news reports. He reminds her that the international cycling competition in Australia is in its final leg. Returning to the ITV guide, she locates the latest coverage and displays it so they can both watch as the son of one of their closest friends crosses the finish line in third place. With a voice command, Curt displays the winning times and statistical data on the race. He can also call up a map of the route and personal profiles of the finalists.

Carol heads for the shower as Curt knocks on Chloe's door to let her know that she has less than 15 minutes before her shuttle arrives. Chloe is scrambling to put the finishing touches on her presentation. She's had to leave out some of the stuff she gathered, but she feels it's good enough as is. She compresses the final production and sends it to her school using the ITV cable link. The link is a free broadband channel maintained by the ITV service for use by local schools and universities. It functions more like a transport system than a typical television channel or online service. Practically everything from homework and course materials to video clips of football games and school board meetings is routed through the link and captured on servers for viewing or using **offline**.

After Carol and Chloe leave the house, Curt settles into the lounge chair in the family theater room and prepares for his weekly study session. He is going through a retraining program to become a **holographic** systems engineer. Holographic movie theaters are the latest rage. These systems project moving three-dimensional images that seem almost real. They are essentially VR systems that don't require people to wear special visors. Theater owners are betting this technology will help revitalize their business, which has been declining steadily since people began installing intimate theaters in their homes. More important to Curt are the opportunities that have emerged for creative engineers in holographic systems development and movie production. In December, he expects to complete his two-year program and to be certified.

What still amazes Curt is how much **distance learning programs** have changed. Even only 15 years ago, when he received his Ph.D. in computer sciences, he could not have imagined the variety and quality of educational opportunities that are presently available. A number of universities had experimented with educational channels in the 1980s and 1990s, but the degree of interaction he currently takes for granted was far beyond the reach of typical families back then. Distance learning programs are now readily accessible, as well as affordable, for nearly everyone.

The programs operate through a combination of the ITV education link Chloe used to ship her homework assignment and the conferencing services provided by the Global Web—(a more advanced version of the old World Wide Web). Curt receives the latest interactive multimedia lectures and demonstrations overnight via the link. This gives him the freedom to participate whenever it's convenient for him.

As Curt watches and listens to today's lecture about holographic modeling techniques on the large wall-mounted TV screen, he uses his remote control to display a diagram from his course materials that compares several advanced data compression models for holographic images. He can have a number of different windows open on the screen at the same time. Curt often uses this capability to watch three or four TV programs simultaneously. He can do this easily because the TV in the family theater is 8 feet wide, 4 1/2 feet high, and about 2 inches thick (about twice the size of the screen in the master bedroom).

Curt now notices that several students have gathered on the Global Web and are discussing the compression models with an assistant instructor. The Web site appears as another window on the TV screen even though it uses a different two-way channel. He remembers another approach he read about recently and inquires about its potential. Curt's question is automatically queued until questions from three other students have been answered. In this way, everyone gets a fair chance to be involved in the discussion. When the study session is over, Curt saves the entire session on the central server. Later in the day, he plans to clip some of the material for his dissertation.

For now, he decides to take a break and relax with his favorite sci-fi adventure. He doesn't like to admit that he still enjoys letting his mind escape into fantasy worlds. His selection of ITV programs for the day is visually displayed on the right side of the screen. With his remote, he launches the show and then settles back in his chair in anticipation of the challenges that await him on Planet Zog.

## Harbingers of the future

Until the 1970s, the living room TV could be used for only one purpose—passively watching network television. Today, the "tube" has many purposes. By attaching various electronic devices and cables, we can use it to play fast-action video games, call up information from online networks, interact with CD-ROM books, view video-cassettes, and select programs from dozens of satellite/cable-TV channels, as well as continue to watch network television. Yet, for all the new options provided by state-of-the-art consumer electronics in the past two decades, we are still making do with analog TV technologies that have remained fundamentally unchanged for more than half a century.

That, however, may not be the case for much longer if the television industry has its way. With a new digital standard, called high-definition TV (HDTV), and a complement of "intelligent" interactive features, the industry expects to fully transform the medium by the end of the next decade. It also expects, in the process, to become a formidable competitor in businesses currently dominated by the telephone, computer, and publishing industries. But, despite all the hype about media convergence, we should not expect the TV sets, telephones, personal computers, fax machines, periodicals, and books scattered around people's homes to be suddenly replaced by a single universal teleputer. The notion that nearly all forms of communication media will fuse into one megamedium is about as fanciful as a popular 1950s vision that nearly all forms of personal transportation would fuse into a single "omnivehicle."

Several omnivehicle prototypes were actually built and demonstrated. These combined an automobile with a boat and an airplane or helicopter. Their enthusiastic inventors envisioned a typical commuter driving along an expressway until he encountered a traffic jam. With the flick of a few switches (in reality the process was much more complicated), he could convert his car into a flying machine and rise above the madding crowd. Or, if he decided he'd rather go fishing that day, he could simply drive his all-purpose vehicle into the nearest river or lake and use it as a boat. Even though several James Bond movies used the concept, the auto/plane/boat vehicle never took off, so to speak. It was not only an ugly and clunky looking vehicle, it was a mediocre car, a mediocre airplane, and a mediocre boat. Likewise, a universal teleputer that attempts to blend all forms of communication media might not be able to perform more than a few of its tasks particularly well. A great deal of technological merging will certainly occur, but, instead of a single teleputer, there are likely to be many varieties of teleputers that are designed to meet specific needs.

## Hidden intelligence

Even though the popular forms of communication media are unlikely to merge into one all-purpose medium, they will undoubtedly borrow technologies from each other as they continue to evolve within their particular media domains. Like instant cameras and automobiles, future TV sets are certain to come loaded with microprocessors, but their new-found intelligence will be mostly hidden behind the familiar flickering screen. Just to process the proposed digital high-definition broadcast signals will require at least 32 megabytes of memory, which is more than most personal computers require today.[2]

In addition to processing broadcast signals, the microprocessors on board will be expected to store and manage scheduling information and personal preferences as well as to simplify remote controls. On-screen instructions should make it possible for people to operate their new digital TV sets without the need for a manual or a remote control with dozens of meaningless buttons. Microprocessors are also likely to provide the essential intelligence for personal video agents that will assist viewers in their search for programs of interest from among the hundreds of channels that will be broadcast globally.

## Death of the medium?

Although broadcast television viewers are certain to be confronted with a range of new options as a result of emerging digital technologies and increasing channel capacity, a growing number of seers are proclaiming that TV's overall power is actually waning and that the medium will be insignificant in the next decade. Futurist George Gilder has gone so far as to boldly declare the death of TV as we have known it. "Whether offering 500 channels or thousands," Gilder believes, "TV will be irrelevant in a world without channels, where you can always order exactly what you want when you want it, and where every terminal commands the communications power of a broadcast station today."[3] In his view, such concepts as "high definition" and "interactivity" are merely cosmetics for the corpse

---

[2]Steven Lubar, *InfoCulture: The Smithsonian Book of Information Age Inventions*. Boston: Houghton Mifflin, 1993, p. 280.

[3]George Gilder, *Life after Television: The Coming Transformation of Media and American Life* (rev. ed.). New York: Norton, 1994, p. 21.

of an industry approaching the end of the road.[4] He contends that interactive information and entertainment media belong to the emerging realm of broadband communication networks and personal computers rather than the outmoded domain of broadcast channels and television sets.

Whether or not television is, indeed, nearing the end of its road is hardly a resolved matter. Commercial radio was declared dead in the 1950s but managed to metamorphose into a profitable new medium serving niche markets. Newspapers and magazines have also been declared dying media at different times, yet both have proved to be more resilient and adaptable than their critics expected. Television appears just as likely to adapt to emerging technologies and changing conditions within the human communication system. No one denies that the next stage of its transformation will be difficult or that its relative importance might be diminished by new media technologies, but, to paraphrase Mark Twain, reports of television's impending death have been greatly exaggerated.

## Next-generation television technology

The needs for more advanced television technologies and standards have been debated as far back as 1939 when RCA demonstrated "live" broadcast TV at the New York World's Fair. Throughout most of the 1940s, CBS tried to convince members of the Federal Communications Commission (FCC) that they should adopt a high-definition monochrome and color standard rather than the more primitive standard supported by RCA. But CBS failed to overcome the law of suppression of radical potential, and RCA prevailed.

By the time World War II ended, tens of millions of dollars had already been invested by U.S. companies in television technologies based on the RCA supported standard. Politicians and economists were counting on television to be a powerful stimulant for the United States' postwar consumer economy, so few government officials were willing to risk any changes in the standard that might delay the medium's introduction or fragment the market.

---

[4]Ibid., p. 11.

Once locked in by the FCC, the **NTSC (National Television Systems Committee)** standard freed the television industry to concentrate its efforts on fulfilling the growing demand for TV sets and programs. The phenomenal success of television far overshadowed its technological flaws. So long as consumers continued to buy TV sets as quickly as they came off the manufacturers' assembly lines and devoted increasing amounts of their time watching the advertising-sponsored programs broadcast by the networks, little thought was given to innovations that might require revising the standard.

However, by the early 1980s, the market for TV sets in technologically developed nations was considered saturated. The introduction of color more than two decades earlier had been the last major innovation, and color sets were already in about 90 percent of U.S. households. For manufacturers, the time seemed right to pursue entirely new TV standards. The supervening social necessity was, of course, to spur a great demand for new sets and equipment that would carry the TV manufacturing industry well into the next century.

## High-definition television

One of the many arguments put forward for developing new standards was the need to correct screen dimensions to match modern films. When television was under development in the 1930s, it was designed to conform with the film format of that period. Hence, the picture tube was landscape oriented with a width-to-height **aspect ratio** of 4 to 3. Unfortunately, by the time television became a commercial medium in the latter half of the 1940s, the motion picture industry was preparing to adapt a much wider format.

Modifying the physical dimensions of the TV picture tube was deemed to be too costly and disruptive for the fledgling postwar electronics industry, so broadcasters were forced to adopt another solution when they began showing Hollywood movies in the late 1950s. They literally squeezed the CinemaScopic films into the narrower TV window through the use of lenses that distorted and truncated the images.

Another argument involved the need to redefine bandwidth capacity. The NTSC standards were based on a belief that bandwidth would always be scarce. However by the 1980s, with compression technology and modern broadcast equipment, the bandwidth allocated for TV proved to have a far greater capacity than anyone could have predicted when the original standards were established. And the low-resolution, flickering images viewers had come to expect from television, and on which Marshall McLuhan had based most of his theories about the medium, in fact, were merely a vestige of primitive electronic technology.

**Forced obsolescence.** Upgrading the standards would dramatically improve the home viewer's TV picture as well as increase the number of channels available. But changing the established standard was not expected to be a trivial task. It would require a television industry agreement, followed by the coordinated replacement of all cameras as well as studio recording, transmitting, and receiving equipment. And, unlike the earlier transition from black and white to color that allowed both technologies to coexist, this change was expected to render all existing TV sets obsolete and force viewers to buy new sets.

Committees were formed in the mid-1980s to tackle various issues relating to the development of a new standard, which came to be known as high-definition television (HDTV). Television manufacturers in Japan, Europe, and the United States recognized that the stakes were high. The market for new broadcasting equipment and TV sets was then estimated to be worth more than $100 billion by the year 2000.[5] Consequently, national pride and competitiveness quickly became issues, as they had when the original standards were drafted.

**MUSE and MAC.** The Japanese, who by this time already controlled the largest share of the television manufacturing business worldwide, were the first to propose a new HDTV standard, which they called **MUSE.** It doubled the number of scan lines per picture and adopted the width-to-height ratio of 16 to 9 used by contemporary films. But to carry the additional picture data, it also required doubling the bandwidth requirements. This meant that MUSE programs could not be transmitted in the bandwidth allocated for existing TV channels.

A consortium of European firms and laboratories invested more than $1 billion in the latter half of the 1980s to develop its own HDTV standard, which was called **MAC.**[6] An intermediate standard that would be compatible with existing European TV sets, called

---

[5]Lubar, *InfoCulture*, p. 278.
[6]Ibid.

PAL, was also developed and implemented. Both European standards and the Japanese MUSE were based on the original analog TV broadcast technology used since the 1930s. While this made sense at the time, it would prove to be a costly mistake.

**Digital versus analog.** Companies in the United States were late entering the game, but in this case it proved to be a significant advantage. By the beginning of the 1990s, it was becoming increasingly evident that more advanced *digital* technologies could be used to provide high-resolution images without doubling the bandwidth requirements. With a digital HDTV standard, U.S. manufacturers recognized they could leapfrog the Japanese and European companies who had already begun to introduce their analog systems. By 1994, the Japanese and Europeans conceded to the superiority of digital technology and were abandoning their analog systems. But the game is far from over.

There is a growing awareness that HDTV is no longer about just providing higher resolution images in a wider format. The real benefits of digital systems are now seen in their ability to economically deliver new services to homes and to provide potentially lucrative new sources of revenue for the television industry. Some industry analysts have begun suggesting that, aside from a wider screen, digital TV sets in the next decade may not offer a picture much better than that offered by existing analog sets. Instead of significantly higher resolution, what they may offer is a wide range of interactive information and entertainment.

**Is the cost too high?** A troubling question that remains unanswered is will these proposed new services justify the added expense? There are growing concerns from consumer groups that the cost of converting may prove to be too high. The National Association of Broadcasters (NAB), an industry lobby based in Washington, D.C., has estimated that replacing today's 220 million outmoded analog TVs with digital sets capable of receiving the new HDTV signals and interactive services would cost viewers at least $187 billion.[7] At a cost of about $1,500 more than the average analog set today,

---

[7]These data were drawn from a Knight-Ridder News Service story by Frank Greven that appeared in the Boulder, CO, *Daily Camera* (January 16, 1996), p. D1.

HDTV sets are likely to be more expensive than home computers with video-capability in the year 2000. As we will discover later in this chapter, the rise of personal computers is calling many assumptions about the future of television into question.

## 500-channel TV

When John Malone, the chairman of the United States' largest cable-TV operator, TeleCommunications, Inc. (TCI), casually mentioned in a 1992 speech that video compression technologies might give cable operators the ability to deliver 500 or more channels, the news media seized on his pronouncement and made it the popular catch phrase for future television. Malone later explained that he had chosen the number somewhat arbitrarily and had not meant for it to be taken literally, but that didn't matter. The image of "500-channel TV" quickly became fixed in people's minds.[8]

**Cable television.** The notion that viewers might one day have access to 500 or more TV channels may have shocked some, but the groundwork for ever expanding channel options had been laid by cable-TV operators beginning in the 1950s. Cable TV (CATV) emerged as a solution to a technical problem. Most early television stations were located in or around large cities. Viewers in small towns and rural areas far from the broadcasting towers were unable to get good reception without installing large, expensive antennas. The idea of erecting a single community antenna and distributing the captured signals by coaxial cable directly into homes made economic sense. By the mid-1960s there were more than 1,500 CATV systems in the United States, each serving an average of about 1,000 homes.[9]

**Satellite television.** Protests from broadcasters, who regarded CATV systems as signal thieves, caused the FCC to put a freeze on new cable operations between 1966 and 1972, but this proved to be only a minor setback. Soon after the freeze was lifted, cable operators began rapidly expanding into urban areas and taking advantage

---

[8]Kevin Maney provides a more detailed account of John Malone's "500-Channel TV" speech and his motivations in *Megamedia Shakeout: The Inside Story of the Leaders and the Losers in the Exploding Communications Industry.* New York: Wiley, 1995, pp. 15–17.

[9]Lubar, *InfoCulture*, p. 257.

of a new source for television programming—communication satellites. Satellites provided not only better reception but a greater number of channels to choose from. They also contributed to the development of premium movie, sports, and news channels that would not be available to "over the air" viewers, such as Home Box Office (HBO), the all sports network (ESPN), and the Cable News Network (CNN).

As satellite communication technologies improved and receiving dishes became smaller and less expensive, cable-TV operators found themselves dealing with a formidable competitor of their own for home delivery—direct broadcast satellite (DBS) services. Initially the DBS dishes were bulky and required some technical skill to install. But since the introduction of digital TV signals[10] and more powerful satellite transmitters in the early 1990s, dishes have been reduced to the size of small pizza pans and are expected to become even smaller in the next decade.

*Narrowcasting.* Cable and satellite TV services can now offer their customers anywhere from 35 to more than 200 discrete channels. In addition to the more well known network and pay channels, there are 24-hour channels devoted to specific areas of interest, such as golf, science fiction, and history. As TV channels have proliferated and become more focused on niche audiences, this form of the medium has come to be known as narrowcasting.

How far the trend toward narrowcasting may go is still a matter of speculation. We should not, however, expect to see a greater variety of entertainment in the short term. Despite the development of lower cost video equipment, quality movies and TV shows will continue to be expensive to produce. Digital surrogates may be able to replace some human actors in some situations, but not entirely. The best writers, directors, and talent will undoubtedly continue to demand and get high fees.

Furthermore, most cable-TV operators have tended to see "500-channel TV" more as a metaphor for time shifting than discrete channel expansion. The same movies, for example, might be broadcast on multiple channels at staggered times, perhaps 10 minutes apart. In that way, a customer who missed the 7:00 P.M. showing might be able to catch the 7:10 or 7:20 broadcasts. This approach

---

[10]Most DBS services capture digital signals and then convert them to analog signals for standard TV sets.

would, of course, quickly consume most of the additional channel capacity without adding any new viewing choices.

***Personal channels.*** Another proposal that has been gaining popularity is to allow customers to create their own personal channels. As the number of viewing options grows, "channel surfing" with remote controls and daily scanning of printed TV guides will become increasingly frustrating and impractical. By using an on-screen guide, as I've described in the scenario, viewers could select the programs they regularly watch and the movies they may want to see, and then have their VCR, or its digital successor, automatically record the programs as they are broadcast and sequence them to match their schedule. Several companies have already begun to offer such services. The next step, already being pursued by a number of technology companies, is to provide viewers with their own "intelligent video agents" that can "learn" their interests and do all the hunting, gathering, and sequencing remotely. In essence, 500 channels' worth of content could be reduced to a single personalized channel from the perspective of each customer.

Even with the ability to create personal channels, viewers will probably continue to have access to the standard lineups provided by the television networks and local stations for at least another decade or two. Just as TV sets are unlikely to be replaced quickly, viewing habits are also not likely to change overnight.

***Offline services.*** Some of the expanded TV channel space might well be used for scheduled video conferences and distance learning programs where two-way, high-speed communications are required. Channel space may also be used for aggregated express, point-to-point deliveries of mixed-media digital products, such as books, newspapers, and music videos for offline consumption. (This potential application is described in greater detail in chapter 9.)

Broadcast textual material is likely to be used to complement TV shows and advertising. For example, viewers would be able to display on demand specific information about the programs or commercials they are watching (or want to watch), such as the titles, names of actors, sports statistics, and product data, as well as current weather, road conditions, sports scores, and other frequently updated information of general interest. Reading large amounts of text on TV sets, however, may not appeal to very many people even with larger, high-resolution displays.

### Broadcasting on the Web

Until the mid-1990s, radio and television businesses had had even less success with interactive services than newspaper and magazine publishers. The text-based consumer online services didn't offer much opportunity for broadcasters to stand out, and the market trials for interactive TV (ITV) services were consistently proving to be expensive disappointments.

The explosive growth of the World Wide Web, however, finally presented broadcasters and producers of pay-TV channels with a propitious opportunity to develop low-cost interactive services that would play to their strengths as well as leverage their extensive video and audio libraries. Two critical factors converged to make this possible. These were (1) the Web's inherent ability to easily link and display all types of digital content—text, graphics, video, and audio; and (2) the increasing ability of home computer users to economically access multimedia content via relatively low-cost high-speed telecommunication networks.

Since the end of 1995, nearly every network, pay channel, and local station of significance has established a presence on the Web. Most provide a mix of promotional materials, schedules, program descriptions, news, behind-the-scenes information, answers to commonly asked questions, and access to fan clubs as well as a limited selection of video and audio clips. Radio broadcasters have also begun providing program information and digital audio clips on the Web. Like publishers, broadcasters have the great advantage of being able to easily and frequently promote their Web sites and to instantly develop cyber communities.

At this stage, the Web sites managed by broadcasters are simply supplementing their radio and television programs. But as cable-TV operators begin offering relatively low-cost broadband access to the Web through such services as the @Home network and Time Warner's Road Runner, a popular and practical version of the interactive TV vision might finally emerge. Hybrid technologies that blend broadcast video programs with Web-based interactive information and transactional capabilities could make distance learning, as described in the scenario, a reality well before the year 2010.

Cable-TV operators are also planning to use their two-way broadband capacity to provide video telephone calls and conferencing, but these services are not expected to be cheap—at least not in the beginning. For a decade or so, consumers are likely to use video calling only on special occasions, much the way long-distance calls were used until the 1970s.[11]

## Intimate home theaters

The most obvious changes in TV sets between now and the year 2010 will be in the shape, size, and clarity of their screens. Television manufacturers are already producing sets with screens that conform to the wide-screen 16-by-9 aspect ratio. These sets, which are still based on the analog NTSC standard, give viewers the advantage of watching movies without the "letterbox" effect that TV broadcasters have begun adopting in anticipation of digital HDTV. Instead of squeezing and truncating wide-screen movies to fit into the original 4-by-3 format, they are now appearing at their full width on TV screens. Viewers with standard TV sets see the movies with a thick black bar above and below the image. With the newer wide-screen TV sets, the black bars disappear.

Manufacturers have also found a growing demand in recent years for TV sets with substantially larger screens. The popularity of these rather bulky and expensive sets seems to suggest that a trend toward intimate home theaters, or entertainment centers, is already under way. As display technologies shift from traditional cathode-ray tubes, which require deep cases, to relatively lightweight, thin-screen CRTs and flat panels, the dimensions of TV screens are bound to expand even further. Digital HDTV screens of the size mentioned in the scenario should not be uncommon in the next decade. Intimate home theaters with these large, high-resolution, thin screens mounted on walls will be capable of providing a viewing experience comparable to that of a small commercial movie theater.

Despite the many popularized predictions that digital technologies will ultimately eliminate the distinctions between producers and audiences, that seems unlikely. Although digital television will, indeed, be more interactive, it is certain to remain an essentially passive entertainment medium. The dominant traits of the broadcast domain are too deeply imbedded in our culture to suddenly disappear. Much of the appeal of noninteractive, linear stories and spectator events has always been in their elements of surprise and the pleasure of being entertained. Moreover, few people either have the

[11]Maney, *Megamedia*, pp. 42–43.

talent or the inclination to create their own stories or to participate in the majority of events that interest them.

### Commercial video and holographic theaters

Owners of movie theaters are also considering automated video projection systems and large flat-screen displays for future theaters. With this approach, movies could be economically broadcast to theaters all across the country from a central location, which would eliminate the need for locally operated projection booths. Ironically, this is the future vision that many people saw for television back in the 1930s. During the Depression years, the notion that people would pay to watch TV programs in public theaters, just as they did for motion pictures, seemed quite logical.

By the end of the next decade, however, commercial theater owners may have another, much more compelling option—holographic movies and stage performances. Laser-based holographic systems might be far enough advanced by that time to create a highly realistic, three-dimensional illusion of "live" performers on stage. Holographic theaters would not require members of the audience to wear special glasses or sensors to fully appreciate large-scale, virtual reality presentations. Such systems might make it possible for concerts and stage productions to be broadcast to theaters all around the world, just like movies, without losing the sense of intimacy and excitement that comes from attending live performances.

A consequence of the shift to commercial video-holographic theaters and intimate home theaters is that, after more than a half century of coexisting, film will finally be subsumed by digital video. Photographic films still yield higher quality images than digital systems, but the distinctions for most consumers will be insignificant within 10 to 15 years, or perhaps even sooner. The development of more advanced digital imaging systems and larger high-definition displays will almost certainly contribute to a rapid decline in the popularity of traditional film for both motion pictures and still photography. Like most older media that have been subsumed, chemical processed film will be relegated to hobbyists and specialized uses.

## Future control and social issues

The conversion of electronic broadcast media to digital technologies is not just about providing higher resolution images or stimulating the consumer electronics market. It is mostly about control. Digital systems give producers greater control over the content elements, presentation, and distribution. For viewers, they provide greater personal control over the scheduling, sequencing, and selection of content. On the surface, these changes can be seen as beneficial, but they are not neutral. While they can be used to enhance and generally improve the quality of television viewing, they can also be used to more easily manipulate and distort the substance of images. The thin membrane that separates reality from fantasy might dissolve entirely if we are not careful in the near future.

## *Manipulation of visual and audio content*

In the nineteenth century and for much of the twentieth, photographic images were regarded as absolutely truthful representations of reality. They could be used as supportive evidence in courts of law and as reliable historical records, but that is no longer the case. While it has always been possible to retouch or stage photos, hints of altering and staging were usually detectable. However, with digital technologies, the manipulations of both still and moving images can be accomplished with such precision that they are virtually impossible to detect.

Despite the ethical concerns of many professional photographers, images are routinely altered today in nearly all forms of visual communication media using digital imaging systems. Usually these changes involve the enhancing of colors or details, but they can also involve substantive changes, such as adding or deleting people from a picture, putting the head of one person onto the body of another, and rearranging the physical elements of a scene.

The motion picture industry has led the way in demonstrating the power of digital imaging systems to create fantastic special effects in recent years. They include the **morphing** of one object or person into another as in the *Terminator* movies, and the merging of present-day actors into archived films of famous people from the past as in *Forest Gump*. Already these capabilities have moved from the special effects studios to affordable software that can be run on most top-of-the-line personal computers. By the next decade, producers should be able to easily digitize living actors, as well as actors from the past, and have them do anything they wish in a movie or television program.

And the manipulation of content is not limited to images. Digital audio systems are also used to alter voices, music, and other sounds.

With digital sound sampling and synthesizers, recording studios can create background music for singers without live musicians and even reproduce the musical styles and voices of artists from the past.

All of these capabilities to alter sound and images have far outpaced the abilities of lawmakers and government regulators to keep up and provide adequate guidance. The chosen solutions to the ethical dilemmas arising from the next stage of the third great mediamorphosis are certain to have as much influence on the development and spread of new media as they will have on the future direction of society and culture.

## Parental control and censorship

Depending on one's point of view, the most disturbing or desirable feature of the Telecommunications Act of 1996 is the so-called **v-chip,** which this law requires manufacturers to build into all new TV sets. The intended purpose of the v-chip is to give parents some measure of control over programs that can be viewed by their children. To make this system work, all TV programs will be required to include specific encoded information about the nature of their content. Through some simple but "child-proof" routine, parents should then be able to instruct the v-chip to block out any programs that contain potentially objectionable material (for example, excessive violence, adult language, nudity, and sexual situations).

How well this system will work remains to be seen, but the precedent set by the v-chip has already raised a number of concerns. For instance: Could a similar approach be used by governments to censor content within their borders that they judged to be objectionable? Could it be extended to block any program or news item that mentioned subjects considered objectionable by certain religious and political groups, such as abortion, homosexuality, and the theory of evolution?

## Zapping commercials

The control issue extends beyond the v-chip. Advanced digital systems are bound to give viewers the power to easily zap commercials. This, too, raises concerns. Unless television evolves into an entirely pay-per-view or subscription-based system, which seems unlikely, advertising will remain essential. If viewers can program their future TV sets to eliminate commercials, the broadcast networks and advertisers can be expected to adapt in some way.

Among their options would be to make their commercials less intrusive and more entertaining. Or they might weave their messages subtly (or not so subtly) into "free" programs, as they were in the early years of television. Infomercials already seem to be trending in that direction. Advertisers could also use feedback channels with future cable systems to include simple, interactive response forms that could be used to immediately order products, register for contests, or request additional information as an added incentive for viewers to not zap their commercials.

The continuing integration of commercial messages with electronic broadcast content may seem innocent enough, but it clearly has the potential for further eroding our ability to critically evaluate the accuracy and credibility of the information we receive as well as for shaping cultural values and priorities. Some have argued that commercial television has already altered our perceptions and values to the point where further integration of advertising messages with editorial content will make no difference. They might be right, but this is still an important issue that should be addressed before there is no opportunity to turn back.

## Isolating tendencies

A number of pundits have expressed concerns that intimate home theaters combined with consumer online services may significantly diminish individual desires to socialize and share experiences in the company of strangers as well as with friends and relatives. While some people may be inclined to "cocoon" somewhat more than they do today, there seems little doubt that they will still occasionally enjoy gathering in large groups for live concerts, plays, ballets, and comedy shows, or collectively watching many of the same broadcast television productions long after their homes have been wired for high-definition, interactive television.

The new media technologies that Bill Gates, Microsoft's cofounder and chairman, has built into his home and expects to see proliferating early in the next century may, indeed, tempt people to stay at home more, but he doesn't think most people will forego opportunities to enjoy the pleasures of the real world. "As behaviorists keep reminding us," he says, "we're social animals. We will have the option of staying home more because the [information] highway will create so many new options for home-based entertainment, for communications—both personal and professional—and for employment. Although the mix of activities will change, I think people will decide to spend almost as much time out of their homes."[12]

## Mediamorphosis within the broadcast domain in perspective

Despite the many diverse and often pessimistic predictions, television seems to be in little real danger of fading away early in the next century. The medium is much too tightly woven into the fabric of our culture and economy to be suddenly eliminated or greatly diminished. Broadcast TV channels might become the "freight trains" of the digital communication age, efficiently carrying vast cargoes of multimedia content into homes at a relatively low cost. But even with that role, the networks and premium satellite and cable-TV channels are likely to continue entertaining large audiences with traditional narrative stories and spectator events. Television viewing may involve a greater range of options but will no doubt remain a shared, relatively passive experience.

As for high-definition and interactive TV, the ultimate winners will, of course, finally be decided in the consumer marketplace. It is quite possible that, when all is said and done, most people may be perfectly satisfied with television technology as it exists. All they may really want is a wider selection of entertainment and more control over viewing times. That's not to say TV sets will remain exactly as they are or won't incorporate some of the same technologies as personal computers. We may well have TV sets with brains and personal computers with virtual versions of Sylvester Stallone in the near future, but there is no reason to believe they will fuse into one universal device or a single megamedium. Both will continue to serve different purposes and involve us in different ways.

There is, however, one fusion that does seem all but certain—the melding of video and film. Next-generation digital imaging technologies and large-format, high-resolution, flat-screen displays can be expected to dissolve the last remaining technological distinctions between these two forms of broadcast media in the coming decade.

---

[12]Bill Gates, *The Road Ahead*. New York: Viking, 1995, pp. 205–206.

The trend toward home TV sets with larger screens is likely to accelerate as thin-screen CRTs and flat panels become more practical and affordable. Intimate home theaters that provide a viewing experience similar to commercial theaters should become commonplace within 10 years. Although the spread of intimate home theaters may cause a significant decline in movie theaters for some period of time, the development of holographic or other virtual reality projection systems should make it possible for them to adapt and evolve by the year 2010.

As we will see in the next chapter, publishers may take advantage of TV's broadband capacity to deliver their digital editions of newspapers, magazines, catalogs, and books directly to homes and offices. They may also incorporate some of the more compelling characteristics of radio and television.

# mediamorphosis within the document domain

Newspaper, magazines, and books are so strongly associated with paper in our culture that they are commonly regarded as old-fashioned media in the age of digital communication. The assumed dependence of these document forms on mechanical technologies and pulp paper is often seen as preventing publishers of print media from adapting and remaining profitable in the face of growing competition from producers of digital media.

Challenging this view has been particularly difficult for newspaper publishers. It requires a solution to the Zenlike question: If a newspaper is no longer printed on paper, is it still a newspaper? This riddle is more difficult for English-speaking people to solve because the term tightly binds *news* to *paper*, but that is just an artifact of the language. For those who speak most other common languages, there is no problem, linguistically at least, separating the newspaper from paper because the word *paper* is not included in the name. The term for newspaper in most languages derives not from the display medium, as it does in English, but from the nature of the content, which is primarily timely news and information. For example, "newspaper" in German is *Die Zeitung,* which has as its root "time" *(Zeit),* in French *le journal* has as its root "day" *(jour),* and in Spanish the root of *el periódico* is "a period of time" *(periodo).*

By defining newspapers as periodic disseminators of timely, general interest information, the paper question is neatly avoided. It also allows us to see that printing presses and paper are just a means to an end. Albeit, for more than 500 years, they have been the most efficient and least expensive means available to publishers for manufacturing and distributing copies of their branded documents to large numbers of customers. But even though newspaper publishers are undeniably in the business of providing information at low cost, the function and importance of newspapers within societies extend well beyond the utilitarian role of information provider or database.

In this chapter, we explore an offline vision of digital publishing that builds upon and retains the familiar attributes of traditional print media, such as portability, portrait orientation, and branded packaging, while incorporating some of the more compelling traits of the interpersonal and broadcast forms.

I have focused this chapter on newspapers because in my view they represent the most complex as well as the most immediately challenged form within the document domain. It should be understood, however, that the concepts and technologies discussed are just as applicable to magazines, books, and nearly all other document forms.

A chronology of major technological developments that have influenced the transformation of newspapers in the past two centuries and that are likely to affect their ultimate transition to digital publishing systems early in the twenty-first century is found in Exhibit 9.1.

### Scenario for 2010.   *The mobile digital document reader*

As Deborah awakens, her body tells her the time should be about 7 A.M., but the digital clock next to her bed argues that it's precisely 4:17 A.M., Tuesday, September 21, 2010. Memory returns slowly. Finally, she recalls that this is San Diego, California, and that she arrived late last night from New York to speak at a conference this morning. There's no chance of falling back to sleep now, so she goes to the microkitchen to start the coffeemaker. Then she picks up her **tablet** and prepares to gather her morning newspapers.

This hotel has equipped its rooms with the latest high-tech amenities. In addition to the microkitchen, Deborah's room has a wall-mounted flat-screen display, a color fax machine that also functions as a printer and copier, and a teledock. With the teledock, Deborah can choose the television programs she wants to watch and then set the time and sequence she prefers. She can also use the teledock to purchase current electronic editions of newspapers, magazines, and books.

About a year ago, she finally decided to buy a tablet to use in her work. The tablet is about the size and shape of a standard printed magazine and weighs about a pound. She can attach a keyboard, but mostly

**Exhibit 9.1** Time line of print media developments, 1800–2010.

| Year | |
|---|---|
| **1800** – | – First experiments with electric current. |
| | – Method for producing continuous-roll paper developed |
| | – |
| | – Steam-powered printing presses |
| | – |
| **1825** – | – |
| | – |
| | – Emergence of "Penny Press" (low-cost, large-circulation newspapers) |
| | – Electric telegraph invented; photography invented |
| | – Telegraphic news (concept of breaking news is born); first rotary press |
| **1850** – | – First newspaper wire service (Associated Press); electromechanical press |
| | – Inverted-pyramid writing style adopted by newspapers |
| | – First telegraphic message between Europe and the United States |
| | – Permanent transatlantic telegraph cable; foreign news bureaus established |
| | – Manual typewriters; newsprint developed |
| **1875** – | – Telephone invented; four-cylinder perfecting press |
| | – Practical photoengraving process developed |
| | – Mechanical typesetting machines (Linotype) |
| | – Monotype system |
| | – Halftone method for reproducing photos; wireless telegraph |
| **1900** – | – Color printing in newspapers |
| | – Offset printing press |
| | – Transcontinental telephone service in U.S. |
| | – Portable radiotelephones |
| | – Broadcast radio "newspapers" |
| **1925** – | – Commercial facsimile telephoto service |
| | – Wirephoto network |
| | – Personal facsimile news services |
| | – Live electronic television introduced at the 1939 World's Fair |
| | – Xerographic process invented |
| **1950** – | – Commercial mainframe computers; radio-facsimile newspapers |
| | – Electric typewriters; transatlantic telephone cable |
| | – Xerographic copying machines; communication satellites |
| | – Phototypesetting; hypertext concept |
| | – Computer editing and typesetting systems; flat-panel displays |
| **1975** – | – Digital page-layout systems; laser printers invented |
| | – Commercial personal computers; videotex services; digital print media |
| | – Desktop publishing; camera-ready computer graphics |
| | – Digital photography and image processing; digital facsimile newspapers |
| | – Emergence of consumer online and Internet publishing |
| **2000** – | – Portable tablet-sized displays; emergence of tablet publishing |
| | – Electronic newsstands and bookstores |
| | – Global distribution networks for digital print media |
| | – |
| | – |

she interacts by touching or writing on the screen. With an electronic pen, she can highlight items, append notes, and work the crossword puzzle, as well as quickly locate items. If she chooses, she can also interact with the tablet by using a selection of voice commands.

Tablets have been on the market for about a decade, but she didn't see their value until there was an extensive selection of material available for reading on tablets. Now she can read the latest editions of her favorite publications almost anywhere and anytime that's convenient for her. Electronic newsstands and teledocks have already been installed in many airports, train stations, hotels, and book stores. Television controllers in homes and offices have also been adapted to provide easy access to digital print media.

Customers continue to have a choice of subscribing or purchasing single copies. Prices are about the same as they are for printed versions, although electronic editions contain more information and provide extra services. With a subscription to an electronic edition, delivery is no longer tied to a single home or office address. This gives subscribers the freedom to access their publications at the office or from any teledock or electronic newsstand. The system works in much the same way as the banks' automatic teller machines (ATMs).

To access the latest edition of the *New York Times,* Deborah inserts her *NYT* card into her room's teledock. These **memory cards** are supplied by newspapers and magazines when customers subscribe to their electronic editions. They are similar in size and shape to credit cards but are thicker and can be used anywhere for as long as the subscription remains active. Each card contains personal data, such as the subscriber's name and address, subscription codes, and preferences, as well as enough storage to hold a complete edition and a personal file of items that the subscriber has "clipped and saved."

On the teledock's touch screen, Deborah enters her personal identification number just as she would at an ATM. In less than a minute, the current edition of the *New York Times* is loaded onto her card. She removes the card and repeats the procedure for the *Financial Times.* To buy a single copy of the local newspaper, which in San Diego is the *Union-Tribune,* she inserts a card that allows her to purchase any electronic publication. This card contains her personal data and digital cash to pay for purchases. After entering her password, the teledock displays a menu of available newspapers. As soon as she touches the *Union-Tribune* option and confirms her selection, the edition is loaded and the fee is automatically debited.

The coffee is ready, so she pours a cup and takes it to the bedside table along with her tablet and newspaper cards. She could use the wall-mounted, flat-screen television in her room to display the newspapers, but she prefers using the tablet to read in the comfort of her bed.

As soon as she inserts the *NYT* card into her tablet, she is told that 14 stories in this edition contain topics included in her personal profile. She is particularly interested in astronomy and space exploration and in news from several South American countries. She has the option of going directly to those stories or just browsing. Since she has plenty of time this morning, she chooses to browse first. She starts with the front page.

The page displayed on her tablet bears a strong resemblance to the front page of the printed edition of the *New York Times*. The only obvious difference is the page size. To preserve the information density of a full-sized printed paper, items that appear on the browsing pages of tablet editions are actually abstracts, or brief summaries. The combination of headlines, abstracts, and graphics organized on newspaperlike pages makes scanning and assessing content quick and easy.

For most stories, the abstracts provide enough information to satisfy Deborah's interests. But when she wants more, all she needs to do is touch the abstract. In an instant, the front page is replaced by the actual story, which can be as long as it needs to be. The story pages appear more like the pages of a book to facilitate reading. These pages can also include images and graphics as well as background and explanatory information.

With printed newspapers, readers often complain that the text is too small. With a tablet edition that is not a problem. If the standard text is difficult for Deborah to read, she can enlarge it to whatever size feels comfortable. If she is too tired to read or she needs to concentrate on some other activity, such as driving a car or preparing a meal, she can also have the tablet "speak" stories to her. She often uses this feature to create her own custom "radio" news reports that she listens to when she's driving to and from her office. With simple voice commands, she can skip to the next story, repeat a segment, or locate another story.

Each electronic edition contains sets of browsing pages organized in sections much as they are in the printed edition. After scanning the front page, Deborah can turn to the next page by touching the page-turning icon or go to another section by touching the appropriate section icon.

As she browses the *Times'* business section, she finds a story about the latest federal surtax. A graphic offers her the opportunity to see how she will be affected. By using the pen to enter her estimated salary and a few other details, the graphic immediately computes and displays the amount of her surtax and shows her how she compares with other taxpayers. She'd like to print the story and graphic later, so she touches the Clip option on the screen. This puts the page in her memory card's personal file. She can also transfer items she has "clipped" from the newspaper to her office computer or send annotated copies to other people by using the tablet's electronic mail feature.

Another story in the business section refers to a news event that occurred last week. She apparently missed the story when it was originally published, so she touches the Library icon. This retrieves the headlines and abstracts for all stories published on this subject by the *Times* in the past month. She discovers that the earlier story was published last Wednesday. The abstract is useful, but she would like to see the full story. By touching the abstract, she is told it will cost 50 cents to retrieve this item from the newspaper's electronic library. That's fine, so she touches the OK button. The tablet's wireless communicator autodials the newspaper and sends the necessary instructions to retrieve her selection from the library's central computer. Within a few seconds the complete story is added to her memory card's personal file.

The lead story in the science section is about the multinational exploration of Mars. By touching an image of the planet, Deborah can watch a 20-second video segment showing views sent only a few hours ago by the robot vehicle as it roved the surface of the planet. Video news clips are now becoming a common feature of tablet newspapers. When touched, some photographs become full-motion video clips with sound, so she can watch and listen to news events as well as read about them. If she missed something, she can replay the clip or freeze an image.

As she "turns" pages, she also encounters a variety of advertisements. Ads in tablet newspapers are juxtaposed with editorial content on most pages just as they are in printed editions. If she is not interested in an ad, she simply "turns" the page.

Advertisers are fully exploiting the opportunities afforded by these digital editions. If she requests it, some ads will speak to her; others display their merchandise with short video clips and animations. More importantly, advertisers are able to deliver a variety of targeted messages that can be matched to each personal profile. With the tablet's wireless communicator, customers can also conveniently order advertised products, request additional information, or take advantage of coupons.

For example, an airline offering discount fares and package deals to South America entices her to explore the possibilities alluded to in its ad.

She is planning to take some vacation time in Peru this winter, so she touches the ad to get more information. The haunting sound of an Andean flute plays in the background as she peruses the spectacular images of Machu Picchu and Nasca. She sees that this is the last day these low fares will be available, so she decides to act on the offer. With the communicator, she can make her reservations immediately from the tablet. Her agent's e-mail address and her credit card numbers and other essential data are maintained in her personal profile. All she has to do is write in the dates and times that she wants to travel and touch the reservation button on the screen. Her personal information is encrypted as well as password protected, so there is no risk of someone else placing orders with her tablet and memory cards.

Deborah will be staying in San Diego for two more nights, so she checks the *Union-Tribune's* Guide section to see what's going on. All articles about upcoming events as well as listings and reviews of restaurants, movies, concerts, books, and so on are always available to tablet newspaper subscribers in these supplemental guide sections. Guides are a blend of newspaper entertainment sections and local telephone yellow pages. She can easily select categories of interest and in some cases even see and hear a sampling of events, places, and productions. As with the airline advertisement, many of the ads in these sections offer reservation and ticket purchasing services by way of the tablet's communicator.

Her presentation is at 8:30, so she decides to take a break from the news to review her speech and check her e-mail. Tablets are used for many purposes, not just for reading newspapers and magazines. She has brought with her several electronic editions of books and scientific journals stored on memory cards. On one of her personal cards she has stored a copy of her speech and supporting graphics. Using the electronic pen, she can make changes in her speech right up to the last minute. At the rostrum, the tablet will serve as her personal prompter. As soon as her presentation is completed, she can easily provide participants and reporters with electronic or printed copies of the final version.

## Gutenberg's legacy

The development of digital publishing systems, such as I have described in this scenario, should *not* be interpreted as foretelling the death of print media. On the contrary, it suggests that print can be transformed into an even more versatile and popular medium for communication in the next century. This hypothesis requires us to accept, however, that print media are not dependent upon pigmented ink and pulp paper or printing presses for their continuing evolution.

After more than 500 years of associating publishing and print media with mechanical printing technologies, it is no wonder it is so difficult for so many people to now separate them in their minds. I have come to believe that much of the current anxiety about the future of newspapers, in particular, can be traced to an often repeated textbook definition that includes among its criteria the statement that a "true" newspaper is produced by a mechanical printing process.[1] Until the 1970s, there was little reason to dispute this definition since mechanical printing was the only practical process available to publishers, as well as the only one imaginable for the foreseeable future.

## Taking the first steps

The emergence of personal computers, the World Wide Web, and portable information appliances in the ensuing years has clearly demonstrated that other economical processes for manufacturing and distributing newspapers are becoming available to publishers. But only by consciously disconnecting print media from mechanical printing presses and pulp paper can we begin to see that the adoption of digital publishing technologies represents a transition, not a termination, for newspapers. Printing, whether manual, mechanical, or digital, is essentially a *production* process—a means to an end—for replicating the written word and images on portable display media.

This is not meant to imply that the transition from mechanical to digital is inconsequential. Just as Gutenberg's inventions ultimately shifted sovereignty over information from the keepers and preservationists to the authors and producers,[2] digital publishing technologies appear to be shifting control from the authors and producers to the distributors and consumers. There is no reason to believe that this shift will have any less influence upon contemporary social, political, and economic systems than the earlier shift had on medieval Europe.

---

[1]Edwin Emery, *The Press in America* (5th ed.). Englewood Cliffs, NJ: Prentice-Hall, 1972, p. 3.

[2]Anthony Smith, *Goodbye Gutenberg: The Newspaper Revolution of the 1980s*. New York: Oxford University Press, 1980, p. 20.

For newspapers, the first phase of this transition began in the 1960s with the introduction of computerized typesetting systems. Since then, publishers have been rapidly converting their labor-intensive industrial age technologies to digital systems. Today, journalists gather, write, and edit stories on word-processing computers linked to high-speed networks, photographers process their photos on digital imaging systems, artists create graphics and advertisements on microcomputers, and designers compose complete pages on sophisticated production systems. Practically everything contained in most newspapers has, in fact, already been converted to a digital form.

While this phase has resulted in significant cost savings for publishers and has affected the lives of those who have been working in the printing and publishing businesses, nearly all the changes have gone largely unnoticed by readers. Newspapers continue to arrive as they always have on the schedules set by the publishers. The printing may be crisper and more colorful, but the ink still rubs off on your fingers. The content may be better written and better packaged, but it remains a delayed slice of time. All that, however, is about to change. In the next phase, digital editions can be expected to overcome these problems and limitations while adding new value for readers.

### Incentives and disincentives

The incentives for publishers to complete the transition to digital systems are great. Today, more than half of a typical publisher's overall costs are associated with manufacturing and distributing, (costs related to press plates, presses, inserting and bundling machines, paper, ink, electricity, facilities, truck leases, gasoline, and labor). Newsprint alone averages about one-quarter of the cost of publishing a newspaper in the United States. No further savings of any real significance can be expected from the adoption of more advanced digital systems by the "front-end" departments—editorial, advertising, marketing, and business. Therefore the only place where publishers can seek substantial savings in coming decades is within the "back-end" departments—pressroom, mailroom, paper handling, and circulation.

There can be little doubt that as soon as digital systems begin to match the quality and cost of mechanical technologies for producing and distributing publications, most publishers will move quickly to make a full transition. But even though digital systems promise great savings in the long run, in the short term they confront established publishing companies with a number of major hurdles to surmount, not the least of which is the strong emotional and financial attachment to mechanical presses.

For more than three centuries, the printing press has been revered by journalists as the sacred symbol of their profession. However, for owners and publishers, the press is much more than a symbol. Since the beginning of the industrial age, the mechanical press has also been viewed as a powerful and nearly insurmountable barrier to entry for potential competitors. Rotary presses are enormously complex pieces of heavy machinery that require a great deal of capital to purchase. The *New York Times* and Rupert Murdock's Australian-based News Corporation each invested close to a billion dollars to build new color printing plants in the early 1990s. Even for small daily newspapers, the cost of new presses can run in the tens of millions of dollars. In most cases, publishers need between 20 to 30 years to recoup their investment.

A consequence of these huge capital investments is that presses can also serve as a barrier to exit for established publishers when technologies and market conditions change. As digital print media diffuse into the general consumer market, publishers who own their own printing facilities will need to protect their investments for as long as they can while fending off a new generation of digital competitors who can afford to sell content and space at a substantially reduced cost to both consumers and advertisers. Until the market for digital print media becomes large enough to risk abandoning their mechanical presses, publishers will be forced to support dual production and distribution operations. Their challenge will be to keep the demand for mechanically printed editions from falling too quickly and thereby turning their presses into expensive albatrosses.

Publishers are not the only ones who must carefully balance the declining value of their capital investments in industrial age technologies with the rising demand for digital print media. Printing press and newsprint manufacturers are already predicting a steadily declining market for their products after the turn of the century. Ironically, by scaling back on their manufacturing capacity or shifting resources into other businesses in anticipation of declining demand, they might well accelerate the final phase of the transition to digital publishing. This is not a remote prospect. If the predictions prove to be wrong and demand for mechanically printed newspapers does not decline, their imposed reduction in supply would doubtlessly result in significantly higher prices that would make digital publishing even more competitive. In other words, the anticipation of a sudden shift from mechanical to digital publishing could turn into a self-fulfilling prophecy.

# Next-generation digital print technologies

When IBM introduced its first personal computer back in 1981, visions of a "paperless" society abounded. Yet, in the years since then, per capita consumption of paper has continued to grow. Instead of replacing paper, the personal computer has, in fact, served as a tool for creating more paper documents. So, it is not surprising that a great many people in the publishing business have been lulled into a false sense of security and are generally skeptical about the future of paperless digital publishing technologies. While digital alternatives to the mechanical printing presses and delivery trucks are beginning to be taken more seriously, the most popular visions of the future among established publishers still tend to include presses and paper.

## *Printing presses in the home*

One of the more enduring visions involves the printing process migrating from large central facilities into homes and offices through the use of "personal presses," such as fax machines. But as futuristic as the idea of using facsimile transmission systems to deliver and print individual editions of publications may seem, neither the technology nor the vision is new. The first protofax was conceived as far back as 1843. By the end of the 1920s, newspapers were already employing facsimile machines to transmit and receive photographs.

Debates about the potential threat or promise of facsimile transmission as a personal news medium have raged on and off again since the 1930s, when radio-delivered fax first became commercial. In a book published in 1938, titled *Television: A Struggle for Power*, the authors articulated a vision of facsimile publishing that has changed surprisingly little in more than half a century.

> Facsimile machines are today literally capable of producing the newspaper in the home, eliminating two of the greatest expenses now

attached to the publications industry, printing and delivery. The effect such a radical alteration in methods must have upon investments in presses, trucks, and buildings is obvious. The effect upon employment is equally apparent.[3]

***Early fax newspapers.*** World War II temporarily halted commercial facsimile services, but the vision of home printing presses lived on. In the late 1940s, a number of U.S. newspapers made significant financial commitments to the development of radio-delivered fax services. The abbreviated editions they created for fax delivery closely resembled their printed editions except for size (that of a standard letter). These fax editions were well designed for that period and often included photos and graphics (see Exhibit 9.2).

However, despite their best efforts, by the early 1950s commercial fax services were all but forgotten by the newspaper industry. The market had proven to be too small and the cost too high. And by then a new electronic medium had diverted the attention of newspaper publishers and audiences—commercial television.

***The emergence of digital fax.*** Facsimile technology evolved slowly in the 1960s and 1970s. Xerox introduced the first generation of all-purpose facsimile machines in 1966, but only a few businesses and institutions could afford them, and those that could tended to use them sparingly. The market remained relatively small, so no one seemed quite prepared for the swift and dramatic market changes that occurred in the 1980s. The adoption of a new international standard for digital fax transmission, based on research by Nippon Telephone & Telegraph, along with an array of new technologies provided much faster transmission speed, greater reliability, and significantly lower cost. Within just a few years, digital fax machines connected by standard telephone lines seemed to spring up everywhere and were being used to deliver all manner of information.

***The revival of fax newspapers.*** The availability of low-cost, digital facsimile machines rekindled interest in fax news services, and the newspaper business rushed to embrace it. But despite the renewed expectations of publishers, history appears to have repeated itself.

---

[3]Frank C. Waldrop and Joseph Borkin, *Television: A Struggle for Power.* New York: Morrow, 1938, p. 52.

**Exhibit 9.2** Example of an early fax newspaper.

The Philadelphia Inquirer
*Facsimile Edition*

BROADCAST OVER WFIL FM

BROADCAST OVER WFIL FM

Vol. D1 No. 3     MAY 7, 1947     8:00 Edition

# SenateRejectsLaborCurb

WASHINGTON. — The Senate dealt its Republican leadership a surprising jolt today when it rejected, by a 44-to-43 vote, a G. O. P. move to toughen the omnibus labor bill by writing in a curb on industry-wide bargaining.

The single vote defeated an amendment backed by Senator Robert A. Taft (R., O.), chairman of the Senate Labor Committee, and Senator Kenneth S. Wherry (R., Neb.), the Republican whip. Sixteen Republican Senators, including a number of "freshmen," bolted party lines on the rollcall.

Sponsored by conservatives of both parties, the proposal would have outlawed the recognition of national labor unions for collective bargaining purposes, with certain exceptions. Its foes trained heavy guns to shatter it the moment it hit the floor.

Senator Wayne Morse (R., Ore.) led off with an assertion that the amendment would "leave only a shell of labor's rights to bargain collectively." Senator Irving M. Ives (R., N. Y.), a Dewey man, denounced the measure as one that would "do little good, whereas it may do great harm."

The upset, altogether unexpected, was the first major defeat suffered by the Taft leadership. There was no way of telling what will happen to the main bill from here out.

Proponents of today's amendment were so confident of victory they failed to make a single speech in its behalf.

## Oklahoma Senator Shot By State Representative

OKLAHOMA CITY. — Representative Jimmy Scott shot Tom Anglin on the floor of the Oklahoma Senate Chamber today.

Scott was seized by eyewitness. Anglin, suffering from a bullet wound in the left hip, was taken to a hospital.

The assailant told police he fired when he thought he saw Anglin, who also was armed, draw a gun. Witnesses said two shots were fired. It was not determined whether Scott had fired both.

The two legislators are from Holdenville. Paul Ballinger, also of Holdenville, said Anglin's law firm was handling a divorce action for Scott's wife.

Anglin, 64, is dean of the Oklahoma Senate. Scott, 35, is serving his first term in the legislature. He was in the Pacific with the Marines

## Phone Strike Cracking; 11 States Report Settlement

WASHINGTON —(UP)—A wave of local settlements putting more than half the 325,000 strikers back to work appeared to have cracked the national telephone walkout today and held out hope for early resumption of normal service.

Official reports reaching here showed that by mid-afternoon settlements had been made locally in 11 States and the District of Columbia, following the strike leaders' surrender of their basic demand for pay raises on a national basis.

Coupled with about 80,000 strikers estimated to have returned to work independently, the new settlements meant that about 175,000 workers were back on the job or had agreed to go back. Union spokesmen said their central organization, the National Federation of Telephone Workers, was "financially exhausted" by the 31-day stoppage.

## UN Assembly Capitulates To Arab Ultimatum

LAKE SUCCESS. — Under threat of an Arab Higher Committee boycott, an extraordinary plenary session of the United Nations voted to extend a formal offer to the Arab group of equal footing with the Jewish Agency in hearings before the UN Political Committee.

The Arab Higher Committee had said it would stand on its decision to boycott the Palestine debate until it was handed the formal invitation by the Assembly itself.

**Source:** From *The Philadelphia Inquirer, Facsimile Edition,* May 7, 1947, p. 1. Reprinted by permission of *The Philadelphia Inquirer.*

The assumption that corporate managers and professionals were eager to receive daily news summaries via facsimile machines has, so far, proved disappointing. Few services have attracted enough paying subscribers to cover costs. And, just as television overshadowed newspaper fax services four decades earlier, the latest attempts have been eclipsed by yet another emerging electronic medium—consumer online networks and the World Wide Web. As a result, most digital fax editions have been abandoned or converted to online services.

However, fax is not the only means available for printing publications or selected information in the home. High-quality color printers attached to personal computers or TV sets are also being evaluated. But even though personal fax machines and printers are steadily becoming more reliable and affordable, they still have a number of limitations that are likely to inhibit their widespread use as "presses" for personal editions of newspapers. In addition to the telecommunication costs, subscribers to fax or printer services must bear the full cost for maintenance and consumables, such as paper and toner. To provide the contents of even a small community newspaper could require between 100 and 200 sheets of paper every day. Even if subscribers are able to tailor publications to satisfy only their most immediate interests, the amount of paper—as well as the amount of time required to print the pages—are still serious impediments.

**The problems with paper.** Paper may well remain the most practical and affordable document display medium for some time, but growing concerns about our environment and waste management could soon make it an expensive liability for print media. Publishers are already troubled by the number of people who claim that "saving trees" is their main reason for not subscribing to newspapers. Countering this perception is difficult. As one of the world's largest consumers of wood fiber, publishers cannot deny that they contribute directly to the cutting and crushing of hundreds of millions of trees each year. Some newspapers, in fact, own forest lands and paper mills.

Even the harvesting of so-called urban forests has not eliminated environmental concerns. The deinking and repulping processes essential to recycling require a great deal of electric power and fresh water. They also produce large quantities of toxic waste that must be carefully treated before disposal. Moreover, since most paper mills are located in remote areas, the bales of recycled newspapers must be trucked or shipped great distances, which consumes oil and contributes to the discharge of hydrocarbons. Even though newsprint might be produced from other renewable sources of fiber in ways that are less damaging to the environment, public perceptions of waste and environmental problems combined with added costs and aggravations could have more impact on the future direction of print media than any emerging technology.

**Digital paper.** One solution proposed by researchers in MIT's Media Lab is to develop an entirely new paper technology that can be re-used or, more precisely, reprogrammed. This material, which they call *digital paper*, would appear to be high-quality paper, but would function more like a thin flat-panel display. They suggest that bound pages made of this material could be used to create "the world's first one-volume library. A book that was *Moby Dick* one day could become *The Iliad* the next."[4]

Researcher Joseph Jacobson explains that the technology under development is an "ink" composed of tiny particles that are black on one side and white on the other. By changing the electric charge underneath them, they can be made to "flip" and create type and images. A microprocessor in the electronic document's spine would program these particles to "set" the desired text, which would remain stable until reprogrammed.[5] Although the concept is intriguing, it is likely to be many years before it could become a commercial alternative to pulp paper.

## *Printing custom publications*

As with fax publications, the idea of building printing presses that could print different versions of newspapers and magazines without stopping to change plates has been around for some time. In the 1970s, several press manufacturers began touting inkjet printing as the solution for the future. This technology literally sprays the images of pages onto paper. While inkjet presses never succeeded in achieving the levels of quality and speed required for printing newspapers, they are commonly used today for specialty publications, catalogs, limited personalizing of magazines, and direct mail advertising.

In 1992, a promising digital printing press called the Electrobook was introduced for custom printing of textbooks, pamphlets, manuals, and catalogs. This new press uses electrostatic imaging technologies closely related to the technologies found in office copiers and laser printers. "Digital electronic imaging" and "electrophotograph-

---

[4]"The Book of the Future," *Frames* (January 1996: 51), 1.
[5]Ibid.

ic printing," as these technologies are properly known, have made it possible for the Electrobook press to bypass the costly and time-consuming prepress operations and on-press preparations required by traditional presses. Pages can be transferred directly from an editor's computer to the press with no intermediate steps.

Since 1992, a number of similar printing presses have been introduced, but the digital press technology required for fast, custom printing of metropolitan newspapers still appears to be an elusive dream. As with inkjet printing, the process is much too slow. Without a major breakthrough, high-speed digital printing systems suitable for daily newspapers won't be available for several decades.

Although creative methods have been found to do limited tailoring of publications with existing technologies, mechanical presses are not expected to evolve to a point where they can print a different publication for every customer. Even if they could, other problems associated with mechanical printing, such as distribution, timeliness, and recycling, would remain.

## Publishing on the Web

While publishers continue to be firmly committed to pulp paper and mechanical printing, the accelerated growth of personal computers, modems, and consumer online networks has stimulated a revival of interest in online publishing. Instead of establishing their own full-service networks, as some attempted to do in the previous decade, the first group of publishers who decided to try again in the mid-1990s chose to play it safe by contracting with one of the existing networks.

This approach may have provided a low-risk point of entry, but it also limited publishers to only those online customers who subscribed to the particular network they had chosen. Each consumer online network employs a different proprietary technology and restricts access to "members only," so the pool of potential subscribers for online publications, which was not excessively large, was seriously fragmented. Publishers found themselves in the position of having to aggressively market their chosen online network as well as their sites within the network. Moreover, since the networks "own" all the subscribers and collect the monthly access fees, publishers had little influence over the operation of the networks, could not easily differentiate themselves, and received only a small percentage of the online revenue for their efforts.

This situation changed radically in 1994. The opening of the World Wide Web and related Internet services to commercial enterprises and general consumer access suddenly provided publishers with another alternative. Even though the Web lacked the organization and many of the popular features of consumer online networks, it gave publishers far greater control over their online presence as well as their destiny. Also, unlike the proprietary consumer networks, the Web is global and accessible to practically anyone with a computer.

By the end of 1995, several hundred newspapers and magazines in more than two dozen countries were publishing their content on the Web. Hundreds of other publishers have announced their intentions to follow with their own Web sites. Given the present momentum and level of financial commitments from companies, institutions, and governments around the world, it seems likely that the Web will evolve into a popular medium for online publishing.

***Positive and negative implications of online publishing.*** There are, however, both positive and negative implications for established mainstream publishers. On the positive side, they have recognized brand names and the ability to promote their online sites extensively in their printed editions. They also have the financial resources to fund a potentially long start-up period, an infrastructure already in place to gather and process information, and the credibility and connections to create instant cyber communities and marketplaces.

On the negative side, online customers have tended to be attracted more to specialized information and interactive services than to the aggregated general interest information provided by established mainstream publishers. With so much "free" information available and so many "cool" sites to explore in cyberspace, customers have been difficult for publishers to hook and hold. Consequently, most newspapers and magazines have had little success attracting paying advertisers or convincing online customers to pay subscription fees for access to their sites. As more people devote more of their time and money to computer-mediated communication, concerns have been raised that traditional print media will suffer over the long term.[6]

---

[6]See Eric Philo, *CyberPublishing: A New Frontier in Content Liquidity.* New York: Goldman Sachs, 1995.

**Mediated knowledge stores.** Although newspaper Web sites are generally regarded as electronic supplements and are seen by most publishers primarily as a means to protect their franchises and build circulation for their printed editions, they may evolve into something quite different. Some publishers are wisely attempting to address the aforementioned problems by adapting their online content and services to the inherent strengths of the Web, which derive from a blend of interpersonal and document traits. Instead of merely replicating their daily newspaper editions online, they have turned their Web sites into community forums and mediated knowledge "stores." These sites offer readers the opportunity to express their opinions and engage the paper's staff and community leaders in interactive discussions. They also provide their customers with a wealth of useful and timely community information that has been validated by journalists and offer convenient connections to other sites and services that may be of special interest.

By becoming the focal points on the Web for people who have an interest in the communities they serve, newspapers may be able to operate reasonably profitable knowledge stores in cyberspace. And even if online publishing does not prove to be a great financial success for established publishers, it could serve as the bridge to a more suitable *offline* form of digital print media.

## Digital print media and portable tablets

To function as a practical alternative to mechanical printing and pulp paper, digital print media will require underlying technologies that are quite different from present-day personal computers and consumer online networks. First of all, they will need to be highly portable and simple enough for anyone to use without having to read a manual. As with traditional print media, digital forms must be comfortable and convenient to read while lying in bed, riding on a subway, dining in a restaurant, or sitting on a park bench. They will also need to integrate some of the more compelling elements of cyber media, such as interactivity, hypertext, and audio/video clips, *without* sacrificing the readability and ease of using paper.

Personal computers are bound to become more portable in the next decade but, contrary to popular wisdom, increased processing power and expanded storage capacity will not make them significantly easier to use or more suitable for reading digital editions of mainstream publications and books. The solution, I believe, lies in the development of a new class of digital devices that will enhance and extend the dominant traits of the document domain. These devices, which I have described in the scenario as *tablets*, in a way take document technologies almost full circle back to their presumed origins in the soft clay of Sumer and Mesopotamia (see Exhibit 9.3).

***A new Renaissance.*** Instead of completely discarding more than 500 years of accumulated printing and publishing knowledge, digital print media developed for portable tablets could lead to a new Renaissance in typographic and visual communication. In this next stage of the third great mediamorphosis, newspapers, magazines, and books will routinely merge the written word and still images with full-motion video and sound in engaging and aesthetically pleasing formats.

Moreover, publications designed for this new document-based digital medium will be capable of retaining their familiar print characteristics and branded identities while adding greater depth and transactional services. Despite the present fascination with the apparently limitless amounts of information that can be found in cyberspace, I am convinced that manageable, branded packages of information that provide an editorial context and have a clear beginning and end will continue to be preferred by most people.

Tablet publications can be just as personal and nearly as interactive as online media without eliminating the judgments and creativity of professional editors and designers. Readers should be able to use intuitive tools built into the tablet editions to quickly locate stories of potential interest. Even though tablet editions will be designed for reading primarily *offline,* wireless communication will make it possible for readers to go online whenever they want or need to.

***The first portable digital newspapers.*** While affordable tablets with high-resolution, magazine-size displays may not be commercially available until the beginning of the next decade, smaller pocketbook-sized information and communication appliances, such as the Apple Newton and Sharp Zaurus, are already finding market niches. Despite the small size of their displays, these handheld devices, which average about $500, are more powerful and have a greater

**Exhibit 9.3** Tablet mockup.

**Source:** Courtesy of Kent State University News Service.

storage capacity than a typical PC had in the early 1980s. Nearly all include modems for both wired and wireless communications.

Although these devices are limited in their ability to display formatted pages, they are considered adequate for reading small amounts of text and possess two essential document traits—portability and simplicity. The importance of these traits was not overlooked by the *Mainichi Shimbun,* Japan's third largest national newspaper. Early in 1996, it became the world's first publisher to begin distributing daily editions specifically designed for reading on a portable electronic display. The digital editions are updated twice a day, five days a week, or more frequently when there are major breaking events. The handheld Zaurus, which is the recommended device, can store up to 18 stories for offline reading. It is also capable of receiving and displaying photos and graphics. The newspaper reportedly expects to reach its goal of 50,000 paying subscribers in 1997.

Other newspapers are also beginning to experiment with the delivery of content to larger portable digital devices. *El Periódico,* a newspaper published in Barcelona, Spain, launched the first market trial of a tablet edition in 1996 using devices called NewsPads developed by Acorn, a British electronics company. Even though the prototype tablets are bulkier and heavier than they would prefer for commercial versions, the newspaper and manufacturer still expect to learn a great deal about consumer acceptance of tablet publishing systems from this experiment.

### Flat-panel technology

The idea that people will be leisurely reading documents on portable tablets by the year 2010 may seem unrealistic given the present state of computer and display technologies, but it is no more fantastic than was the 1980 vision of people routinely using mobile cell phones, fax machines, and CD players. While the timing may be off by a few years either way, most executives of computer and consumer electronics companies are now reasonably confident that tablets suitable for displaying and interacting with digital print media will become ubiquitous in the next decade.

*The Dynabook.* The vision of thin, lightweight displays that can be used as portable information and communication media has been around for some time. However, the credit for conceiving the first portable information appliance is usually given to Alan Kay.

As a young computer scientist at the Xerox Palo Alto Research Center (PARC) in 1972, Kay created a cardboard model of a device that bore little resemblance to the huge mainframes and terminals most people then knew as computers. He called it a Dynabook and described it as a "dynamic media for creative thought."[7] According to Kay, it was to be a personal "self-contained knowledge manipulator in a portable package the size and shape of an ordinary notebook." It would have "enough power to outrace your senses of sight and hearing" as well as "enough capacity to store for later retrieval thousands of page-equivalents of reference materials, poems, letters, recipes, records, drawings, animations, musical scores, waveforms, dynamic simulations, and anything else you would like to remember and change."[8]

The Dynabook idea had been gestating in Kay's mind since the late 1960s when he was a graduate student at the University of Utah. So when he was invited to join the distinguished team of scientists who were forming Xerox PARC, he saw it as an opportunity to develop a working version of his dream. But despite his best efforts, Kay failed to win management support. Instead, the PARC team decided to pursue a project that would lead to the development of what became the world's first desktop personal computer—the Alto. More than two decades would pass before lightweight portable computers that could function as Kay originally envisioned became an "overnight success"—demonstrating once again the delayed adoption principle of mediamorphosis that transforming technologies always take longer than expected to become commercial successes.

*Liquid-crystal displays.* The development of the transforming technology considered most significant to the creation of portable computers and tablets—the liquid-crystal display (LCD)—also conformed to this principle. In 1964, George Heilmeier, a researcher at RCA's laboratories, accidentally discovered that images could be formed by applying an electric current to liquid crystals. Normally, this curious organic material is opaque and reflects light. But when a small electric current is applied, the crystals realign in such a way that they appear transparent.

Heilmeier immediately saw a number of practical applications for his invention and proceeded to build simple liquid-crystal devices

---

[7]Douglas K. Smith and Robert C. Alexander, *Fumbling the Future: How Xerox Invented, Then Ignored, the First Personal Computer.* New York: Morrow, 1988, pp. 84–85.

[8]Ibid.

that could display letters and numbers. Today, LCDs are found in watches and pocket calculators, automobile dashpanels and kitchen appliances, scales and exercise equipment, stereos and cameras, and thousands of other products. They have also become the best-selling display technology for laptop and handheld computers.

In the past 15 years, however, nearly all development efforts have focused on achieving high resolution at high power to compete with CRTs. Even though flat-panel displays are certain to eventually replace picture tubes, TV sets have not been the largest or most lucrative market. Worldwide demand for lightweight, flat-panel displays has been driven almost entirely by a need to create, read, and interact with text-based documents while traveling or telecommuting. Unfortunately, the qualities that make displays suitable for full-motion video have not been entirely compatible with those needs. For example, screen **resolution,** or sharpness of the image, is not a critical issue for viewing moving images, but it is crucial for reading text. Consumer acceptance of a digital display medium for reading documents will depend on the development of portable displays with a contrast and resolution near that of ink on paper.

***Digital ink on plastic paper.*** Technologies that could meet this standard are under development at a number of institutions and enterprises. One of the most promising is based on a material developed at Kent State University's Liquid Crystal Institute in Ohio, called cholesteric liquid crystals. As with ordinary liquid crystals, cholesteric crystals change their state from opaque to transparent when an electric current is applied. But unlike the liquid crystals used in current-generation displays, cholesteric crystals hold their state. In other words, they do not require constant refreshing or power to maintain an image on a screen. They also have several other advantages over other forms of liquid crystals. These crystals do not require polarizing filters[9] or backlighting. This gives displays made with cholesteric crystals the potential to match the contrast of ink on paper in ordinary light without consuming excessive amounts of power. Other advantages include the ability to use lighter weight

---

[9]Polarizing filters are used with all contemporary LCDs to organize the light that passes through the liquid crystals. This significantly reduces the viewing angle and the amount of reflected light we can see on the display's surface.

242 / Chapter Nine

and more durable plastic instead of glass and lower-cost manufacturing processes. If this emerging form of digital ink on plastic "paper" lives up to its promise, it could make low-cost tablets possible by the end of this decade.

**Practical applications of tablets.** Tablets will have a vast number of practical applications early in the twenty-first century beyond displaying digital editions of newspapers, magazines, and books. They are likely to be used by students and teachers to read and interact with course materials; by factory workers as electronic clipboards and manuals; by executives for viewing and distributing memos and reports; by salespersons for presentations and order entry; by attorneys to utilize depositions and documents in court; by repair persons and installers to access up-to-the-minute schematics and instructions; by public speakers as prompters and notepads; by stock brokers and commodities traders to process orders; and in nearly every other situation where paper is used today for storing, displaying, capturing, and distributing frequently changing, timely information.

Just as people don't think about the computer chips in their instant cameras when they take pictures, owners of tablets will not give much thought to the microprocessors behind their displays when they read and interact with digital documents. And instead of having to wrestle with the confusing proprietary technologies typical of computer systems, customers are likely to make their buying decisions for tablets based on the manufacturer's brand-name reputation, functionality, price, and other common variables. Tablets will probably be sold in consumer electronics stores along with digital TV sets, compact disc players, and minicams. While the initial price might be more than a thousand dollars at the end of this decade, by the year 2010 the range of prices will probably be comparable to other common consumer electronics, such as portable TV sets and mobile CD players.

## Memory cards and offline publishing

Unlike the current generation of Internet and consumer online services, customers will not have to remain connected to a communication network in order to read and interact with digital documents on their tablets. As soon as a publication has been captured and stored, customers would be free to move about. They will be able to read comfortably in an easy chair, go to a coffee shop, or take the "publication" with them on an airplane.

Removable, interchangeable memory devices, such as memory cards conforming to **Personal Computer Memory Card International Association** (PCMCIA) standards, are likely to be used for storing and transporting digital editions of publications and other personal documents. Early in the next decade, memory cards can be expected to store at least as much content as present-day CD-ROMs at an affordable price. In 1996, commercially available PCMCIA cards employing solid-state "flash" technology were already capable of storing the equivalent of about 50 million characters (50 megabytes) and could be rewritten more than 100,000 times.

Slots for these memory cards are being built into all types of portable information appliances as well as into most personal computers. In addition to storing large amounts of information, memory cards can be used to provide wireless communications and many other functions that are commonly performed by peripheral devices attached to personal computers. For example, in 1995, several companies began marketing cellular telephones and modems that conformed to the PCMCIA standard. With these devices, portable computer users can send and receive data from almost any location.

*Electronic newsstands.* With tablet publishing systems, subscriptions to newspapers and magazines should no longer be tied to home or office addresses. By using memory cards, subscribers to tablet editions could have their subscriptions fulfilled anywhere and at anytime that is convenient for them through a global network of electronic newsstands similar to automated teller machines. People should also be able to purchase single copies of publications from these machines to read on their tablets. By the year 2010, electronic newsstands may be routinely found in airports, train stations, large hotels, shopping malls, and bookstores, as well as in homes and offices.

With electronic newsstands and personal teledocks, as described in the scenario, the process of delivering digital editions could be almost entirely automated. As soon as a memory card is inserted into the newsstand or teledock, the machine should identify the customer and determine if the card contains a valid subscription. If so, it would quickly seek out the publication and load the current edition onto the card. If the card does not contain subscription information for a specific publication, the machine could offer the customer a menu of available publications to select from. After the card is loaded, the publication or book could be read on any tablet. At the moment the card is inserted into the appropriate slot on a tablet, the front page of the document would be displayed. Since nearly all interactions will take place locally within the tablet, customers should not experience any delays or interruptions caused by an overloaded system.

*Low-cost delivery.* An offline approach could take advantage of relatively low-cost broadcast technologies to deliver highly compressed editions to many locations at the same time. The enormous capacity of digital television channels and fiber-optic telephone lines should make it possible to capture mixed-media editions of publications and books in well under a minute. Also, these technologies could keep the total cost to consumers for tablet editions comparable to or even less than the printed editions.

Standard digital wireless communications could be used with the tablet to easily and simply handle most customer needs for electronic mail, transactions with advertisers, and requests for additional information. Because the file sizes for these occasional online interactions would likely be relatively small, the time and cost should also be small.

## Future control and social issues

As with electronic broadcast media, digital systems can be expected to provide both producers and consumers with greater control over the forms of print media. They will make it possible for publishers to economically package and distribute information that is more current and tailored than their mechanically printed editions as well as to add value through feedback and transactional services. For readers, electronic editions will provide more convenience by allowing subscriptions to be fulfilled (or single copies to be purchased) almost anywhere and at anytime; greater access to background, explanatory, and archived material; the ability to personalize and search content; two-way communication for immediate interactions with editors and advertisers; and a display medium that is cleaner and less damaging to the environment than ink printed on paper. But with greater control also comes a need for greater responsibility and accountability as well as the potential for increasing social fragmentation and invasions of privacy.

The vision I have presented of tablet publishing is based on the assumption that most people early in the next century will still prefer general interest forms of print media that are mediated and packaged by professional editors, retain their brand-name identities and editorial context, and, most of all, are portable, familiar, and easy to read and browse. This is not, however, the only possible future for digital print media. Others have taken the position that most familiar characteristics of contemporary newspapers and magazines may not matter to future generations.

### The daily me or the daily us?

At about the time Knight-Ridder was beginning to develop Viewtron, researchers at MIT's Architectural Machine Group (the Media Lab's predecessor) were conceiving their own version of digital print media, dubbed "NewsPeek" by its principal designers, Alan Kay, Walter Bender, and Nicholas Negroponte. NewsPeek was designed to demonstrate how textual material drawn from various wire services and databases might be blended with video clips from television to create custom "newspapers" for personal computers and video disks.

However, NewsPeek fell far short of Negroponte's grand vision of an intimate medium—which he called the *Daily Me*—that would know individual readers well enough to provide them with completely personalized editions. He envisioned an entirely computer-mediated system that would automatically select material—without the assistance of human editors—from all available news sources based on a dynamic profile of each reader's interests.[10] Personal calendars and electronic mailboxes would also be incorporated into the news pages, so that the main headlines of the *Daily Me* might read: "This Morning's Meeting Has Been Canceled" or even "Today Is Your Mother's Birthday."

---

[10]A more complete description of NewsPeek can be found in Stewart Brand, *The Media Lab: Inventing the Future at MIT.* New York: Viking, 1987, pp. 36–39.

The vision that CMC technologies employing advanced personal agents will ultimately empower individuals to bypass, and perhaps replace, traditional information and entertainment gatekeepers has strong appeal within some groups. There are already a number of services providing individually tailored content via the Internet, but these are highly specialized services that focus primarily on business and technology subjects.

A more all encompassing *Daily Me* presents a much more difficult problem for CMC systems. But with more powerful microprocessors and a significant increase in telecommunication bandwidth, some version of the *Daily Me* is bound to emerge before the year 2010.

While widespread replacement of mainstream newspapers and magazines, which I call the *Daily Us*, by the narrowly focused *Daily Me* seems unlikely, there are possible social and political implications from even a partial shift to this form of media within future societies. Where the *Daily Us* attempts to broaden our perspectives and provide a dynamic context for introducing new subjects of importance and potential interest to nearly everyone within diverse communities, the *Daily Me,* by design, limits perspectives and restricts exposure to new ideas, issues, and topics. Media professionals and scholars have expressed serious concerns about the *Daily Me* vision for this reason. Many have argued that without the community-focused, civic-minded *Daily Us*, we might find ourselves living in an even more individually isolated, fragmented, and dangerous world.

Such fears, however, may be somewhat overstated. Similar doomsday arguments were made with the emergence of the telephone, film, radio, and television. While those who adopt advanced cyber media technologies might become less dependent on mainstream publications for their general news and information, they are unlikely to reject these document forms entirely if the principles of mediamorphosis continue to apply. As the coevolution and coexistence principle suggests, newer forms coexist with older forms rather than replace them.

And even with more advanced CMC technologies, the *Daily Me* may not emerge as the appropriate solution for the vast majority of consumers. It takes time and skill to process raw data, validate it, and turn it into useful and credible information. The Web and consumer online networks have shown that some people are willing to work harder, take more time, and pay more to get highly personalized information, but they are the exception, not the rule. Surveys and experience have shown that readers want digital alternatives to be easier, less time consuming, and no more expensive than existing print media. To be widely adopted, the agent-based *Daily Me* technology will have to become much easier for people to set up, manage, and use than anyone is contemplating at this time. For most people, the idea of seeking answers in seemingly "infinite" databases is about as appealing as getting lost in a huge cave network with only a small flashlight. Print publications, on the other hand, are perceived to be reasonably manageable, understandable, and affordable packages of information with obvious beginnings and ends.

## Preserving the social function of newspapers

Rather than serving as passive repositories of aggregated information that quietly await one's commands, newspapers actively distill and sell current "slices of time" in convenient, portable packages. As community information mediators, they are expected to fairly and objectively report, investigate, analyze, explain, filter, validate, organize, put into context, and make sense out of often conflicting information gathered from many diverse sources. Within most democratic societies, they also have a tacit responsibility to serve as government "watchdogs" and to alert citizens to malfeasance and threats to their freedoms and civil rights.

Interestingly, nearly all *Daily Me* visions tend to eliminate one of the most appealing pleasures of reading a newspaper—the element of surprise. The joy of discovering stories about subjects we didn't know we were interested in until we encountered them is difficult for a computer-mediated service to provide. Typically, the most interesting and talked about stories are not the top stories of the day or the ones that might match individual profiles.

Even more important, of course, are the socially significant stories to which the *Daily Us* routinely expose us. Stories about welfare legislation, global warming, civil rights violations, political corruption, and AIDS may not be the most popular subjects but we still need to know about them. While we may ignore or give little attention to many stories that appear in mainstream media today, we cannot entirely avoid them as would be possible with the *Daily Me*. Mainstream newspapers provide a social context and help to establish the relative importance of events and issues as well as contribute to a general understanding of the world in which we live. The computer-mediated *Daily Me* has a long way to go before it can do all that for less than a dollar a day.

### Providing answers to readers' questions

Proponents of the *Daily Me* vision generally assume that people would prefer computer-mediated services because nearly every story could be accompanied by a Give Me More button. Presumably each of the "more" stories that followed would provide readers with additional Give Me More buttons, which could be extended until either the reader or the information was exhausted. But as often as this assumption is presented, it is somewhat curious that a rather obvious question is rarely asked—Where does all this additional information come from?

Contrary to conventional wisdom, all information that may be of interest or importance to individuals does not exist in online databases. And much of what is stored and available is not in a useful form. If the daily offerings of every news service were made available to *Daily Me* subscribers, they would soon discover that their Give Me More buttons provided them with dozens, or perhaps hundreds, of *nearly identical* stories, photos, and graphics.

In reality, the range of questions people typically have about news events is not as great as it may seem. And editors are generally able to anticipate most questions readers might ask about news events. They work with researchers and graphics editors to develop background material, nugget boxes, maps, informational graphics, and other explanatory devices, and then package them with related stories. Of course, space constraints often prevent editors from publishing this additional material every time an important or continuing story appears.

In the tablet version of the *Daily Us,* as described in the scenario, editors would be able to regularly link the most appropriate background and explanatory items to a story and then promote them with visual clues and headlines. This approach would assure that the additional information would be available and updated when readers want it—without overwhelming them every day. And they could get the answers to most of their questions without the necessity of posing questions or spending their time searching through redundant and irrelevant material.

## *Maintaining personal privacy*

When we read a mechanically printed newspaper or magazine, no one watches over our shoulders to observe which stories and ads we take an interest in or how long we linger on a page. But, with the World Wide Web and consumer online networks, all of our interactions and transactions can be easily monitored and recorded by the service providers. The ability to collect precise data on subscribers' interests, reading or viewing patterns, and buying habits is, in fact, the feature of online publishing that is most frequently touted to potential advertisers.

In theory, online interactive marketing should promote mutually beneficial relationships between consumers and producers. Advocates for this "one-to-one marketing" approach suggest that it will only expose consumers to those products and services they are most likely to want while significantly reducing the producers' cost per household for advertising.

However, despite repeated assurances that personal data collected by online service providers will be used responsibly, concerns about potential abuses and violations of privacy are growing. The specter of governments, giant multinational corporations, or criminals using cyberspace to manipulate and control citizens and consumers has already become a popular theme with authors and screen writers.

With the offline tablet approach, privacy would be a nonissue because nearly all of the interactivity would take place locally within the portable information appliance *after* the digital publication is retrieved. Personal usage data might be collected and stored within the device, but the individual could maintain control over its use. The only time subscribers to tablet editions would give up some of their personal privacy is when they make transactions or interact through the wireless communicator, the equivalent of making routine credit card purchases at a store or over the telephone.

## *Extending brand-name identities*

Newspapers may look rather alike but nearly all possess and cultivate strong brand-name identities. National publications are instantly recognized wherever they may appear. Even if their nameplates are obscured, they can be easily distinguished from other publications in newsstands and coin boxes. Most local and regional publications are also just as easily identifiable within the communities they serve. Loyalties to individual newspapers have weakened somewhat since the 1960s, due in large part to changing lifestyles and increased mobility, but communities and advertisers continue to depend on and support their local papers.

Tablet editions of the *Daily Us* would build on the established brand-name identities of newspapers by retaining the familiar nameplates, section and department headings, typefaces, and design elements found in the mechanically printed editions. Thus, even though the pages would be a different size and shape, enough of the characteristics would be preserved that most readers would have little difficulty recognizing the identity of the newspaper.

In the *Daily Me* vision, visual identities of established publications are not considered important. Readers would be able to aggregate their news and information from many sources and even design their own publications down to the choice of typefaces. News on demand, like video on demand, would allow customers of the *Daily Me* to pay for only the content they select. Instead of subscribing to a specific newspaper in order to read their favorite sports columns, for example, *Daily Me* customers would buy the columns directly from the columnists or syndicates for a few cents per day. Although this vision is appealing to many people, the deconstruction of publications and loss of brand-name identities may come at a much higher price than the few cents per item *Daily Me* customers might pay.

For example, each publication possesses a unique style and personality to which readers generally attach specific degrees of credibility and reliability. The context in which information is presented provides essential clues to the nature of the content. That is, while people find the supermarket tabloids with their outrageous headlines and stories entertaining, most can easily differentiate between these publications and mainstream newspapers. For instance, a story about the discovery of alien life on another planet would certainly be taken much more seriously if it appeared in the *New York Times* than if it appeared in the *National Enquirer*. Stripped of their identifying characteristics, however, one's ability to critically evaluate the legitimacy and accuracy of the story would be seriously impaired.

Newspapers already are professional aggregators of information and advertising. Most nonlocal content comes from other sources, such as wire services and syndicates. Editors are essentially "hired" by the paper's subscribers to gather, filter, validate, and organize information that reflects the general interests, concerns, and needs of the communities they serve. In the newspaper medium, the "program" is not the individual story or the favorite column—the program is the newspaper. Thus, instead of deconstructing publications or blurring their identities, digital forms of print media may need to preserve and extend brand-name recognition.

## Mediamorphosis within the document domain in perspective

In recent years, newspapers have been frequently portrayed as dinosaurs on the verge of extinction. Because of their historic dependence on printing presses and paper, many people assume they will be unable to compete with new forms of electronic media and therefore will eventually die out. That assumption, however, underestimates the adaptability of newspapers and their importance in both contemporary and future societies. Far from dying in the next century, they are likely to metamorphose into an even more versatile and popular communication medium. But to do so, they must complete their transition to digital publishing systems.

Since the 1960s, publishers have been steadily converting their labor-intensive mechanical production equipment and processes to digital technologies. Today, the last vestiges of the industrial age in the newspaper business are the printing presses and delivery trucks. Although print media that rely on mechanical presses and pulp paper can be expected to coexist with digital print media for many years, there will come a time, perhaps within a human generation, when publishers will be compelled for financial, competitive, and environmental reasons to finally abandon their industrial age publishing technologies.

While the World Wide Web, consumer online networks, and facsimile systems have provided publishers with opportunities to develop electronic outlets for their content, these services are unlikely to emerge as the digital successors to mechanical printing presses and pulp paper. Just as with the early videotex services, they still lack several important attributes.

To successfully compete with existing and newer forms of media, electronic editions of newspapers will require underlying digital technologies that build upon the essential traits of the document domain—portability, portrait-oriented pages, and the ability to be easily browsed. As we have seen in this chapter, the emerging technology with the greatest potential to propagate these traits is the flat-panel display. By the end of the next decade, displays with a contrast and clarity comparable to pigmented ink printed on pulp paper should be commonplace.

Lightweight, magazine-sized tablets using advanced flat-panel technologies will offer consumers an inexpensive, reliable, and easy-to-use medium for displaying and interacting with all forms of digital documents from personal correspondence and calendars to textbooks and course materials. Tablet editions of newspapers, as well as magazines and books, will ultimately incorporate audio/video clips and transactional services without sacrificing the readability of the printed word.

# hype and reality

Americans have always had a peculiar fascination with new inventions and technological innovations. For most, the fascination has not been so much with the details of how the devices work but with the opportunities and benefits they might yield. The announcement of practically every major "discovery" or "breakthrough" in the past two centuries has been immediately followed by a deluge of wild speculation and hyperbole proclaiming the birth of a new era or a revolution in the making. So hungry are the media and their audiences for stories about the promise of things "new" that in recent years the hype has begun to precede and overshadow the formal announcements.

Separating the reality from the hype has been made significantly more difficult by the ascendancy of image over substance. A growing number of companies are becoming masters at leaking stories about speculative future products to evaluate market reactions and demand as well as to thwart potential competitors. In more than a few cases, companies have touted products they had no serious intention of ever producing, just to enhance their image. This practice is now so common in the computer and telecommunication industries that most preannounced products have come to be known by the disparaging term *vaporware.*

In this chapter, we will attempt to look beyond the hype to examine some of the realities and challenges that lie ahead for mainstream media enterprises, schools of mass communication, advertisers, and society as a whole. We will also seek to put the present transformation of mass communications in perspective.

# The great cyber stampede

Since the spring of 1994, hardly a day has passed without at least one story in the mainstream media extolling the virtues of "going online" or calling attention to the phenomenal growth of the Internet and consumer online services. Nearly everyone, it seems, is becoming convinced that the future, as well as fame and fortune, are to be found in the ethereal frontier known as cyberspace.

As I read these stories and watched the "special reports," I found myself conjuring up images from the famous Oklahoma land rush. When the U.S. government announced that it would be opening the Oklahoma Territory to settlers in 1889, the newspapers and magazines of the day actively fanned the excitement of readers by providing glowing descriptions of the bountiful land and incredible riches that awaited those who were brave enough to make the trek. Thousands of farmers and would-be farmers who were captivated by these stories were joined by almost as many merchants and more than a few con-artists in what turned into a wild and reckless stampede across relatively unsettled grasslands. Each of these settlers, who came to be known collectively as Sooners, was determined to stake a claim to the choicest acreage before anyone else could grab it, and many died trying.

The majority of those who managed to grab and hold onto a piece of land soon discovered that the stories they had read had not been exactly truthful. While much of the soil was indeed rich and capable of producing good crops, life on the prairie was extremely harsh and lonely. Most of the early settlers had to build their homes out of sod and make do with few amenities and limited contact with the outside world. No doubt there were beautiful days, but the Sooners also had to contend with bitter cold winters and scorching hot summers, severe thunderstorms, violent tornadoes, consuming prairie fires, and apocalyptic dust storms as well as irascible cattle ranchers and cowboys who saw the farmers' fences as a threat to their way of life. A few decades later, some of those early settlers, or their offspring, did manage to become fabulously wealthy—when oil was discovered beneath their farms. But, for most, the promised land was greatly oversold.

After spending nearly 20 years of my life exploring and occasionally tilling the fallow bits of the online frontier, I can't help but feel empathy for the "Cyber Sooners" who are now stampeding onto the Internet and other networks in search of a new promised land. Many, I'm sure, will soon discover that cyberspace has also been oversold.

By the fall of 1995, the gap between expectations and reality had already widened to the point where more than a few of the computer network pioneers who had long championed computer-mediated communications were beginning to question the vision of cyberspace as it was being presented by mainstream media and Hollywood. Clifford Stoll, an author and astronomer who has been involved with the Internet since its inception, eloquently describes the current situation and his concerns in *Silicon Snake Oil*:

> It's an unreal universe, a soluble tissue of nothingness. While the Internet beckons brightly, seductively flashing an icon of knowledge-as-power, this nonplace lures us to surrender our time on earth. A poor substitute it is, this virtual reality where frustration is legion and where—in the holy names of Education and Progress—important aspects of human interactions are relentlessly devalued.[1]

Stoll's criticism is directed not so much at the reality of the Internet as at the hype that has surrounded it. Few would disagree that as an infrastructure for global interpersonal communication and information dissemination, the Internet is becoming invaluable. Or that this medium holds great potential for uniting the world and channeling human endeavors toward solving the many critical problems threatening our future. But, as with all great transformations, there are darker sides that are not always immediately apparent. Choices made at the outset can have a significant influence on the paths new media will follow. Media commentator Howard Rheingold suggests that the future course of CMC may be determined within a relatively brief period of time: "The late 1990s," he says, "may eventually be seen in retrospect as a narrow window of historical opportunity, when people either acted or failed to act effectively to gain control over communication technologies."[2]

------

[1]Clifford Stoll, *Silicon Snake Oil: Second Thoughts on the Information Highway.* Garden City, NY: Doubleday, 1995, p. 4.

[2]Howard Rheingold, *The Virtual Community: Homesteading on the Electronic Frontier.* New York: Harper Perennial, 1994, p. 300.

# The future of mass communication

For all established mass media companies, the next stage of this third great mediamorphosis is certain to be painful. A century ago, carriage makers and their suppliers were faced with many of the same difficult decisions confronting media professionals today. When the first gasoline-powered automobiles appeared in the early 1890s, few carriage makers believed they would ever replace reliable horse-drawn carriages. Most argued that automobiles were merely expensive toys for the rich and that suitable highways and gasoline stations would take generations to build. Others literally backed the wrong horse, convinced that steam, not gasoline, would be the future energy source.

Yet, despite the physical obstacles and the natural tendencies of established companies to resist change, the gasoline-powered automobile spread rapidly throughout the world. Within three decades most companies that had been building carriages and their accouterments converted to automobiles and auto accessories, shifted into other fields, or went out of business.

Today, nearly all leaders of established media enterprises have already come to accept that their businesses are about to be profoundly changed by emerging digital technologies and shifting cultural expectations. At this juncture, many paths appear to be possible. Exactly where they may lead and at what cost, however, is still beyond anyone's ability to see clearly. Thus, media companies are placing bets on as many possible routes as they can afford. Most of these paths, though, are certain to lead nowhere or to merge with other paths. Only a few will link the present with the future, and even they will take mainstream media companies through many unexpected twists and turns.

Whichever routes ultimately lead to successful new forms of communication media in the twenty-first century, media professionals can take some comfort from the historic patterns of technological change brought to light by the principles of mediamorphosis. For instance, no matter how promising or threatening any vision of new media may seem, the *delayed adoption principle* reveals that implementation and widespread adoption will take much longer than most visionaries predict. Typically, the process has required at least a human generation. The *coevolution and coexistence principle* has also shown that older forms of communication are capable of coexisting with newer forms for long periods of time. Instead of dying out as newer forms emerge, the *survival principle* suggests that older forms will adapt and continue to evolve within their media domains.

These principles are not intended as justifications for complacency, however. Although new media technologies have typically required several decades to move from laboratories to the marketplace, we have seen that diffusion can occur quickly once a new medium is perceived by individuals and societies to meet their needs or desires at an affordable price. Established media companies that are caught unprepared to adapt in a rapidly changing environment may not survive for long.

Also, despite the many popularized visions of a new era in which all forms of mass communication will be ultimately replaced by more intimate forms of computer-mediated communication, there seems little real support for this belief. Digital technologies will certainly give individuals greater control over the content and scheduling of mainstream newspapers, magazines, television, and radio, but they are unlikely to bring about the demise of mass media. Mass media have evolved and become essential within modern societies because they fulfill human needs for shared information and entertainment and because they provide the cultural glue that bonds large communities of diverse people with common social, political, and economic interests.

Although the popular forms of communication can be expected to adapt and propagate their dominant trait, that does not mean that every existing media enterprise will survive the transition to digital language. Many may, in fact, suffer the fate of the carriage makers who were slow to change. To survive and prosper, established communication companies must use digital technologies to become more accessible and useful to their readers, viewers, and listeners.

## *Print media and the business of publishing*

For newspaper and magazine publishers, the mediamorphic transformation from mechanical printing presses and pulp paper to digital print media offers numerous opportunities to create and profit from a wealth of new products and services. But competing with an array of nontraditional information providers and cyber-savvy entrepreneurs while simultaneously defending their franchises and reeducating their staffs will present enormous challenges. Publishers who own their own printing presses and production facilities will have the added burden of protecting their enormous investments in industrial age technologies as they convert to digital print media.

However, when one considers that manufacturing and distribution account for at least half the costs associated with printed newspapers and magazines, electronic publishing holds the key to dramatic reductions in operating expenses and corresponding increases in profitability. Some of the savings in manufacturing and distribution costs will need to be shifted into the editorial and advertising departments but, even then, the pretax margins for electronic editions should be higher than for mechanically printed and distributed editions.

Publishers' brand names may be their most valued asset in this period of transition. Even in cyberspace, the identities of information sources will continue to be significant. Each publication possesses a unique style and personality to which readers attach degrees of credibility and reliability. As we noted before, the context in which information is presented provides essential clues to the nature of the content.

While online publishing on the World Wide Web and consumer online services has provided newspapers and magazines with a relatively low-cost point of entry for digital delivery of their content, I believe offline publishing on portable tablets will prove to be the most popular form of digital print media in the next decade. Unlike online networks, tablet systems extend and enhance the dominant traits of the document domain. There can be little doubt that people will continue to prefer publications, books, and other documents that they can read anywhere and at anytime. Portable, branded packages of information mediated by professional editors may have an even greater appeal among consumers after cyber media become widely available.

Whether future newspapers will be published on paper or on some new electronic display medium is not the most significant issue, however. What does matter will be their continuing ability to conveniently and responsibly inform people in the communities they serve; to provide accessible forums for public discourse and the exchange of diverse viewpoints; to validate and make sense out of disparate and often conflicting reports; to facilitate the sharing of information and experiences that strengthen community bonds; to expose malfeasance and sound the alarm when our freedoms, communities, and lives are endangered; and to continue delighting and surprising readers with the unexpected and offbeat. To do all of this, at the lowest possible cost, newspapers must also continue to provide an effective, affordable and compelling marketplace where buyers and sellers can be easily brought together.

### Broadcast media and the business of broadcasting

For radio and television broadcasters, the transition from analog to digital systems is expected to improve on-air and off-air efficiency as well as presentation quality. But it has also raised serious concerns among media professionals and critics alike as to the impact it may have on content quality. New technologies that are financially justified by reductions in staffing have already had an impact on broadcast news operations. A 1995 survey found that many professionals fear TV news departments will soon reach a critical point in staffing where station managers will have to decide whether to continue uncovering and reporting news or simply "processing" news— replaying newscasts and regurgitating information from outside sources.[3]

External pressures are also squeezing budgets for news operations. And as digital technologies make it possible to significantly expand the number of radio stations and TV channels, competitive pressures will increase. The situation is expected to become even more difficult for broadcast TV networks and stations in the future. While television continues to be seen as the most compelling medium by advertisers and ad agencies, new digital technologies will make it easier for viewers to zap commercials and avoid advertising messages altogether. Other uses for the TV set, such as video games, information services, and distance learning, will also continue to cut into passive audience viewing time.

On the positive side, broadcast entertainment is likely to remain popular in all societies. What television viewers seem to want is greater control over viewing times rather than the ability to interact with programs or choose from a greater array of options. Digital technologies should be able to give viewers that control without

---

[3]For more details see *The Future of News: Defining the Issues.*
Washington, DC: Radio and Television News Directors Foundation, 1995.

adding complexity. More advanced digital displays that are less bulky, offer sharper images, and larger wide-screen formats may encourage people to install intimate home theaters, which could further enhance the appeal of broadcast TV programs and movies.

## Schools of journalism and mass communication

Digital technologies will undoubtedly help to meet growing consumer demands for more tailored information, but they will not eliminate the need for human judgment and analysis. If anything, the need for media professionals is likely to increase substantially in coming decades. But next-generation journalists are certain to need expanded skills in such areas as abstract writing, digital audio and video editing, and hypermedia navigation as well as a much better understanding of information and communication sciences.

The Internet and consumer online networks will be essential tools for harvesting information and identifying new sources, but their use will still require basic research and analytical skills in addition to corroboration and validation. With the continuing convergences of print, audio, and video technologies, contemporary distinctions between print and electronic broadcast media are bound to become outmoded.

The goals for all journalism educators and students during this period of transition should be to focus attention on content development and community interaction, not just technology. As the *opportunity and need principle* reveals, technology is not what drives new forms of media. People do not buy information technologies—they buy content, usefulness, and convenience at the point when they perceive value to match the cost.

Society and mass communication will change in unexpected ways, but we can be reasonably certain that the needs and desires for timely, reliable, and contextual information about the world in which we live will remain strong. Humans are inherently interested in the public occurrences within their communities and are curious about communities other than their own. They enjoy exchanging information and interacting with other humans, and they feel excitement and pleasure when something new is learned or experienced. Fulfilling these human needs and desires is, to a large extent, what journalism and mass communication are all about.

## *Advertising and the business of mass marketing*

However mass media may evolve in the next two decades, advertising will remain the key to their success. Those who suggest that digital information and entertainment should be sold without advertising fail to recognize that advertising actually provides essential information in our culture. Also, advertisers subsidize the costs associated with gathering, packaging, and disseminating information for general audiences.

Digital technologies are likely to merge the familiar strengths of broadcast and print advertising while integrating some of the interpersonal features of cyber media. Unlike TV commercials, ads in digital media might not intrude on or delay readers and viewers. They might function much more like storefront windows in a shopping mall. Readers and viewers could simply "walk" by the ads that don't interest them, just as they walk by stores in malls. But when a "window" ad hooks a prospective customer, he or she would only have to touch or select the ad to enter the merchant's "store." Once through the electronic "doorway," the customer might encounter a brief video or audio clip similar to a TV or radio commercial. After that, customers could select several layers of additional information.

Most merchants are likely to include transaction forms that customers can use to purchase items, make reservations, request additional information, or send in comments. Through electronic mail, merchants could return confirmations and answer questions. This would allow merchants to easily assess the effectiveness of their ads and know more about their customers. It would also serve to create more of a one-to-one marketing relationship between merchants and customers, without invading privacy.

No one, of course, can predict with absolute certainty which of the new mixed-media advertising and marketing models emerging from the transformation of mainstream media will be the most successful. Current trends strongly suggest, however, that new forms will need to be more personal, more interactive, and more accountable than contemporary forms. Yet, experience has also shown that advertisers and customers alike have always gravitated to the forms of media that are the most convenient, intuitive, and cost effective to use.

## Audiences, customers, and users

Digital print media in the next decade will have the potential to be richer and more diverse than possible today. But their most appreciated quality is likely to be greater convenience. Subscribers to digital publications, for instance, will not have to leave their homes or hotel rooms to locate a newsstand or wait for delivery. Newspapers won't accumulate on doorsteps and magazines won't fill up mailboxes when subscribers are out of town, and they won't have to be sent to recycling stations. The ink won't rub off on customers' hands, and inserts won't fall out on the floor.

For those who are frequent travelers, the ability to pack several newspapers, magazines, and books, as well as personal papers, speeches, and reports on credit-card-size memory cards and read them on portable, easy-to-use tablets will not only be more convenient, it will help save their overstressed backs as well. Ultimately, digital print media will likely give travelers access to their regional newspapers as well as their other favorite publications, from nearly any hotel or airport in the world. Electronic editions of books would also be readily available and would rarely go out of "print."

With digital broadcast media, individuals will gain greater control over the scheduling and sequencing of programs, but they are unlikely to significantly change their viewing and listening habits. Most people are still likely to prefer linear, noninteractive forms of broadcast entertainment. As large, thin-screen display technologies become more affordable, intimate home theaters with a viewing environment comparable to commercial movie theaters should become commonplace. This may encourage commercial theater owners to develop and install new technologies, such as holographic projection systems, which can provide audiences with shared virtual experiences.

Interpersonal cyber media will extend telephony and provide users with a wider range of possible interactions with other people as well as with digital agents and avatars that act as surrogate humans. Although computer-mediated communication systems will give users greater access to databases of information, as well as to other people throughout the world, they are unlikely to replace mainstream media as the primary sources for general interest information anytime soon. For even with more advanced digital technologies, the process of gathering, sorting, selecting, evaluating, and validating will require more time, effort, and expense than most people will be willing to devote. For this reason, I believe most people will continue to rely on professional journalists, information managers, and producers for the majority of their information and entertainment.


## Keeping the future in perspective

Amidst all the fanfare and general excitement that surrounds the development of new media, there are those who question whether the promised gains will ultimately outweigh the certain losses within our culture. Such questions are never easily answered.

When European printers began producing Bibles in languages other than sanctified Latin, the Roman Catholic theocracy feared that the spread of Gutenberg's invention might lead people to challenge the Church's authority, which it did. By the end of the sixteenth century, reformists had severed spiritual ties to the pope and established the Protestant religions. If it were possible for a Roman Catholic bishop in the mid-1440s to travel two centuries into the future, he would almost certainly declare that the printing press was, indeed, the work of the devil.

In the years immediately following the American Revolution, Thomas Jefferson was a staunch supporter of newspapers and the radical new concept of a free press. But when he experienced the unbridled power of the press during his presidency in the early 1800s, his attitude changed, and he wrote: "I deplore . . . the putrid state into which the newspapers have passed and the malignity, the vulgarity and the mendacious spirit of those who write them."[4]

In the 1930s, scholars worried that governments and subversive groups would turn television into a powerful tool for spreading propaganda and manipulating public opinion. Many were also concerned that TV would lead to a breakdown in social norms and values. Some even speculated that the divorce rate would escalate because housewives would neglect their household chores to watch TV. Still, whatever disruption to traditional social values television has caused, the alarmists certainly overstated their predictions.

---

[4]Quoted from a letter written by Thomas Jefferson to Walter James in 1813.

The rapid growth of the Internet is now stirring many of the same fears. Governments are worrying that they will lose control over sensitive information and will be unable to monitor financial transactions across state and national borders. Parents worry that their children might be exposed to hard-core pornography and accosted by pedophiles. Also of concern is who will have access to information in the future.

Where once people spoke of the haves and have-nots in terms of financial wealth, now they often speak of them in terms of information access. Even though schools and public libraries may continue to provide free or low cost access to the Internet and other consumer online networks, they are not available all the time. And while computer technologies are certain to become more affordable and easier to use, interactively accessing and processing information from electronic databases and online services may not appeal to a broad cross section of people.

Already there are growing concerns that African Americans and Hispanics may be left out of the electronic loop. A U.S. Census Bureau survey of 55,000 households in 1993 found that about 37.5 percent of whites were using computers at home and at work compared with 25 percent of African Americans and 22 percent of Hispanics. The survey also estimated that 26.9 percent of white adults had a personal computer at home, compared with 13.8 percent of African American adults and 12.9 percent of Hispanic adults.

What to do about these serious concerns is another matter. Despite the many expressions of concern and efforts to manage change, no one has ever succeeded in anticipating all of the possible outcomes or in controlling the effect of new information technologies upon social systems. The truth is that societies have always been affected and transformed by new forms of media. Whether the outcome is seen as good or bad depends, to a great extent, on the viewer's perspective.

I must also emphasize that however apocalyptic or beguiling the technologies and visions described in this book may seem, I do not believe new media technologies alone will save or kill contemporary media companies. New technologies merely facilitate change and create opportunities. The challenge for established media companies and professionals will be in learning how to create, manage, and deliver mixed-media content on the emerging digital tollways in a convenient and easy-to-use form. To survive, they must adapt to a changing and often confusing world where people will have greater personal access to mixed-media information, but will need, even more, the assistance of people they can trust to help them validate and make sense out of it.

In the rush to cash in on emerging forms of digital communication, media companies and professionals should not lose sight of their implicit responsibility to keep people informed about social developments, government activities, and community affairs, regardless of their race, gender, age, education, financial status, or level of technical skills. The mainstream media must continue to serve as community builders and forums for public expression as well as marketplaces for businesses and individuals.

Rather than focusing entirely on individual needs, media scholar Jay Rosen argues that mainstream media should make a greater effort to enhance the capacity of communities to understand and deal with common problems. To pursue individually packaged content that is limited to narrow sets of personal interests is to destroy the very essence of social systems and cultures.

Without concerted efforts by media companies and professionals to assure the quality of their information and to provide more of what people need and want at an affordable price, the next stage of the third great mediamorphosis will yield an empty chrysalis. As the age of digital communication bursts forth, I believe the most valued characteristics of future mainstream media are likely to be their credibility and connections to the communities they serve.

# acronyms / abbreviations

## a

**ABC** American Broadcasting Corporation
**AI** artificial intelligence
**AM** amplitude modulation
**AMLCD** active-matrix liquid crystal display
**ANSI** American National Standards Institute
**AOL** America OnLine
**API** 1. American Press Institute; 2. application program interface
**ARPA** Advanced Research Projects Agency [an agency of the United States Department of Defense (pronounced "are-pah")]
**ARPANET** Advanced Research Projects Agency Network (pronounced "are-pah-net")
**ASCII** American Standard Code for information interchange (pronounced "as-key")
**AT&T** American Telephone and Telegraph
**ATM** 1. Adobe Type Manager; 2. asynchronous transfer mode; 3. automated teller machine
**AV** audio/visual

## b

**BASIC** Beginners All-purpose Symbolic Instruction Code (pronounced "basic")
**BBS** bulletin board system
**bit** binary digit (pronounced "bit")
**bps** bytes per second
**Bps** bits per second

**byte** binary digit eight (pronounced "bite")

## c

**CATV** community antenna television (now known as cable TV)
**CBS** Columbia Broadcasting System (USA)
**CD** compact disc
**CD-I** compact disc interactive
**CD-ROM** compact disc read-only memory (pronounced "cee-dee-rom")
**CMC** computer-mediated communication
**CPU** central processing unit
**CRT** cathode-ray tube

## d

**DOS** disk operating system (pronounced "dos")
**DPI** dots per inch
**DRAM** dynamic random-access memory (pronounced "dee-ram")
**DVD** digital versatile disk

## e

**EDI** electronic data interchange
**e-mail** electronic mail
**EPROM** erasable programmable read-only memory (pronounced "ee-prom")

# f

**fax** facsimile transmission
**FCC** Federal Communication Commission
**FM** frequency modulation
**FTP** file transfer protocol

# g

**GUI** graphical user interface (pronounced "gooey")

# h

**H&J** hyphenation and justification
**HDTV** high-definition television
**HTML** hypertext markup language
**HTTP** hypertext transfer protocol

# i

**IBM** International Business Machines Corporation
**IC** intergrated circuit
**IP** Internet protocol
**ISDN** Integrated Services Digital Network
**ISO** International Organization for Standardization (pronounced "ee-soar")
**ISP** Internet service provider
**ITV** interactive television

# k

**kHz** kilohertz (million cycles per second)
**knowbot** knowledge robot

# l

**LAN** local area network (pronounced "lan")
**laser** light amplification by stimulated emission of radiation (pronounced "lay-zur")

**LATA** local access and transport area (pronounced "lattah")
**LCD** liquid crystal display
**LED** light-emmitting diode

# m

**MAC** 1. Apple Macintosh Computer; 2. European analog high-defintion television standard (pronounced "mack" in both instances)
**MAC-OS** Apple Computer Macintosh-operating system
**MHz** Megahertz (million cycles per second)
**MIPS** million instructions per second (pronounced "mips")
**MIT** Massachusetts Institute of Technology
**modem** modulator/demodulator
**MS-DOS** Microsoft Corporation-disk operating system
**MUD** multiuser dungeon, multiuser dimension, or multiuser domain

# n

**NAA** Newspaper Association of America
**NAB** National Association of Broadcasters
**NAPLPS** North American Presentation Level Protocol Standard (pronounced "nap-lips")
**NBC** National Broadcasting System (USA)
**NCSA** National Center for Supercomputing Applications
**NII** National Information Infrastructure
**NTSC** Natioal Television Systems Committee

## o

**OS** operating system

## p

**PAL** 1. phase alteration line (European color TV standard); 2. programmable array logic (pronounced "pal" in both instances)

**PARC** Xerox Palo Alto Research Center

**PC** personal computer

**PCMCIA** Personal Computer Memory Card International Association [Standard]

**PCN** personal communication network

**PDA** personal digital assistant

**PDL** page description language

**PIA** portable information appliance

**PIC** portable information communicator

**PIN** personal identification number (pronounced "pin")

**pixel** picture element

**PPV** pay-per-view

**PROM** programmable read-only memory (pronounced "prom")

**PSDN** packet-switched data network

## r

**R&D** research and development

**RAM** random-access memory (pronounced "ram")

**RCA** Radio Corporation of America (USA)

**RFI** radio frequency interference

**RGB** red, green, blue (usually refers to digital color monitors)

**RISC** reduced instruction set computing (pronounced "risk")

**ROM** read-only memory (pronounced "rom")

## s

**SIMM** single in-line memory module (pronounced "sim")

**SQL** structured query language

## t

**TCP/IP** transmission control protocol/Internet protocol

**TIFF** tagged image file format

**TV** television

## u

**UHF** ultra-high frequency

**Unix** uniprogrammed version of Multics [a multitasking, multiuser operating system] (pronounced "you-nix")

**URL** uniform resource locator

## v

**VAN** value-added network

**VBI** vertical blanking interval

**VCR** video cassette recorder

**VDT** video display terminal

**VHF** very high frequency

**VHS** Video Home System

**v-mail** voice mail or video mail

**VON** voice on the net (pronounced "von")

**VR** virtual reality

## w

**WAN** wide-area network (pronounced "wan")

**WORM** write once, read many times (pronounced "worm")

**WWW** World Wide Web

**WYSIWYG** what you see is what you get (pronounced "wizzy-wig")

## g

# j

Jacobson, Joseph, 233
Jacquard, Joseph-Marie, 84, 85
Jefferson, Thomas, 263
Jobs, Steven, 17
journalism schools, 260

# k

Kahn, Robert, 181
karioke singing, 58
Kay, Alan, 239–40, 245
Kennedy, President John F., 111
Kent State University Liquid Crystal Institute, 241
kilobyte, 73
Knight-Ridder, 143, 148, 150, 151, 152, 153, 157, 245
Knight-Ridder Graphics Network, 2
Knight-Ridder Viewtron. *See* **Viewtron.**
**knowbot** A contraction of knowledge robot. One of the first primitive agents. Developed in the mid-1980s by Vinton Cerf and Robert Kahn at the Corporation for National Research Initiatives (CNRI), 181. *See also* **agent.**
knowledge stores, 236

# l

**landscape orientation** The orientation of a display medium such that its width is greater than its height. Usually referred to by artists and publication designers as *horizontal orientation,* 38
language, 47. *See also* **digital language;** oral communication; spoken language; written language.
  as agent of change, 24, 50, 53
  digital, 24, 33, 53
  expressive, 54–56

mediamorphic role of, 53–80
  standardization of by publishers, 66
Lanier, Jaron, 184
**laser** A device that produces an intense beam of parallel light at precisely defined wavelengths. With ordinary light, emitted photons scatter in all directions from the source. The photons that emerge from a laser source are highly focused, or coherent, so they remain confined to a tight beam over great distances, 187
**laser printer** A printing device that uses a laser beam to transfer text and images to paper, 187, 221, 233
**law of suppression of radical potential** A social, political, or economic "brake" that can delay or stifle the development of a new media technology or concept. Coined by Brian Winston, 20–22, (in China and Korea) 63, 127, 203
libel laws, 123
  consumer online services and, 126
licensing, 124
  of radio frequencies, 124
  of transmitters, 124
*Life,* 70, 131
**light-wave communication** Any of several methods for transmitting information as pulses of light through networks of optical fiber, 54, 186–88
**linear** Events or content elements that flow sequentially from beginning to end, 38, 41, 47
**link** (1) A hypertext connection between computer files. (2) A connection between computers and/or peripheral devices. 3) A message sent via electronic mail, 104, 182. *See also* **electronic mail.**

development of a large number of related technologies and that contributes to a significant change within societies and cultures, 24

**transistor** A miniature device that can function as a high-speed switch in an electric circuit. Usually made by introducing chemical impurities into pure silicon or other crystalline material. Invented at Bell Labs in 1947, 100. *See also* **chip.**

**triode** A three-element vacuum tube used to detect and amplify radio signals. *See also* **audion; vacuum tube.**

two-way wireless communication, 89, 166, 210

typographic age, 63–66, 99

# u

**ultra high frequency (UHF) band** The region of the radio spectrum above 300 MHz that was assigned by the Federal Communications Commission in 1947 for use by television broadcasters. The FCC originally anticipated that eighty-two channels could be fit into the UHF band using the standard 6-MHz TV bandwidth, 98

unmediated communication, 45

**user** A person who uses a computer device or computer-mediated communication service. Also called an *end user*

# v

**vacuum tube** An electronic device that resembles a light bulb, used in early computers and electronic devices. With the exception of cathode-ray tubes (picture tubes), vacuum tubes have now been replaced by transistors and other miniature electronic components, 96, 100. *See also* transistor.

vaporware, 253

**v-chip** A special computer chip for TV sets developed to allow selective filtering of programs containing violent, sexual, or otherwise offensive scenes by viewers, 214. *See also* **chip.**

VCRs, 48, 54, 133, 135, 197, 198, 209

**vertical blanking interval (VBI)** The usually blank spaces that separate the individual frames of broadcast TV programs, 140, 141

**very high frequency (VHF) band** The region of the radio spectrum below 300 MHz assigned by the Federal Communications Commission in 1947 for use by television broadcasters, 97

Victrola, 90

video cassettes, 48, 201

**video clip** A brief full-motion video recording that can be incorporated into a multimedia presentation, 44, 77

video compression technologies, 207

video conferencing, 54, 77, 209, 210

videodisc players, 135, 197

video games, 54, 133, 162, 169, 200, 259

development cycle, 11–12

**video mail** An electronic messaging service that provides moving video images, usually with audio, 77, 171

video messaging. *See* **video mail.**

video-on-demand, 7

videophone, 140, 210

British research on, 140

unpopularity of, 185–86